The Boundary Politics of Independent Africa

Written under the auspices of the Center for
International Affairs, Harvard University

Boundary and territorial disputes in Africa, 1957-1972

Numbers are keyed to the Appendix list of boundary disputes
Shaded areas represent disputed territories and boundaries

Saadia   The Boundary Politics
Touval   of Independent Africa

Harvard University Press
Cambridge, Massachusetts
1972

Contents

v

In the late 1950s and early 1960s it was widely believed that the borders of the new African states would give rise to many bitter conflicts. This expectation has not been borne out. Conflicts there were, but only in a few instances did they assume major proportions. This book attempts to explain why the expectation of widespread conflict proved false, and why some of the disputes that did erupt underwent rapid and extreme fluctuation from phases of mild disagreement to phases of violent conflict and of reconciliation.

The expectation of widespread and bitter conflicts after independence was shared by African leaders as well as by outside observers. Former President Kwame Nkrumah of Ghana, for many years regarded as one of the principal spokesmen of African nationalism, warned in 1958 against the dangers inherent in the colonial "legacies of irredentism and tribalism." On another occasion, he stated that unless Africa united, it would face conflict, as had Europe in the period after 1815. The concern of knowledgeable academic observers was reflected in the views of Professor R. J. Harrison Church, the noted British student of African geography, who stated in the mid-1950s that "the unrealistic boundaries need revision," and that "some African peoples will not tolerate much longer their division by such lines."[1]

This expectation of boundary and territorial conflict stemmed in large measure from the assumption that tribes and ethnic groups divided by boundaries would seek to unite, to become members of the same state, or to form a state of their own, and that they would therefore challenge the boundaries dividing them.* The appearance in the 1950s of the Ewe and Somali unification movements seemed to lend substance to this expectation. Actually, however, the assumption of inevitable conflict was derived mainly from the numerous irredentist and secessionist movements of Europe, hence the frequent references to the danger of "Balkanization." Whether consciously or not, the predictions that boundary conflicts would plague Africa after independence were based on an analogy with the course of recent European history. Had this analogy proved correct, the history of post-independence Africa would have been chaotic, since literally hundreds of African tribes and ethnic groups are divided by international borders.

To be sure, almost all African states have at one time or another been involved in some border dispute, or have had to contend with separatist sentiments in some section of the population. But a mere listing of such conflicts suggesting the existence of almost universal disputes, would be misleading. It would be misleading because it would overshadow the most significant element in the situation, namely, that the policies of the great majority of African states reflect their respect for existing borders, and that only four states have opposed the principle or have claimed exemption from it. Furthermore, while disputes have been numerous, really serious disputes, deeply affecting the parties concerned or involving bloodshed, have been few.[2]

The record of disputes displays much variety. Some territorial claims reflected deeply rooted values, related to a state's self-image. Others appeared to be merely the outgrowth of bad relations between neighbors: with improved relations, the border or territorial claim was abandoned. Some disputes were resolved by the conclusion of boundary agreements. Others were suspended without solution. Still others continue active. In some disputes, the struggle was merely verbal, and the parties pursued their goals by an out-

*In this study *border* and *boundary* are used interchangeably to refer to the line separating sovereign states, while *frontier* refers to a zone near the boundary. *Dispute* and *conflict* are also used interchangeably.

pouring of angry speeches. A few led to much bloodshed and protracted fighting, sometimes affecting hundreds of thousands, and even millions, of people.

In reviewing this record, and in seeking answers to the numerous questions which arise, we shall focus our attention upon states, rather than boundaries. To quote a classic work on boundary problems: "Il n'y a pas de problèmes de frontières. Il n'est que des problèmes de Nations."[3] The location of a border may complicate state relations and perhaps make them worse, but the principal factors determining the policies of states on boundary problems are not geographical, but political—in both the domestic and international sense.

In the domestic sphere, boundary politics in one of its aspects involves state-building. But, whereas most studies of state-building are concerned with "national integration," or with the formation of the domestic political system—the "inside" content of the state—this study is concerned with problems of the "outer crust," of the political boundaries of the states. To be sure, if integration runs into difficulty and certain sections, tribes, or areas wish to secede, the crust may break. I have been concerned, therefore, with disintegration or separatism to the extent that they affect interstate relations.

A study of the international politics of African boundaries requires a discussion of regional systems, of the African continental system, and of the global system of international politics. I have not attempted, however, a theoretical "system-analysis," nor have I discussed the entire range of regional, continental, or global politics. This study is confined to tracing interactions on the limited issue of boundary and territorial problems.[4]

It may be useful at this point to make clear the classification of disputes which has been used throughout the book. This classification is based on the assumed principal "cause" of the dispute. To be sure, most disputes do not have a single cause. Nevertheless, they can usually be categorized according to their most prominent features. In this study, for example, a basic distinction has been drawn between disputes which concern fundamentals of self-image and touch on "core values," and disputes which do not affect issues held to be vital for a state's existence.[5] Claims which concern "core values" of self-image can themselves be divided into those which focus upon ethnic distinctions and those which emphasize historical continuity.

The two subcategories can themselves be divided. Ethnic disputes are not all alike. Somalia seeks to unite all members of the Somali "nation" within a Somali nation-state. The Ewe unification movement, on the other hand, sought to incorporate the divided Ewes within Togo, but did not claim that Togo should be an Ewe nation-state. The separatist movement in the southern Sudan rests upon a basic distinction between the Negro South and the Arab North. But the South, for which independence is claimed, is multitribal, and does not form an ethnically homogenous entity. Claims which emphasize historical continuity can also be divided— into those pertaining to precolonial situations, and those based on a colonial border. Morocco's claim to Mauritania and parts of Algeria is an example of the former; the Togo and Cameroon claims are examples of the latter.

The book is divided into two parts. Part One presents the background and setting of boundary politics. The manner in which the boundaries were drawn is discussed and the proposition that the process was uniquely artificial and arbitrary is reexamined in the first chapter. The second chapter discusses some of the sources of status-quo and revisionist policies. It reviews the ideological background, and examines the possible influence of the internal environment of states upon their propensity to pursue either irredentist or status quo policies.

Part Two reviews instruments of policy. The attempts of the parties to disputes to use African organizations and conferences as instruments for the promotion of their goals are examined in Chapters 3 and 4. The various forms of force employed in boundary conflicts, and the limitations of this instrument are discussed in Chapter 5. The role of friends and allies and their impact on the course of the disputes is the subject of Chapter 6. In Chapter 7 a taxonomy of negotiations and outcomes is offered. Negotiations which ended in

deadlock are also discussed in this chapter. The suspension
and termination of disputes by disengagement is the subject
of Chapter 8. Disengagement in the Somali conflicts, which
ostensibly concern "core values" on which, by definition, no
compromise is possible, is examined in Chapter 9. Negotiated
settlement of contentious boundaries is the subject of
Chapter 10.

The book closes with a discussion of future prospects. No
predictions are offered, but I have examined there the factors
which might bring about the eruption of new disputes, the
revival of suspended conflicts, and the prospects for deescalation or settlement.

Some limits to the scope of the study were necessary. I
have not attempted to record case histories as such. The historical record of some disputes is reviewed extensively but
only for purposes of illustration. The study focuses only on
governments and organized movements and does not discuss
the attitudes and behavior of peoples or frontier populations.
Governmental policies toward separatist populations or
frontier tribes have been excluded as well. These subjects
merit a separate comparative analysis.

In preparing this study I received help and encouragement
from many sources. A grant from the Social Science Research
Council, in 1965-66, enabled me to revisit Africa and to engage in library research in Europe. In 1967, the Center for
International Affairs at Harvard University enabled me to
spend several months at the Center to continue my work.
Additional assistance was subsequently provided by the
Faculty of Social Sciences at Tel Aviv University.
I have been much aided in this project by others. Several
individuals holding official positions, in Africa and elsewhere,
helped me with information and with criticism. I am unable
to list their names, but am grateful to them. For informative
conversations on the Somali problem I am much obliged to
Al Castagno, John Drysdale and I. M. Lewis. The late George
Bennett was helpful by criticizing an earlier draft of Chapter
1. Special thanks for helpful comments on earlier drafts of
the manuscript are due to Rupert Emerson and I. William

Zartman. Harvard's Center for International Affairs, in addition to financial assistance also provided me with the invaluable editorial counsel of the late Mrs. Marina S. Finkelstein, the Center's Editor of Publications. I am most grateful to her for her sensitive criticism and careful editing of the manuscript. I am also indebted to Mrs. Judith A. Auerbach, of Harvard University Press, for her expert and thoughtful editorial assistance.

Portions of some chapters in the book appeared earlier in different versions. Thanks are due to the *Journal of African History* and Cambridge University Press for permission to use material from my article "Treaties, Borders, and the Partition of Africa," *Journal of African History*, 7, no. 2 (1966); to the Scandinavian Institute of African Studies and Professor Carl G. Widstrand for permission to use parts of a chapter I contributed to a volume edited by Professor Widstrand entitled *African Boundary Problems* (Uppsala: Scandinavian Institute of African Studies, 1969); and to the editors of *International Organization* and the World Peace Foundation, for permission to use materials from my article "The Organization of African Unity and African Borders," *International Organization*, 21, no. 1 (1967).

Saadia Touval

February 1972
Princeton, New Jersey

Part One. The Background

Chapter **1** *The Drawing of Colonial Boundaries*

It is a common assertion that African borders are unique in their arbitrary and artificial character. They are, of course, artificial, but in this they do not differ greatly from international borders elsewhere. All borders are artificial, in the sense that they are humanly contrived divisions of landscapes often indistinguishable from either side, and that they often restrict contact between peoples who may, on both sides of the line, speak the same language, profess the same religion, possess common cultural traits, and engage in similar economic activities. In this respect, there is probably no great difference between international borders in Africa and international borders on other continents.

The charge of artificiality is sometimes intended to refer more narrowly to the relatively recent and "imposed" origin of African borders. It is suggested that since they were imposed and imposed recently, African boundaries did not crystallize "naturally" under the impact and influence of slow social, economic, and political developments. That is certainly true, yet many of the "respectable" European boundaries are also the result of a specific decision and of a very tender age, dating from 1913, 1919, or 1945. In fact, the majority of African borders were drawn before 1910.

The more important criticism of African borders usually refers to the manner in which they were drawn. It has been said that the boundaries of Northern Nigeria were determined by the distances that Frederick D. Lugard, the British colonial administrator, was prepared to walk before he sat down. In a similar vein it was said that Queen Victoria gave Mt. Kilimanjaro to "Cousin Willie," the German emperor, as a birthday present, and that explains why the mountain and its inhabitants are now part of Tanzania. In more serious vein critics assert that the borders have been drawn in disregard of the wishes of the local population, of local circumstances such as ethnic distribution, of economic needs like land and water use, and of communication patterns. The image has often been of European statesmen, thousands of miles from Africa, parceling out the territories among themselves by drawing lines on inaccurate outline maps of the continent.

There are two ways in which boundaries can be considered arbitrary and unreasonable: (1) because they were drawn in total disregard of local circumstances; and (2) because they were imposed upon Africans by outside powers.

Two kinds of boundaries can be distinguished in the process of boundary-making. The first involves boundaries between territories possessed by different European powers, labeled here as "boundaries established by international agreement." The second concerns boundaries separating territories belonging to the same European power. These shall be called "unilateral boundaries," because they were set by the unilateral act of one government.

BOUNDARIES ESTABLISHED BY INTERNATIONAL AGREEMENT

In colonial Africa the ultimate decisions on the allocation of territories and the delimitation of borders were always made by Europeans. Nevertheless one may ask whether Africans were completely passive and whether international borders in Africa differ in this respect from borders elsewhere. The image of Africans as passive victims in the partition of the continent is widely held but it would be more accurate to describe African societies as naive, rather than passive. They did not foresee the consequences of the coming of the Europeans, but the Europeans did not know, either, where this road would lead.

In the partition and conquest of Africa during the last decades of the nineteenth century, the European powers were aided by some African societies and resisted by others. Taking advantage of African rivalries, the Europeans often used African societies to help them establish control.[1] In the process, Africans often participated indirectly in the allocation of territories and the making of boundaries. A convenient way to examine their participation is through the treaties concluded between representatives of European powers and African rulers at the time of border delimitation. The treaties can of course be questioned on moral and legal grounds, but their usefulness here is limited to one *political* aspect of the treaties—the link they provide between African societies and the allocation of territories and delimitation of borders by the European powers.

The European powers and the African societies concluded the treaties for different motives. European motives were manifold, but foremost among them was the expectation that such treaties would help to support their requests for international recognition of territorial claims.[2] African motives for making treaties with European powers also varied. Often the Africans had no choice, but probably in a great number of cases the European emissaries obtained their treaties through the combined effect of coercion and inducement, of the stick and the carrot. The threat of punishment varied and so did the inducements. Some of the inducements were monetary and economic, gifts of money or promises of trade. Often the inducements were of a political and military nature, and represented advantages which the African ruler hoped to use in his relations with his own African rivals.

Despite translation and explanation of the treaties, the African chiefs did not fully grasp their meaning. No doubt many chiefs signed treaties they did not understand, but since some chiefs refused to make a treaty, and others signed only after pressure or persuasion, it can be assumed that the meaning of the undertaking was not beyond the comprehension of the chiefs in general. Many chiefs must have been aware that, by attaching their signature to the paper produced by the white man, they were signifying the establishment of some new and different relationship with him. African rulers were usually unacquainted with European political institutions and diplomatic practice, but this does not mean that they were politically innocent. African societies did not exist in a political vacuum, and their leaders usually had political experience gained in dealing with neighboring societies, with superior or subordinate tribal authorities, and with rival groups or individuals. Thus, when European emissaries came and offered inducements in return for treaties, their offers often fell upon politically sensitized ears. Although most African rulers probably did not fully comprehend the meaning of the treateis, they felt their political significance, and often tried to take advantage of the inducements offered. The relationships thus formed can in some measure be regarded as alliances.

The African rulers hoped for a variety of political benefits from the treaties. Some hoped a precarious status quo would be strengthened in the face of pressures from Africans and Europeans alike. Others may have had more far-reaching plans to strengthen their position in conflicts with rival African rulers. Still others, like the ruler of Buganda, attempted to make use of special treaty relationships with European powers to preserve their own rule over rebellious subject peoples. In other cases European alliances served the opposite purpose in helping to throw off a superior's yoke. Sometimes African rulers tried to preserve as much of their independence as possible by remaining "nonaligned" and playing off European powers against each other.

In fact until very recently, issues of boundaries and political identity were argued by some *African* groups on the basis of treaties that had been concluded with colonial powers at the time of the "scramble." In the 1950s and 1960s the Somalis charged that by concluding the 1897 boundary agreement with Ethiopia, Britain had violated the treaties of protection it had concluded with northern Somali tribes in 1884-1885. In their appeals to Paris in 1959 and 1960 against incorporation into the new states of the Ivory Coast and Dahomey, respectively, the Sanwi "kingdom" in the Ivory

Coast and the chief of Agoué in Dahomey both cited treaties they had concluded with France. And in Uganda before independence, the Buganda tribal ruler tried to use the 1900 agreement with Britain to argue for the preservation of his kingdom's special status.[3]

Although African chiefs often tried to use their alliances with European powers to help them attain political or military goals, this does not mean that the Africans were necessarily pleased with the situation in which they found themselves. The situation was not of their making, and often not to their liking, but they were not passive victims. Rather, they often tried to make the best of a difficult situation.

What was the effect of such treaties upon the territorial settlements that resulted from the territorial scramble? Only when a European power decided to do so were earlier treaties taken into consideration. Sometimes, a decision by a European state to take into account or invoke a treaty between itself and some African ruler was prompted or influenced by an appeal from the Africans concerned, yet the decision as to whether a treaty should be taken into consideration was ultimately a European one.

In evaluating the effect of prior treaties upon territorial settlements, only territories that were disputed between European governments will be considered. However, treaties involving territories not in dispute probably helped to win general recognition of the primacy of the European power which had made the treaties. This is one manner in which treaties played a role in determining territorial allocations.[4]

In situations of dispute, when a European government bolstered territorial claims by referring to treaties concluded with African rulers, its argument was usually twofold: that it had acquired rights through the treaty, and that it had entered into obligations toward an African society which it could not honorably relinquish. Both arguments can, of course, be questioned, and can be regarded as hypocritical. But it is important to remember that in disputes the treaties were often used to justify territorial claims.

Treaties were also useful for the bargaining advantages they conferred in territorial negotiations. If a power had obtained a treaty with the ruler of a territory, the territory could be

"ceded" to another power in return for a counterconcession.
Weak claims included those for which no treaties existed, or
for which the treaties were contested as faulty. The value of a
concession for abandoning such weak claims was much
smaller, and the counterconcession which could be elicited
from the rival power was commensurate.[5]

Also, the limits of the territory being claimed could sometimes be established by reference to the borders of an African
polity with which the power claiming the disputed territory
had entered into treaty obligations. Perhaps one of the more
interesting (though unsuccessful) attempts to delimit an international boundary by reference to the limits of a traditional African polity concerned the border between Angola
and Northern Rhodesia (now Zambia). In 1891 Britain and
Portugal had agreed that a section of the border between
their respective possessions in Central Africa would follow
the western border of the Barotse Kingdom. However, a difficulty soon developed because the two sides disagreed about
the westward extent of that kingdom's territories. In 1903
the dispute was submitted to the arbitration of the king of
Italy. The arbitrator's decision to set the border along
straight lines of geographic longitude and latitude was made
only after he had concluded that it was impossible to establish the true limit of Barotse authority, and that a border
along tribal lines was impracticable.[6]

Naturally, when a European government invoked treaty
obligations toward Africans in territorial negotiations it acted
in its own interest. But in such cases the European state usually considered that its own interests were best served by
trying to preserve the territorial integrity of African polities
and to prevent the allocation of parts of traditional domains
to rival European powers. In this way, therefore, indigenous
African political circumstances sometimes indirectly influenced border delimitations. Sometimes the question of treaty
obligations was raised by the Africans concerned, who
appealed to the European government to honor them. Such
appeals were often to no avail. A report from 1892, for example, illustrates the attitude of a chief whose territory had
been divided between the Gold Coast and Togo:

I myself gave myself and people to the Governor it is not
the Governor that asked me . . . If the Queen says she
does not like me I take my freedom . . . I gave it to you
whole, now you want to divide my land . . . If the English
want to "dash" any of my people to their friends they
must first come to me and we will talk.[7]

The vicissitudes of the king of Kiama in Borgu (northwestern
Nigeria), and his appeals to his British "protectors" who had
forsaken him (1895), are additional examples of unheeded
appeals.[8]

On other occasions African appeals did prove effective. A
case which received considerable attention at the time was
that of Chief Khama of Bechuanaland. In 1895 Khama and
two other chiefs visited London to appeal against the British
government's intention to transfer his territory to the rule of
the British South Africa Company. The three chiefs were
received by the colonial secretary, Joseph Chamberlain, and
reached an agreement by which a strip of territory claimed
necessary for the construction of the Rhodesian railway was
ceded to the company; the rest of Khama's territory remained a British protectorate.[9]

Ethnic considerations sometimes determined boundary
delimitation even when the colonial powers recognized no
treaty obligation to allow for them. An example is the transfer of some 5,000 square kilometers from Tanganyika to
Ruanda-Urundi in 1923. The original border between
Tanganyika and Ruanda-Urundi had been drawn in 1919 in
such a way as to facilitate the construction of a railway linking Rhodesia and Uganda through British-held territories (the
Cape-to-Cairo scheme). The scheme had required partitioning
the Kingdom of Ruanda between Britain and Belgium, and
the population had protested strongly. As a result, the problem was placed before the League of Nations' Permanent
Mandates Commission, whose chairman, Marquis Reodoli,
reported that the border was "hardly justifiable from the
point of view of the well-being, political order, stability, and
economic development of an African community already

well organized." Consequently, in 1923 Britain and Belgium concluded an agreement for the adjustment of the border so as to incorporate all of Ruanda into Belgian territory.[10]

Boundary treaties sometimes provided for "individual self-determination." According to such arrangements, individuals living in a territory that was being transferred from one colonial ruler to another could choose which territory they wished to reside in. It was thus acknowledged that the interests of the population might be affected by the transfer of territory from one authority to another, and an attempt was made to alleviate the hardship of those whose livelihood or other interests were tied to a particular colonial government, European language, or culture. European governments acceded to such arrangements for a variety of reasons but treaty obligations toward the Africans were sometimes invoked as justification.[11]

Boundary agreements also often included provisions to minimize local hardships caused by new divisions. Agreements for a special boundary regime that would enable people on both sides of the line to pursue their normal economic activity, cross the boundary for work, cultivate the land, have access to water, and the like, were common not only in Africa, but in Europe and elsewhere. A frequent provision in African treaties concerned the nomadic peoples, who were given permission to cross the boundary with their stock for grazing purposes, and sometimes to spend a considerable part of the year in neighboring territory.[12]

In addition to considering the needs of local societies and political structures, efforts were often made to arrive at other rational delimitations of territorial boundaries. Such rational delimitation was greatly hampered by the inadequate information on local conditions available to the boundary-makers. Nevertheless, the assumed needs of colonial territories often figured prominently in boundary negotiations. The most obvious of these needs involved economics and communications. In the light of subsequent developments, when boundaries prove to have been satisfactory, they seldom come to our attention. But some of the wrong decisions have been subject to considerable criticism. The ludicrous shape of the

Caprivi strip, for example, resulted from an Anglo-German agreement that German Southwest Africa should have free access to the Zambezi, which people at that time believed would become an important communication route between the interior and the Indian Ocean. The agreement was obviously based on inadequate geographical information. But the purpose was reasonable—to benefit the territory of Southwest Africa.[13]

Boundary negotiators, aware of their inadequate knowledge of local circumstances, often included provisions in the boundary treaties for sending a demarcation commission to the area, with some authority to deviate from the line delimited in the treaty. Such commissions were assigned the task of surveying the boundary area and demarcating the boundary on the ground while taking account of local circumstances. The commissions sometimes deviated from the line agreed in the treaty in order to enable villagers to have access to their land or water, or to avoid splitting villages into two, and of course to conform to the configurations of the landscape. Modifications recommended by such commissions were of a minor nature but they nevertheless constituted an attempt to take local conditions into account and to diminish the hardships caused by the border.[14]

UNILATERAL BORDERS

Unilateral borders divided territories belonging to one colonial power. The determination of these borders did not involve a process of negotiation between rival sovereign governments, but resulted from the unilateral decision of the government exercising control over both territories. Obviously under such circumstances the bargaining power of African societies was minimal, and their opportunities to influence the delimitation of the boundary were much more restricted than in cases where rival European powers competed for African support.

Unilateral boundaries were changed or modified much more frequently during the colonial period than boundaries established by international agreements. This frequency of modification reflected the desire of colonial administrators and governors to improve boundaries which, in the light of experience, they regarded as inconvenient.

Between 1890 and 1947 Mali, then known as the French Sudan provided an example of frequent changes in French Africa. French Sudan was established in 1890 as a distinct administrative entity. In 1899 it was abolished and dismembered, and parts of it were attached to each of the neighboring territories. In 1902 a new colony under the name of Senegambia and Niger was created. In 1904 the western parts of the colony were detached, and its name was changed to Upper Senegal and Niger. The eastern part of the colony was detached in 1919 and included in the new colony of Upper Volta. Consequently, the reduced territory of Upper Senegal and Niger was renamed French Sudan. In 1932 Upper Volta was abolished, and two of its *cercles* comprising some 50,000 square kilometers and containing approximately 700,000 inhabitants were attached to Sudan.* In 1944 parts of four *cercles* were transferred from Sudan to Mauritania. In 1947 the two *cercles* acquired in 1932 from Upper Volta were detached from Sudan and returned to Upper Volta, which was reconstituted as a separate territory.[15]

Different reasons and criteria determined these border delimitation and boundary modifications. Sometimes they were political and reflected the political preferences of the government in the mother country. Other changes stemmed from local administrative or economic considerations.

Upper Volta illustrates the diverse considerations that might prompt boundary changes. The territory was first constituted in 1919. It was abolished in 1932, and its administrative divisions were absorbed by the neighboring territories of Sudan, Niger, and the Ivory Coast. In 1947 it was reconstituted as a separate territory, and the districts previously annexed by each of the neighboring territories were separated from them and reincorporated into Upper Volta. The decision, in 1919, to establish the territory of Upper Volta was made for administrative reasons, a result of changes to introduce greater reliance on traditional institutions—induced by a revolt in Niger in 1916. The decision to abolish it in 1932

*A *cercle* is a French administrative division.

was made because of difficulties brought about by the economic depression, and in response to the pressures of French economic interests in the Ivory Coast. Characteristically, however, the decision was explained as designed to benefit the local populations: "The populations that were joined to the colonies of Sudan and Niger were by their character, affinities, interests, and geographic proximity naturally oriented in that direction. The largest part of the disbanded colony, containing the heaviest rail and coastal development, and consequently the greatest concentration of wealth, was attached to the Ivory Coast."[16]

The reestablishment of Upper Volta in 1947 was motivated mainly by the desire of the French government to limit the spread among the Mossi people of the Rassemblement Démocratique Africain (RDA), the interterritorial political party in French Africa, which at that time maintained links with the French Communist party.[17] The Mossi's influential traditional ruler, the Moro Naba, had earlier turned down RDA requests for Mossi support. At the same time the Moro Naba had appealed to the French to detach the Mossi from the Ivory Coast. When the French granted the ruler's request, the Mossi became the single most influential tribe in Upper Volta. They supported a political party of their own, the Union Voltaique.

The Kenya-Uganda border illustrates certain other considerations. In 1902 the Eastern Province of Uganda was transferred to Kenya, then called the East Africa Protectorate. The transfer was decided upon for administrative reasons, as Sir Clement Hill, the superintendent of the African Protectorates administered by the British Foreign Office, believed that this measure would allow closer supervision of the area than was possible while it was under Uganda's administration. He also considered it desirable that the entire territory then traversed by the Uganda railway be placed under one administration.[18]

The transfer called for the delimitation of a new border. At first, a new border following natural boundaries was considered by Sir Clement, sitting at Whitehall, but his studies of the problem in London had little effect, and in the end the border was delimited by local officials who had considerable

knowledge of the frontier area. They agreed that the interterritorial border should coincide with ethnic boundaries.
When they came to apply this principle, however, disagreement developed over whether the criterion should be a purely
"scientific" classification of tribes, or whether the "political
connections" among various tribal subunits should be considered. The prevalence of intertribal raiding suggested that administrative criteria would be desirable as well. For the purposes of maintaining law and order, tribes involved in frequent conflict with each other were to be placed under a
single administration. It was an indication of the weight given
to administrative considerations that the boundary which
finally emerged was "merely provisional." It was amended in
1910 after effective administration had been established in
the region and additional administrative experience attained.[19]

The expansion and migration of tribes raised similar questions for border delimitation. For example, in the 1900s
the pastoral Suk expanded from areas wholly within Kenya
into Uganda, clashing there with the Karamojong upon whose
traditional grazing grounds they encroached. The respective
district commissioners of Kenya and Uganda were instructed
in 1916 to prepare a joint recommendation for a Kenya-
Uganda border that would coincide with the Suk and Karamojong border. The commissioners were unable to agree on a
line, however, since the Ugandan district commissioner
argued that historical Karamojong claims to land occupied by
the Suk should be respected, and the Kenyan district commissioner asserted that the existing spread of Suk migration
should be the decisive factor.[20]

The initiative and proposals of one colonial governor were
usually met by the opposition and counterarguments of another governor from the neighboring colony. In 1949, for
example, the high commissioner of French West Africa suggested to the governor of French Sudan a transfer to Upper
Volta of the Sénoufo-inhabited areas of Sudan. The governor
opposed the transfer for several reasons: (1) it was desirable
to maintain the administrative organization of the territory,
which had already undergone numerous changes; (2) histor-

ically, the area in question was part of Sudan; (3) politically,
the transfer might weaken the Sudanese Progressive party
(PSP) affiliated with the French Socialist party, and
strengthen the RDA, which was linked with the Communists; and (4) the transfer would harm the economy of
Sudan.[21] The arguments reflect the variety of principles and
criteria that were considered relevant for a decision on
boundary changes.

Changes in boundaries frequently also stemmed from certain assessments of the needs of various territories. The assessments were not made with concern for the needs of an independent state. They were made by colonial governors whose
view of the requirements of their territory would, of course,
be quite different from that of the government of a sovereign
state. But, even so, the needs and concerns of the colonial
government would often be similar to those of *any* government charged with the administration of a particular territory. This was particularly so with problems stemming from
local administration and from the needs of the population
living near the boundary. Tribal and ethnic groups were often
split by the boundary, or the population needed access to
land, water, and grazing. Negotiations between colonial
governors who were subordinate to the same Ministry of Colonies at home centered around the same kinds of issues raised
in negotiations between independent states. The agenda in
1949 of a proposed conference between the governors of
Sudan and Mauritania provides an illustration: (1) respect for
the 1944 border; (2) migrations of nomadic tribes; (3) control over Mauritanians in Sudanese territory; (4) taxes to be
paid by Mauritanians in Sudan; (5) the proposal to install a
Mauritanian mission at Kayes in the Sudan and the powers to
be conferred on such a mission.[22]

The resolution of such problems between colonies belonging to the same European power was easier, of course, than
the resolution of such problems arising between independent
states. But, more important, since the resolution of conflicting interests was made by the decision of a single government, it was often possible to devise and impose solutions
which were based to a considerable extent on local needs (as
understood by the colonial administration).

ARE AFRICAN BORDERS EXCEPTIONAL?

The argument that the borders in Africa were drawn in disregard of local circumstances implies that better borders could have been devised. This is undoubtedly true, but it is doubtful whether any criterion or formula for good borders exists. For example, had the borders of West Africa been drawn in accordance with ethnic and cultural criteria, the states in the area would have been formed in layers parallel to the coast. While such states would have been marked by a larger measure of cultural homogeneity, they would have fared poorly in economic terms. The more uniform climate would have restricted the opportunities for developing a diversified agriculture, and their access to the sea would have depended on the state controlling the coast.

As it happened, most borders resulted from neither a whimsical stroke of the pen, as is sometimes suggested, nor careful studies. Borders evolved in several stages: claims and recognition of spheres of influence, allocation of territories, initial delimitation of boundaries, and, finally, alteration and modification of boundary lines, stemming from studies by boundary commissions and from administrative experience. The gradual process afforded opportunities to correct mistakes made at a previous stage, and served to diminish greatly the arbitrary nature of the borders.

The boundaries were not necessarily convenient and they were not always made with the welfare of the local population in mind. The criteria for selecting many borders may have been inadequate or they may have been misapplied, or the decisions may have been based on erroneous information. But attempts to take local conditions into account *were* often made. The decisions were often *reasoned* and considered and reflected a compromise between conflicting interests and diverse concepts and criteria.

Some comparisons with European borders can be made. African borders are probably more arbitrary than boundaries in Europe—there is a difference in degree, but not in the process itself. European borders, too, were often determined by international conferences at which the local populations were able to exert only a minor influence, if any. They were often determined by the interests of the great powers and the rivalry between them, rather than by the interests or needs of the populations directly affected: the boundaries drawn for the Balkans in 1878 and 1913-1914 are glaring examples. More recent examples are the Russo-Polish and Polish-German borders determined by the Soviet Union, the United States, and Great Britain during World War II conferences. President Roosevelt's view of the procedure for determining boundaries was not atypical: "The President said that, after all, the big powers would have to decide what Poland should have and that he, the President, did not intend to go to the Peace Conference and bargain with Poland or the other small states."[23]

It is true that in innumerable cases the governments of the European states in question did have a major influence on border delimitation; in Africa, native influences were of less importance. Yet, an element of coercion was almost universally involved, since most borders were drawn following a war or as a result of other pressures exerted by one state against another.

BOUNDARIES IN PAN-AFRICAN IDEOLOGY BEFORE INDEPENDENCE

The views of the Africans themselves about their boundaries were not much influenced by historical or comparative analyses, but rather by the political context in which such views were formulated. The most remarkable African pronouncement on boundary questions was undoubtedly the call at the All African Peoples Conference in 1958 for the "abolition or adjustment" of borders. The antecedents for this appeal lie in the early Pan-African movement, from the 1920s to 1945.

Edward Wilmot Blyden (1832-1912), the Liberian statesman of West Indian birth who is regarded as one of the founders of Pan-Africanism, frequently called for the preservation of African social institutions, customs, and values. Yet his attitude toward the colonial partition of the continent was ambivalent. According to his biographer:

> Blyden chose to believe that the partition was "an act of Providence" and was ultimately for the good of the Africans. He stated this view most explicitly in 1903: "Our country has been partitioned in order . . . of Providence, by the European powers, and I am sure that, in spite of what has happened, or is now happening or may yet hap-

pen, this partition has been permitted for the ultimate good of the people, and for the benefit of humanity." It was not that he naively believed in the altruism of Europe. He recognized that Europe was attempting "to utilize Africa for her own purpose," but he clung to the transcendental belief that "Providence used men and nations for higher purpose than they themselves conceived."[1]

World War I and the peace settlement, which stimulated African political consciousness in general, also awakened some interest in boundary problems. This interest was limited mostly to West Africa, where the partition of the German colonies of Togo and Kamerun between Britain and France affected the educated and commercially active sections of the population, and especially the Ewe people, who now found themselves divided into three sections, in French Togo, British Togoland, and the British colony of the Gold Coast.[2] Their sense of grievance against this partition received expression in 1920 by the National Congress of British West Africa, a loose organization of the educated elite which was active in the postwar years.

At its inaugural meeting at Accra in March 1920, the National Congress adopted a number of resolutions, concerned mainly with self-government, the franchise, and other reforms designed to extend the rights of the African population. Among the resolutions were two brief paragraphs concerned with boundary problems, under the title, "The Right of the People to Self-Determination":

the Conference views with alarm the right assumed by the European powers of exchanging or partitioning countries between them without reference to, or regard for, the wishes of the people.

this Conference condemns specifically the partitioning of Togoland between the English and the French Governments and the handing over of the Cameroons to the

French Government without consulting or regarding the wishes of the peoples in the matter.[3]

The resolutions also called attention to an ethnic aspect of the new boundary, stating that sections of the Fanti and Ga tribes and "the ancient capital of the Paramount Chief of Awuna" had been placed in the Togo sphere allocated to France. Thus, in addition to the explicit claim that the local population should have a voice in the shaping of borders, the Congress also implied that boundaries ought to conform to ethnic divisions. Finally, in view of the subsequent evolution of African attitudes, it is significant that the resolutions sought assurance that the integrity of the four British West African Colonies would not be disturbed.[4]

But the Congress did not discuss the general question of African boundaries, and concerned itself only with local grievances, for which it acted as a spokesman. These local grievances were expressed in terms of universal principles of national self-determination; that peoples and territories should not be disposed of arbitrarily and that ethnic groups ought not to be divided by international boundaries. The principle of self-determination was one of the topics discussed by the 1920 conference, and it was also invoked by Joseph Casely Hayford, a founder and leader of the Congress, in his book, *United West Africa*, published in 1919.[5] The apparent absence of these ideas in earlier Pan-African thinking and their appearance during 1919-1920 should be attributed to their acceptance in Europe at the end of World War I. They began to influence political thinking in Africa as well.*

*It is interesting to recall in this connection that David Lloyd George, the British prime minister, had preceded the Congress in advocating the application of self-determination to the African populations conquered from Germany during the war. He is reported to have spoken in this vein as early as 1917 and to have reiterated this view in a speech on January 5, 1918, saying that "the general principle of national self-determination is . . . as applicable in their cases as in those of occupied European territories." (See H. W. V. Temperley, *A History of the Peace Conference of Paris*, II (London: Oxford University Press, 1920), 227.) His motives were, of course, not the same as those of the African nationalists. He apparently hoped that by invoking for the Africans the right of self-determination Britain could legitimize its retention of the German territories in Africa it had conquered during the war.

The Congress did not label itself as Pan-Africanist, yet it was Pan-Africanist in its goal of unity for the British West African territories. Indeed, its very existence as an interterritorial nationalist movement was an expression of Pan-Africanism. To what extent the Congress influenced subsequent Pan-African thinking is hard to determine, but some indication of a link between the Congress and the Pan-African movement was provided by George Padmore, one of the most influential ideologues of Pan-Africanism in the 1940s and 1950s, who said of Casely Hayford, the Congress leader, that "although an ardent Gold Coast patriot . . . Mr. Hayford had a clearer social vision and wider conception of Pan-African nationalism than most of his political contemporaries."[6]

In the development of Pan-Africanism an important role was played by the conferences organized by W. E. B. DuBois after World War I (in Paris, 1919; London and Brussels, 1921; London and Lisbon, 1923; and New York, 1927). The main concerns of these conferences were racial equality and humane colonial policies. Boundary questions or the effect of boundaries on African lives did not attract attention.[7] These issues were not to be raised again until the Pan-African Congress held in Manchester, England, in 1945.

While the leadership of the Pan-African conferences held after World War I was primarily American and West Indian, by 1945 Pan-Africanism had become transformed into a movement led primarily by Africans, and concerned primarily with African problems. Moreover, the demand for independence was beginning to be heard. It is not surprising then that the 1945 Congress devoted some attention to boundary problems, although it did not concern itself with the question of African boundaries in general. Boundary problems in only two areas were raised: West Africa and Ethiopia.

The Congress passed a resolution about West Africa which stated inter alia "that the artificial divisions and territorial boundaries created by the Imperialist Powers are deliberate steps to obstruct the political unity of the West African peoples."[8] This resolution was the first formal condemnation of colonial borders in terms which were subsequently to receive wide currency: it emphasized the double theme of the artificiality of the borders and their obstruction of unity. But the resolution referred only to West Africa and not to the continent as a whole. Furthermore, it did not call for the abolition or the revision of boundaries. In this, it differed from the formulation of Pan-African views which was to take place in 1958.

It is interesting to speculate about the possible reasons for the insertion of the sentence on boundaries in the resolution. Padmore's published account of the Congress (in *Pan Africanism or Communism*, and *History of the Pan African Congress*), contains no reference to any discussion of boundary problems or political unity. At least part of the origin of the boundaries clause can be traced to the Ewe problem. Thus, the criticism of the boundaries is contained in the Congress resolutions on West Africa, and the main speaker at the second session, on Imperialism in North and West Africa, held on October 19, was Dr. Raphael E. G. Armattoe, an Ewe physician and poet, active in the Ewe unification movement. Although there is no reference to the Ewe problem, or to the question of Togo reunification in the summary record of Armattoe's speech, his presence at the Congress undoubtedly increased awareness of the Ewe discontent at their division. Keeping in touch with developments in their homeland, delegates of Gold Coast (Ghana) origin must have been aware of the resurgence of the Ewe unification movement taking place at that time. Also, the *Ewe Newsletter* had begun publication in May 1945, under the editorial guidance of Daniel Chapman, then a teacher at Achimota (the school which produced many of the Gold Coast elite), and subsequently a senior Ghanaian official. While advocating the unification of all Ewe under British administration, the *Ewe Newsletter* had in June 1945 written that "the real truth of the matter is that it is impossible to set up a satisfactory frontier anywhere between the lower Volta in the Gold Coast and the lower Mono on the western border of Dahomey."[9]

The chairman of the session on imperialism in North and West Africa at the Congress was Kwame Nkrumah, and it is probable that he played a leading role in formulating the resolutions on this subject. Nkrumah's participation raises the possibility that the phrasing of the resolution may reflect the beginnings of his preoccupation with the idea of unity, rather than a narrower concern with merely the Ewe problem. Most probably Nkrumah's interest in African unity and sympathy for Ewe unification coalesced. Both points of view were subsumed under the resolution.

As for Ethiopia, its boundaries were mentioned in the Additional Resolution on Ethiopia which stated that:

1. This Congress condemns the suggestion that parts of Massawa and Asmara should be put under international control.
2. In the interest of justice as well as of economic geography this Congress supports most heartily the claims of the Somalis and Eritreans to be returned to their Motherland instead of being parcelled out to foreign powers.
3. This Congress demands the immediate withdrawal of the British Military Administration from Ethiopian soil.[10]

It is easy to discern the background of this resolution. Some delegates prominent at the 1945 Congress had been active in organizations established in Britain to support Ethiopia after the Italian attack on that country in 1935. As the most ancient independent African state, Ethiopia had a special place in the hearts of African nationalists, and much attention was paid to its international problems. After World War II, when the question of the disposal of the Italian colonies arose and Ethiopia laid claim to Eritrea and to Somalia, many African nationalists supported its claim. Another issue at that time was Ethiopia's demand for the withdrawal of the British Military Administration, established in Ethiopia during the war; Britain was delaying because it was then interested in regrouping the Somali-inhabited territories under a single administration. This would have entailed the separation of the British-administered region from Ethiopia.

The echoes of this controversy, and of Ethiopia's postwar claim to Italian Somaliland, found expression in the discussions at the Congress dealing with Ethiopia and the black republics, held on October 17. Peter Abrahams, who represented South Africa at the conference, said in the debate: "the Somalis with whom I came in contact while working my way from Africa in 1941 looked upon Ethiopia as their motherland." He explained that one of Ethiopia's greatest needs was an outlet to the sea, and that "the Federation of Somaliland with Ethiopia would provide that outlet to the sea" which Ethiopia required.[11]

The boundaries in West Africa and the question of Ethiopia's borders were treated by the Congress as two separate issues. They were linked only by their criticism of imperialism, yet both boundary questions were of only marginal interest to the Congress. Only later did boundary issues rise to prominence. As independence approached, the attention of political leaders was increasingly drawn to the tasks of national integration. Among the ramifications of the problem of national integration were boundary questions and relations with neighboring states.

DOMESTIC SOURCES OF POLICIES

Since World War II only four African states have embarked upon irredentist policies: the Somali Republic, Morocco, Ghana, and Togo. Their irredentism, challenging the legitimacy of existing boundaries and of the resultant territorial apportionments, has caused five conflicts: between Somalia and Ethiopia, Somalia and Kenya, Morocco and Algeria, Morocco and Mauritania, and between Ghana and Togo.[12] In addition, a number of border disputes have arisen between states which, in principle, had accepted the status quo but disagreed over the interpretation of documents delimiting borders. Such disputes continue to erupt from time to time. A few have been resolved, some were simply discontinued without a solution, and some continue to disturb relations between neighbors.

Irredentism cannot be ascribed simply to the existence of a border cutting across an ethnic group, since obviously very few of the hundreds of peoples so divided have adopted irredentist or separatist attitudes. The argument that nationalism causes irredentism leaves unanswered the question of why some states are more nationalistic than others. The advocacy of the status quo cannot be explained merely by the inclination of states to preserve what they have. There is another side to the advocacy of the status quo, namely that states refrain from claiming territory from their neighbors. The explanation that the majority of states are "satisfied" and therefore accept the status quo is also not sufficient. Why are they "satisfied?" Nor is it clear why two states are prompted to engage in a border dispute and then, after a period of bickering, prompted to resolve the issue by a compromise that they could have reached long ago, or to drop the matter as if it had never existed.

Answers to these questions can be sought in a number of ways. One obvious course of inquiry would be to consider the boundaries themselves. Can the presence or absence of conflict be explained by their "artificial" or "arbitrary" nature? To what extent can we attribute state policies to a boundary's interference with economic activity, or cutting across ethnic groups and communication lines. Implicit in this approach is the assumption that the location of borders, taken together with facts of economic or human geography, is in *itself* a major factor. In other words, the boundaries themselves can be "good" or "bad," conducive to peace or to conflict. During the first half of this century, such an approach was very common in European literature on international politics. It was expressed eloquently by Lord Curzon, who said that borders are "the razor's edge on which hang suspended the modern issues of war or peace," and that borders have an "overwhelming influence" in the history of the modern world.[13] This is essentially a geopolitical approach to international politics, and as such it is deterministic in character.

Without denying the influence of the location of the border, it should not be given too great a weight in comparison with other factors that also influence the behavior of states. No doubt the annual need of the Somali tribes to cross the border from Somalia into Ethiopia for grazing, and the consequent friction between these tribesmen and the Ethiopian authorities, have contributed a good deal to the conflict between the two states. But grazing arrangements could have been made without the issue becoming a major territorial dispute. Somalia, however, chose to pursue irredentism, and therefore did not merely seek arrangements for transfrontier grazing. Similarly, the dispute between Mali and Mauritania cannot be explained solely by pointing out that nomadic tribes cross the border in pursuit of their livelihood, and in the process clash with the inhabitants and authorities on the other side. Morocco's interest in the mineral resources of Tindouf was undoubtedly a factor influencing Morocco's policies in its dispute with Algeria, but the Moroccan territorial claims also had much deeper and more extensive roots. The mere location of the line drawn by France just to the west of the rich Tindouf area was only one factor among many and not even the most salient. More basic reasons, social and political, rather than geographic, explain these and other border disputes.

In the search for clues or answers, it is tempting to attribute revisionist policies to states which have adopted a radical ideology, and status quo policies to conservative states. However, no such correspondence exists. Morocco, generally regarded as pursuing a conservative policy both domestically and internationally, is among the revisionist states. Prior to the 1969 coup Somalia was not, and Togo still is not, known for revolutionary radicalism. Algeria, on the other hand, which prides itself on its radicalism in both domestic and international affairs, is among the staunchest advocates of the territorial status quo and of the sanctity of the boundaries imposed by the colonial powers. Ghana under Nkrumah was the only example of coincidence between radicalism and territorial revisionism. Explanations for the attitudes of states to their boundaries should be sought in other directions.[14] The ethnic composition of the African states, their political history, and their internal politics were the more important factors influencing state policies on boundary and territorial problems. Personalities, in some cases, also seem to have exercised a decisive influence on boundary politics. More complete explanations of the internal determinants of state policies would also require an analysis of decision-making processes, but, unfortunately, available information on decision making is incomplete and uneven.

Some Explanations of Status-Quo Attitudes

Nationalism and tribalism. In drawing analogies between
European and African boundary problems it is assumed that
the ethnically heterogenous composition of African states
would give rise to problems similar to those of national
minorities in Europe. The indiscriminate use of the term "nationalism" in describing both European and African political
movements has served to confuse the issue further. A comparison of European and African nationalism, and of
European national minorities and the ethnic components of
African states will explain the contrast between the European
experience of numerous boundary conflicts and irredentist
movements caused by divided peoples, and the African experience, in which such divisions have thus far caused relatively few boundary conflicts.

In Europe, nationalism was a political movement of ethnically homogenous nations. Where such nations did not possess their own states (nation-states), the nationalist movement waged a struggle for the creation of a nation-state. This
struggle sometimes led to movements of separatism and
irredentism, whose goal was the secession of national groups
from states in which they were a minority, and their union
with other members of the nation in a single nation-state.

In Africa, nationalist movements usually did not coalesce
around ethnic nations, but rather around the population of a
given colonial territory. These populations were in most cases
ethnically heterogeneous. Most African nationalist movements first developed among an educated class made up of
members of diverse ethnic groups who joined together in the
hope of taking over the government of the territory from the
colonial ruler. In Europe the nationalist struggle was waged in
the name of an ethnically defined "nation"; in most African
cases the struggle was waged in the name of a territorially
defined population. Most European movements aimed to
establish separate nation-states; in Africa the goal was usually
independence within the existing territorial-administrative
framework. A few exceptions exist: the Somalis, and perhaps
some Ewes, Yorubas, and Ibos, did seek to establish nation-
states, but, in general, the concept of a nation-state has been
irrelevant to Africa.[15]

To be sure, tribalism is prevalent in most African states. The processes of development and modernization tend to facilitate national integration on the one hand, and to create circumstances conducive to the growth of tribalism on the other. While society is being transformed, and new nontribal links and groups take shape, the process also induces group consciousness of all kinds, including tribal consciousness.[16] Yet tribalism is different from the political movements of minorities in European nation-states. In most African states, *all* the ethnic groups within the state are "minorities." They do not all have equal influence, but the absence of a single dominant group makes maneuver possible, and even a disadvantaged group can increase its share of power if it manages its political alliances skillfully.

The element of cultural oppression which stimulated national consciousness among many European minorities is absent in most African states. In Europe minority groups were expected to lose their special identities and either to assimilate into the dominant group, or at least to identify with its values and symbols, because these became the values and the symbols of the state. In Africa, with a few exceptions (notably Ethiopia, Somalia, Sudan, Mauritania), there have been no attempts to impose the culture of any single ethnic group upon the rest of the population. In Europe, the cultural heritage of the dominant ethnic group was used to cement and strengthen the nation-state, but in most black African states the realities of ethnic heterogeneity have prevented the use of tribal cultures as instruments of integration. On the contrary, reference to the cultural heritage of tribes is considered as hindering the achievement of the generally accepted goals of national integration and state-building.[17]

There is also an important difference between tribalism and separatism. Tribalism seeks to increase the tribe's influence within the state; separatism rejects membership in the state and aims at secession. Tribes may be possessed of a highly developed sense of group identity and be fiercely engaged in the internal political struggle, yet be devoid of secessionist sentiments, and refrain from aiming at unity with kinsmen across the border.

The Bakongo are an example of a tribe that chose to seek

political influence through participation in the intertribal politics of the existing state, rather than trying to unify its members in a nation-state. In 1950 a group of Bakongo formed the Bakongo Alliance (ABAKO), for the "unification, conservation, development and expansion of the Kikongo language." In view of ABAKO's frequent references to the "golden era" of Bakongo history, when a Kongo kingdom had dominated the region, and in view of the Bakongo division among the Belgian Congo, French Congo, and Angola, it seemed that ABAKO might develop into a movement aiming at Bakongo political unification.[18] This did not happen. The Bakongo assumed a leading role in nationalist agitation for the independence of the Belgian Congo. With independence, they received an important share in the ruling coalition of the new state and Joseph Kasavubu, former president of ABAKO, was elected president of Congo.

In addition, certain practical economic interests may take precedence over the symbolic, but materially uncertain, goal of political unity. An example are the Yorubas, who are divided between Nigeria and Dahomey. In the 1950s some Yoruba personalities in Nigeria proposed that the Yoruba-inhabited areas in Dahomey be joined to Nigeria. This idea was not supported by the Dahomeyan Yorubas. Their lack of support for national unification probably stemmed from the fact that they had become integrated into Dahomey's economic and administrative life. Some of them had learned French but did not speak English. Transfer to Nigeria would have required many adjustments on their part and would have placed them at a disadvantage in relation to the English-speaking Nigerian Yorubas. Thus, while retaining close social and cultural links with the Nigerian Yorubas, the Dahomeyan Yorubas were indifferent to the idea of political and administrative unity.

Another illustration, from a politically less sophisticated group, concerns the Suk tribe in East Africa. In 1932 a section of the tribe was transferred from Kenyan to Ugandan administration. When consulted in 1934 about whether the administrative line which placed them inside Uganda and separated them from the Suks of Kenya should be abolished, the Suks of Uganda replied in the negative, although abolition would have entailed their reunification with the Suks in Kenya. Their reason was probably a practical, economic one: the elimination of the administrative line would have enabled the Kenya Suks to gain equal access to the grazing grounds in Uganda, thus diminishing the share of the Uganda Suks.[19]

Governmental perceptions of state interest.   The ethnic composition of the African states has been an important influence in shaping governmental attitudes and policies on boundaries. Boundaries may be likened to the external shell of the state. Since the majority of African states have not yet attained internal cohension, it is in their interest to preserve this shell intact. In many cases, the maintenance of the status quo has come to be associated with the self-preservation of the state. It was feared that, were the right to secede granted to any group or region, such a grant could stimulate secessionist demands from additional regions or groups, and thus threaten the disintegration of the state. The danger of such disintegration has been vividly exemplified by the secessionist movements that have sprung up in several states.

In the Congo Republic (Leopoldville), secessionist sentiment was strong in the 1950s among the large Bakongo tribe. After the Congo emerged to independence in 1960, Katanga province proclaimed its independence from the Congo. Ethiopia, too, has been troubled since the end of World War II by secessionism among its Somali population in the south, and among sections of the Eritrean population in the northeast. In Ghana, Ewes claimed the right to secede and join their brethren in Togo. In the Ivory Coast, the Sanwi people rose in 1959, claiming the right to secede. In Kenya's coast province, on the eve of independence, there was sentiment favoring separation and reunion with Zanzibar. Furthermore, a strong secessionist movement has existed among the Somalis in northern Kenya. In Mali, the Touareg tribe rose in revolt in 1963, refusing to recognize the government's authority. The Sudan has been torn by civil war because the black population in the south has since 1955 claimed the right to secede. Uganda's unity has been threatened both before and after independence by separatist sentiments among the important Buganda people who possessed, until

1966, a measure of autonomy in their Buganda Kingdom. And, most recently, the Ibo people in Nigeria tried to secede and establish an independent Republic of Biafra.

The interest of states in preserving the status quo is reflected also in the qualms many states have shown about annexing regions or tribes from neighboring states. In Europe separatism and secession were often encouraged by nation-states, which acted as poles of attraction. In other cases, nation-states developed irredentist aspirations and claimed the right to unify all members of the nation within a single state. In Africa, with a few exceptions, there are no nation-states to act as poles of attraction, or to give rise to irredentism aiming at national unification. Ethnic groups may develop grievances against the government; but neighboring states usually do not claim them as "lost brothers." Certain tribes may lack a feeling of loyalty toward the state in which they live, but they have no loyalty to any other state.

African governments have not normally aimed at unifying tribes divided by a border in part because they feared that support for the aspirations of any tribal group would open the government to charges of tribal favoritism. The addition of any population to the state would alter the delicate political balance between tribes and for that reason would be opposed by all groups, which would fear the diminution of their influence. Thus, for example, concern over the possible increase in the influence of the dynamic Fang people has been a factor restraining both Gabon and Cameroon from claiming the neighboring Spanish territory of Rio Muni. Similarly, internal political considerations were an important factor behind the Nigerian government's opposition to suggestions, in the early 1950s, by some politicians belonging to the Action Group (the main political party at that time, in the Western Region, dominated by Yorubas), concerning the annexation of the Yoruba-populated area of Dahomey.

Since states are in a sense defined by their boundaries, the self-image of the newly independent became associated with their colonial borders. This association is exemplified by disputes concerning boundaries which had been altered during the colonial period. Both Togo's irredentism and Cameroon's claims have aimed at the restoration of boundaries as they were during the German colonial period. Boundary changes during the colonial period contributed to the Somali disputes and the Mali-Mauritania dispute, and inspired claims by Egypt against the Sudan and by Congo-Brazzaville against Gabon. Tanzania's demand for the alteration of its boundary with Malawi was preceded by the spread of a myth among Tanzanians, according to which Britain had after World War I moved the border from the middle of Lake Nyasa to the Tanzanian shore.[20] To be sure, not all boundaries which were altered during the colonial period have become subject to dispute, but boundary changes in several cases led to a state's uncertainty about its identity.

Commitment to the status quo was inconsistent, however, with the anticolonial nationalist ideology current in Africa. The ideas and values prevalent among nationalist leaders at the time of independence predisposed them to view critically the international borders inherited by their states. Their anticolonial nationalism led them to resent all the arbitrary impositions of colonial rule, borders included. For those who wished to abolish the entire colonial legacy, a logical corollary would have been to reject the colonial borders as well. The myth of pre-colonial unity, and the Pan-Africanist aspiration for unity, also pointed to the rejection of colonial borders.

Advocacy of the right of self-determination, a corollary of anticolonial nationalism, could also have led to the rejection of colonial borders. It is significant then, that most African interpretations of the right of self-determination, and in particular of who is entitled to it, have differed markedly from some European interpretations of the right of "nations" to self-determination. As Rupert Emerson has pointed out, most African leaders, like most colonial nationalists, chose to interpret this right as applicable to the colonial territory as a whole, within the inherited boundaries. No *section* of the population, however defined, was considered entitled to this right.[21] Yet, this restriction of the right to self-determination was also inconsistent with the prevailing anticolonial ideology.

The fragility of the new states was thus accompanied by the added weakness of their anticolonial revisionism. In order

to lessen their vulnerability, states were impelled to seek new
ways to establish their legitimacy, or to borrow Rousseau's
oft-quoted phrase—to transform "strength into law, and
obedience into duty."

In Europe, legitimacy was for a long time derived from the
ruling dynasty. In the nineteenth century, nationhood began
to be accepted as the legitimizing principle, and it is still
widely regarded so today. But since most African states were
neither nation-states nor dynastic states, they could neither
avail themselves of nationhood as a legitimizing principle nor
be legitimized by the dynastic principle. In the insecure and
precarious situation of the new states the absence of a legitimizing principle was an added weakness. It rendered insecure
not only the government but also the existence of the state.
But, whereas the government could in the short run justify its
position and authority because it had come into power
through the efforts of the nationalist movement, the existence of the state and its territorial extent could not in the
long run be legitimized by this device.

Because the African states had to define themselves according to colonial boundaries the majority of them realized that
they had a mutual interest in establishing respect for the
status quo. Since most states are vulnerable to external incite-
ment to secession, it was obvious to the majority of states
that reciprocal respect for boundaries, and mutual abstinence
from irredentism, would be to their advantage. This principle
calls to mind the formula of the Peace of Augsburg in 1555,
except that in contemporary Africa, nationality and not
religion was at issue: *cuius regio eius natio.*

Sources of Revisionist Attitudes and Policies

If support for the status quo by the majority of states
stemmed from the rarity of "tribal irredentism" and their
precarious inner political balance, it follows that in the
revisionist states these conditions did not prevail. Some revisionist policies were in fact associated with tribal irredentism or separatism, and furthermore, the revisionist states
were able to legitimize their statehood by calling on ethnic
nationhood or history, and were therefore not under the
same compulsion to legitimize themselves by pointing to

their inherited boundaries. The Somalis are probably the outstanding example of irredentism in Africa. Somali nationalism is based on an ethnic-cultural definition of Somali nationhood embracing all Somalis—those living in the Somali
Republic as well as those in Ethiopia, Kenya, and the French
territory of the Afars and Issas (formerly known as French
Somaliland). Somali nationalism thus resembles European
forms of nationalism. The irredentism of the Somali Republic, which aims at the unification of all Somalis within
one nation-state, is complemented by separatist sentiments
among the Somalis of Ethiopia and Kenya. Thus, Somali nationalism differs significantly from most other African
nationalist movements.[22]

As a state, the Somali Republic has acted as a pole of
attraction to the Somalis living outside its boundaries. It has
actively pursued irredentist policies and encouraged separatism among the Somalis of Ethiopia and Kenya. Somalia
could afford to pursue an irredentist policy because it is a
nation-state. The cohesion of its population is much stronger,
and it is much less threatened by disintegration than is true in
the majority of African states. Not being as fragile or as open
to disruptive challenges, Somalia is also not open to the same
inducement or pressure to accept the norm of respect for
colonial boundaries. The legitimizing principle of the Somali
state is Somali nationhood, and not the norm of reciprocal
respect for the status quo.

Morocco is another irredentist state. On the grounds of
historic rights, it has claimed territory from Algeria and has
wished to annex Mauritania. In justification, Morocco has
argued that its historic borders were violated by French
colonialists, who usurped part of its national territory.
Moroccan irredentism can, like Somalia's, be explained by
the fact that it too can afford to ignore the norm of respect
for existing borders. The existence of the Moroccan state is
legitimized by the principle of the continuity of the historic
Moroccan state, rather than by colonial boundaries or a
nationalist movement. In this sense, Morocco too is an exception among African states, possessing a legitimizing principle
which others do not. It is significant, however, that Morocco
has refrained from resorting to the principle of self-determina-

tion in justification of its claim to Mauritania. Indeed, on several occasions Moroccan leaders have even asserted that the principle of self-determination was not applicable to Mauritania. Writing in his party's newspaper, for example, the Istiqlal leader Allal el Fassi has stated that the universal application of the principle was absurd; its application to Mauritania would be as unacceptable as asking the populations of Liverpool or Marseilles whether they wished to be English and French.[23]

The appeal of Moroccan irredentism among certain groups in Mauritania was largely traditional and dynastic rather than ethnic. Some Mauritanian groups considered themselves bound by an obligation of loyalty to the Moroccan throne and lacked a sense of loyalty to Mauritania as a political entity. Yet it is probable that consciousness of ethnic links with Morocco also played a role in the initial rallying to Morocco of some groups, which sought in an association with Morocco a guarantee against possible incorporation into a Negro-dominated West Africa federation. The Reguibat tribes were an important group who initially supported Morocco. They were probably influenced by economic interests—their nomadic existence necessitated seasonal migrations to grazing grounds in Morocco and the Spanish Sahara, and they were accustomed to trade at the markets of southern Morocco.

Perhaps it is fortunate that only a few of the contemporary African states can trace their statehood to precolonial times, since streaks of irredentism can be discerned in other historic states as well. Ethiopia, for example, deeply conscious of its historic continuity as a state since ancient times, claimed Eritrea and Somalia after World War II. Ethiopia justified its claim by arguing that Eritrea and Somalia had been part of Ethiopia in historic times. Yet, with the advent of African states to independence, Ethiopia's policy and general attitude have changed, and it has become an ardent advocate of the status quo. The change was probably influenced by the ethnic basis of Somali irredentism. Although a historic state, Ethiopia is far more fragile than Morocco because it is ethnically heterogeneous. Since the revisionist principle held implications which could endanger Ethiopia's integrity, if not its survival as a state, it was very much in Ethiopia's interest to establish acceptance of the status quo as the prevailing norm in Africa.

The Ghana-Togo dispute is more complex. It originated in the ethnic nationalism of the Ewe, who had been divided after World War I between British and French jurisdictions and demanded the unification of the Ewe people. When it became doubtful that the principle of ethnic unity could advance their case in the United Nations, the Ewe leaders in the 1950s redefined their aspirations as the reunification of the two Togolands. The Ewe's main instrument in their struggle was the Togo Republic (formerly French Togo), which, after its attainment of independence in 1960, espoused an irredentist policy, justifying the claim for the reunification of the two Togolands by an historic argument— the restoration of the boundaries as they had been during the period of German rule.

The attitudes of the population in British Togoland varied. The plebiscite held in 1956 indicated that the majority of Ewes favored the merger of their territory with French Togo, whereas the northern tribes preferred association with Ghana. The attractiveness of unity with French Togo for the Ewes in British Togoland can be explained in part by the leading position which Ewes occupied in French Togo. This same image of Ewe dominance served to repel the northern tribes, while the traditional ties of some of those tribes with Ghana influenced their vote in favor of unity with Ghana.[24]

Togolese irredentism boomeranged, however, since it helped to provoke a Ghanaian counterclaim. Ghanaian irredentism can be viewed as a defensive reflex against Togolese claims, and also as an expression of Nkrumah's commitment to an anticolonial Pan-Africanist ideology. The Ewe and Togolese claims were of course a serious threat to Ghana's territorial integrity and to its desire to integrate former British Togoland into the Ghanaian state. Given the intensity of the Ghanaian commitment to the Pan-African ideology, Ghana could not respond to the Togolese challenge by proclaiming the sanctity of colonial borders. Instead, Ghana chose to counterattack, arguing that the best means to Ewe and Togolese unity was to join Ghana and become part

of it. In Ghanaian eyes, the annexation of the Togo Republic
by Ghana had the double advantage of removing the threat of
Togolese irredentism and of being in accord with Pan-African
ideology. As Ghana saw it, this would have been a step toward the abolition of the colonial legacy and toward the
greater unity of Africa.

The dual source of Ghanaian revisionism—in Pan-African
ideology and Ghanaian state interest—is reflected in a White
Paper explaining the 1960 constitution:

> The Government ask the people, by voting for the draft
> Constitution, to show that they believe in the unity of
> Ghana and reject any form of federalism . . . The draft
> Constitution, however, is not based upon any form of
> nationalism. The Government realise that the present
> frontiers of Ghana, like so many other frontiers on the
> African continent, were drawn merely to suit the con-
> venience of the Colonial Powers who divided Africa
> between them during the last century. The object of the
> draft Constitution is to provide firm, stable and popular
> Government in Ghana so that Ghana can assist in achiev-
> ing a union of African states and territories. Apart from
> facilitating the entry of Ghana into a union of African
> states and territories, the draft Constitution is also
> designed to enable peoples who are at present outside
> Ghana but who are linked by racial, family and historical
> connections with Ghanaian peoples to join them in one
> integrated state.[25]

Ghana also entertained irredentist claims against the Ivory
Coast. It seems plausible to attribute this to a combination of
factors. One was the mere fact of the "availability" of the
Sanwi separatist movement in the Ivory Coast, which offered
itself to exploitation. Nkrumah belonged to the Nzima tribe,
which was closely related to the Agni people of Sanwi.[26] The
third factor was the fundamental political antagonism
between Nkrumah and Félix Houphouët-Boigny, president of
the Ivory Coast. And, finally, Pan-African ideology provided
justification for altering the colonial boundaries, and thus
"reuniting brothers separated by colonialism."

The existence of the Sanwi movement also calls for an explanation. The Ivory Coast government has been from time to time troubled by opposition of a tribal character, and by protests against the predominant position of the Baoulé, President Houphouët-Boigny's tribe. The Sanwi movement, rooted in the 40,000 Agnis of the Aboisso region was the most persistent and best organized of such protest movements. Its origins can be traced in the administrative history of the region and in the social and economic competition between the Agni and the Baoulé. The Agni, who had signed a treaty with France in 1843, had been accorded preferential treatment by the French administration, which had continued to recognize the king of Sanwi even after recognition of the traditional authority of chiefs had been generally withdrawn. However, during World War I, in protest against manpower levies imposed by the French government, many Agni migrated to the Gold Coast, some even advocating the transfer of their region to the Gold Coast. The Agni argued that by imposing the levies France had violated the 1843 treaty. Consequently, the French administration dismembered the Sanwi state. This measure led the Agni to focus their political demands on the reestablishment of the Sanwi state, a measure which the French administration conceded in 1943. The first to acquire European education, the Agni lost their economic and social primacy as education and European economic activity spread to other tribes, notably the Baoulé. When political organizations began to be formed after World War II, the Agni generally refused to join the Baoulé-dominated Ivory Coast Democratic party (PDCI), and supported instead the rival Progressive party. As the PDCI became the standard bearer of the Ivory Coast independence movement, the Sanwi felt alienated and turned to separatism.[27]

The Sanwi case illustrates the complex causes of separatism. Mere tribal antagonisms have not produced separatism. The Sanwi case and other separatist movements, suggest that separatism has occurred when ethnic differences coincided with economic, social, or political issues of conflict. Thus, Katanga's attempt to secede from the Congo (1960-1963), though nourished by tribal antagonisms, had roots in the administrative and political history of the province and it was further stimulated by the economic differentiation between Katanga and the rest of the Congo. The southern Sudan's separatism has deep roots in the historical antagonism between the Negroes and the Arabs and in memories of Arab slaving expeditions. These traditional differences between the north and the south were further reinforced by the practices of the British administration and by the conflict between Islam and Christianity. The roots of Biafra's secession from Nigeria can be traced to the economic and social competition between the Ibos who had emigrated from their home region and the people among whom these Ibos had settled. The Targui movement in Mali, which contained separatist tendencies, was caused in part by the Targui feeling of racial superiority over Negroes, from among whom the Touareg had traditionally taken slaves. It was sparked by the "Negro" government's attempt to impose economic and administrative measures upon the Touareg designed to integrate them within the Malian state.

These examples suggest that although separatism has been relatively rare in Africa thus far, it may yet develop if differential rates of economic and social progress intensify tribal antagonisms and produce feelings of discrimination and alienation among ethnic groups.

Inconsistencies, Regimes, Personalities

Basic postures have been examined—attitudes favoring the status quo, irredentism, and separatism, but states have often taken actions that deviated from general patterns of behavior or from established principles. States do not always act on principle; they may pursue contradictory goals, they may be tempted into actions that run contrary to the principles they espouse. Furthermore, policies are not pursued at an even pace; irredentism may rise or subside. States which in principle accept the status quo may become involved in a bitter border dispute with a neighbor, or they may lend assistance to secessionist movements, despite their awareness that such acts tend to disrupt confidence and may boomerang to damage their own security. It is doubtful whether a meaningful general theory explaining such inconsistencies can be devised. But a few factors can be examined which have influenced state policies, and which provide partial explanation of a variety of acts which have deviated from established patterns and principles.

A number of border disputes may, for example, stem from wide and deep political antagonism between governments. Such antagonism usually originates in reasons unrelated to the common border, but once relations have deteriortated and governments view each other with hostility and suspicion, secondary disputes, including boundary disputes, develop. The primary conflict between the governments may have had a variety of causes: personal antagonism between leaders, competition in the African arena, one government's support of opposition groups against the other, and a chain of mutual suspicions and subversion. When such relations lead to border disputes, these border disputes are an inadvertent by-product, or symptom, of another conflict. At the same time, boundary claims that arise in this manner may serve as a lever for the exertion of pressure intended to extract concessions in matters unrelated to the boundary. A few examples will illustrate the process.

Egypt's territorial claims against Sudan in 1958 can be interpreted in two ways. They can be viewed as a symptom of the fundamental tensions between the two countries, stemming from Egypt's age-old drive for influence over the upper reaches of the Nile and its displeasure at Sudan's rejection of union with Egypt. Another interpretation is that the Egyptian boundary claims were intended as a lever to extract concessions from Sudan on two matters then under negotiation: the compensation claimed by Sudan for the flooding of the Wadi Halfa region that would result from the construction of the Aswan Dam and the consequent need to resettle the local population; and the revision of the 1929 Nile Waters Agreement, requested by Sudan. Negotiations on this last question had become deadlocked in January 1958, a few weeks before the border dispute erupted. The dispute may thus have been both a symptom of underlying tensions and a move in the bargaining process.

Another border dispute, that between Ghana and Upper

Volta (1963-1966), was ostensibly over the interpretation of documents and maps defining the border, but its deeper cause is to be found in the growing antagonism between the two governments. Ghana was disappointed at Upper Volta's reversal of its rapprochement with Ghana, initiated in 1961, and at the close links Upper Volta had established with the Ivory Coast. For its part, Upper Volta suspected the Ghanaian government of supporting subversion against it. Within this atmosphere the two governments apparently developed a genuine difference over the interpretation of documents. This subsequently became aggravated as Ghana tried to use the problem to demonstrate to Upper Volta its capacity to cause trouble, whereas Upper Volta used the dispute to embarrass Nkrumah by portraying Ghana as expansionist.

The Dahomey and Niger dispute over Lété island also illustrates the influence of a number of factors, including the importance of personalities. Ownership of Lété island had been contested by the French administrators of the two territories during the colonial period, and the dispute was inherited by the independent governments of Dahomey and Niger when they became independent in 1960. But as long as Hubert Maga had been president of Dahomey, the excellent personal relations between him and Hamani Diori, president of Niger, had assured close collaboration and harmony between the two states. A number of minor incidents stemming from the disputed ownership of the island did not mar the friendly relations. The fall of President Maga in 1963 disrupted this harmonious relationship. Niger began to suspect the new Dahomey regime of aiding the subversive Sawaba party. In these circumstances, longstanding tensions over the presence and prominence of Dahomeyans in the civil service and in private firms in Niger, and over Dahomey's position astride Niger's communications with the world, began to embitter relations between the two states. The vehemence of the dispute over Lété island was merely a symptom of the antagonism that had developed between the two governments on other subjects.

The dispute between Tanzania and Malawi also seemed to be a symptom of political antagonism. The location of the

Tanzania—Malawi border on the Tanzanian shore of Lake Nyasa was long resented by Tanzania, although the border had been accepted. In fact, the 1964 resolution of the Organization of African Unity (OAU) pledging respect for existing boundaries had been introduced by President Nyerere. In 1964, however, antagonism between the two governments had begun developing. The demand, formally raised by Tanzania in 1967, to move the boundary to the middle of the lake can be regarded as merely another expression of this antagonism. Had relations been better, it is likely that Tanzania would not have demanded the modification of the border. Instead, it would probably have been possible for the two governments to agree on practical measures to enable the inhabitants of the Tanzanian shore to use the lake.

To the extent that relations between states depend upon the sympathy or antipathy regimes harbor toward each other, these relations can change with changes in regimes. Where a border dispute has existed, a change in the regime of one party may open the way for a settlement. The reverse may also happen: where both neighbors had been committed to the status quo, a change in regime may lead to the development of a border dispute. Both personal and ideological factors may play a role in such policy shifts.

The overthrow of President Nkrumah in 1966 is an example of a change that opened the way to the settlement of Ghana's border disputes. The coup was followed by the renunciation of Nkrumah's policies by the National Liberation Council. The new government made special efforts to resume normal relations with neighboring states and to reassure them that Ghana harbored no territorial ambitions.[28] A notable gesture was the extradition to the Ivory Coast of the leaders of the Sanwi separatist movement, who had been brought to Abidjan by a Ghanaian goodwill mission.

The reverse process—of a change in regime leading to the development of a border dispute—is illustrated by the Dahomey-Niger dispute which erupted after the overthrow of President Maga of Dahomey. Sudan's increased friction with Ethiopia and Chad, after 1965, can also be attributed to the change in its regime. During the military regime of General Abboud, Sudan's relations with Ethiopia and Chad had been relatively smooth. Following the revolution of October 1964, Sudan's policy changed. Sudan's toleration on its territory of bases of the Eritrean separatist movement led to conflict with Ethiopia, and permission for the formation of a Chad government-in-exile in Sudan produced friction with Chad.

The pressures of domestic politics must also be considered. Pressure groups expressing African economic interests are not much developed, but tribal interests are often of primary importance in African politics. The delicate balancing of tribal interests has in most states apparently exercised a moderating influence, restraining governments from embarking upon irredentist policies that might upset the existing tribal balance, or that might expose the government to charges of tribalism.

Nevertheless, in some instances tribal influences have intensified border friction. In the Somali case, for example, the Darod tribe has occasionally criticized the government for not pursuing Somali territorial claims vigorously enough. The Darod's special interest in these claims can be explained by the dependence of sections of the tribe upon grazing land and water in Ethiopia, and by the fact that the annexation of the Somali-inhabited portions of Ethiopia would increase the numbers and weight of the Darod in the Somali Republic.[29]

Aggressive foreign policies and the external involvement of states often represent the efforts of a government to divert attention from domestic shortcomings and to unite public opinion in the face of an "enemy." It seems that such considerations have in fact contributed to a few border disputes.

The growth of political opposition in Morocco has been regarded as one factor influencing King Mohamed V of Morocco to make irredentism a major issue and goal of Moroccan policy. Until 1958, Morocco has pressed its boundary claims in quiet negotiations with France. Although the Istiqlal party had agitated for the restoration of Morocco's legitimate boundaries, the king had refrained from committing himself publicly to such a goal. Only with the growth of internal opposition did he publicly embrace irredentism, in a speech at M'Hamid, in the south, in February 1958. As a result of the king's commitment, irredentism became a major issue and a device for uniting the nation behind the king and his government in the face of an external enemy. The Moroccan desision, in May 1963, not to attend the summit conference in Addis Ababa seems to have been influenced by the election campaign then in progress, in the course of which the government had been accused of preparing a "sell-out" by normalizing relations with Mauritania.[30]

Domestic politics may also have influenced some actions by Somali governments. According to A. A. Castagno, when the Somali government was threatened by a vote of no confidence in the National Assembly, in April 1962, it was saved in part by "the mounting acrimony between Ethiopia and the Republic, to which the Premier responded vigorously.[31]" Similarly, the eruption of serious fighting along the Somali-Ethiopian border in January and February of 1964 has been attributed by commentators to the proximity of the general elections in Somalia. The vehemence of the Dahomeyan position in its dispute with Niger in 1963 has also been linked with the need to suppress the discontent in the north of the country over the overthrow of President Maga.

Nevertheless, in view of the internal difficulties which African governments often face, it is interesting that border and territorial disputes are not more frequently initiated or aggravated for domestic political reasons. There are two explanations. One is ideological. The sentiments of Pan-African solidarity exert a moderating influence upon inter-African relations. Significantly, in Somalia and Morocco, Pan-Africanism is considerably weaker than the ideologies with which the irredentist sentiment had initially been associated. Somali irredentism is a product of Somali nationalism, which developed independently, and outside the mainstream of African thinking. Traditionally, Somalis have regarded themselves as racially distinct, and perhaps even superior, to Negro Africans. They associated themselves with Pan-Africanism relatively late, after Pan-Somali nationalism had already been embraced by all sections of the population. In Morocco, the standard bearer of Moroccan irredentism has been the Istiqlal party, whose ideological roots are Islamic rather than Pan-Africanist.[32]

Ideology has also served in another way to reduce inter-African conflict. The external enemy to which attention can be diverted from internal problems has been identified as imperialism and "neocolonialism." It is significant that in some territorial disputes, African governments have blamed the former colonial power and emphasized the colonial origin of the problem, rather than accusing the neighboring African state of responsibility. Both Morocco and Tunisia initially blamed France for usurping and dismembering their territories. Somalia blamed Britain. Only subsequently were accusations leveled at neighboring African governments, but they remained tempered by references to the primary responsibility of the colonial power. Such an apportionment of blame accorded with Pan-African ideology and helped maintain ideological consistency.

Expediency is a second explanation for the fact that African states have seldom resorted to border disputes as a diversion from domestic difficulties. Experience has shown them that quarrels with neighbors can be dangerous, because the territory of the neighboring state can become a base for the opposition and for organizing subversive activities against the government. Thus, instead of diminishing internal pressures, border conflict with a neighbor may stimulate external support for the domestic opposition and thus strengthen it. For this reason too, neighbors had better be left in peace.

Somewhat paradoxically, then, the domestic fragility of most African states has induced caution in the relations between neighboring states. On the other hand, relative cohesion—ethnic, traditional or ideological—has enabled states to pursue irredentist policies.

Part Two. The Politics

The conferences after 1957 differed significantly from the Pan-African conferences, reviewed earlier. The differences can be traced to the impact of independence: increasingly, concrete problems and policies came to preoccupy the conferences, with abstract ideological discussions gradually receding into the background.

The frequency of high level conferences, and the effort invested in them by African states and organizations, suggest that participants regarded the conferences as important instruments in the conduct of foreign policy.

It may be that the importance attached to these conferences and to the adoption of formal resolutions and declarations comes in part from the political style that the nationalist movements had adopted under colonial rule. From the African point of view, it was through the formation of organizations, the mobilization of African support, and the influencing of public opinion in the mother country, that independence had been attained. By the time of independence, this style of political action had become a habit. Since it had been successful within the colonial framework, African political leaders continued to use it in the conduct of their foreign policies. In addition, the conferences provided the new states with opportunities to assert their status of sovereign statehood and assisted them in crystallizing their personalities.

Much of the conference activity during this period revolved

around Nkrumah's aspiration for Pan-African leadership and his vision of the political unification of the continent, both of which were regarded by most African leaders as challenges. The situation in the Congo and the war in Algeria also attracted much attention. In this context, with the exception of Katanga and Mauritania, boundary and territorial problems seldom came to occupy the center of the stage. Nevertheless, border and territorial problems were raised in the proceedings and included in the resolutions. Interested parties believed it essential, for the record, to state their position regarding the boundary questions that concerned them, since failure to do so might in the future weaken their stand over the issue in question. The mention of an issue by one party challenged its adversary to respond. Sometimes parties to disputes tried to obtain the endorsement of their point of view through formal resolutions. They regarded such resolutions to be at the least propaganda achievements. More important, states hoped that the semblance of international judgement represented by a conference statement would serve to legitimize their goals.

In a sense the conferences played a dual role. They were the institutional mechanisms through which states sought to promote their objectives. At the same time, they influenced state behavior because they were part of the environment in which states operated. As institutional mechanisms, the conferences were created and used by the organizers, and unless the organizers (usually states), are considered as prime actors, the conferences are meaningless. Yet the conferences also created an atmosphere, and helped in propagating ideas. In a few cases the atmosphere of unity at conferences intoxicated the participants to the extent of influencing their attitudes. In this sense, the conference itself, as an institution, came to play a role, though limited, in influencing the course of inter-African politics.

The conferences varied greatly in type. An obvious distinction is between governmental and nongovernmental conferences. However, the organizations participating at the nongovernmental conferences usually served as governmental instruments. Further distinctions can be made between exclusively African gatherings and others that included non-African participants. Conferences also differed according to their political coloring, aims, prestige, procedure, and management.

The procedural rules of governmental conferences usually reflected strict respect for the sovereignty of states. Resolutions were adopted either on the basis of consensus or by a formal vote requiring a qualified majority. On the other hand, at conferences of the Afro-Asian Peoples' Solidarity Organization (AAPSO) and of the All-African Peoples Conference (AAPC), resolutions were often adopted by acclamation, without being submitted to a formal vote. Some resolutions were of a declaratory character expressing the feelings of solidarity among the participants and often containing something to everybody's taste, while others were formulas arrived at after hard bargaining and reflecting the interests and pressures which participated in the process.

Here, only the territorial and boundary questions that were discussed by the more important conferences will be analyzed. The questions to be examined are of two kinds. The first category concerns the substance of views and policies. Do the resolutions of conferences reflect any consistent pattern, or general consensus regarding the maintenance or revision of existing boundaries? If so, can any evolution in the thinking about borders be detected? Another question is, whether any differentiation between attitudes of different kinds of conferences can be discerned? The second category of questions focuses on the process of conference politics. What were the alignments that emerged? What was the impact of other issues, such as the recurring crises in Congo, upon alignments? What was the influence of the links of the former French colonies with each other, and with France? In other words, how did the impact of different issues and different interests converge to produce certain alignments and formulas on border problems?

THE FIRST AFRO-ASIAN PEOPLES' SOLIDARITY CONFERENCE, CAIRO, DECEMBER 1957

The Afro-Asian Peoples' Solidarity Organization (AAPSO) was formally not a governmental organization. Its conferences were attended by representatives of political parties

and movements, rather than by governmental delegations.
But the attendance, character, and resolutions of its conferences were influenced by the fact that they were managed by
an uneasy coalition of Egypt, the Soviet Union, and China.
After 1963, mainly as a result of the disarray caused by the
Russo-Chinese struggle and the Chinese-Indian border war of
1962, the importance of the AAPSO declined.[1]

The first AAPSO conference, held in Cairo from December
26, 1957 to January 1, 1958, addressed itself to a wide range
of contemporary issues, with an emphasis on their anticolonial and anti-western aspects. Boundary problems were
not among the main topics of the conference, but a few of
them were referred to in resolutions adopted under the
general heading of "Resolutions on Imperialism." The resolutions varied in their degree of support for the revision of
boundaries.

Most explicit in its endorsement of irredentist claims was
the resolution on Morocco, which stated that "the Conference strongly supports the demand of Morocco for the return
of areas still dominated by imperialism in order to ensure the
unity and complete independence of Morocco." The definition of the areas in question was left ambiguous: it was not
clear whether the resolution was intended to be a blanket
endorsement of all Moroccan claims, or only the expression
of partial support for the same. Support for Moroccan irredentism at this time was interesting because it anticipated by
a few weeks the public espousal of irredentist claims by the
Moroccan government. Significantly, the Moroccan representation at the conference came from the Democratic Independence Party, led by Mohamed Ouazzani. He was a rival of the
Istiqlal party's leader, Allal el Fassi, who was the main
protagonist of a "Greater Morocco." Allal el Fassi himself is
reported to have denounced the conference as being dominated by Communists.[2]

Somewhat less explicit was the resolution on Somaliland,
which stated that "the Conference supports the struggle of
the Somali people for their independence and recognizes
their right to self-determination." The omission of any reference to Somali unity is significant, but the reference to "the

right to self-determination" was ambiguous, and could be interpreted as implying support for secession as an expression of self-determination.

The resolution on the Cameroons called on the Afro-Asian countries to help the people of the Cameroons in their struggle for "unification and independence." Here was an explicit call for unification. But the term was absent from the resolution on Togo, which expressed concern over the forthcoming plebiscite in French Togoland, and did not refer to the unification issue. In addition to these references to African border problems, the call for the unification of divided national territories was present in the resolutions on Yemen, Indonesia, Okinawa, Goa, Korea and Vietnam.

These issues of boundary and national unification were merged into a common theme by Sharaf Rashidov, a vice president of the Supreme Soviet, who headed the Soviet delegation, and subsequently wrote an essay describing the conference. According to Rashidov, the gathering had been deeply moved by the delegate from French Somaliland who had in his speech asked whether it was possible to divide a human heart into five parts, as the imperialists had done to his country. Rashidov said that "this speech was full of meaning. For not only the people of Somali are deprived of the opportunity of reuniting . . . but so were the peoples of French Equatorial Africa, Cameroons, Taiwan, India, Indonesia, Yemen, Okinawa, Vietnam and Korea."[3]

This common theme was also given expression in a formal act, the Declaration of the Afro-Asian Peoples' Solidarity Conference.[4] This declaration called for "respect for the sovereignty of all peoples and the integrity of their territories." The phrasing is characteristically ambiguous—no criteria for the definition of "peoples" or of their territories are suggested. Although the text could be interpreted as supporting the status quo, it is clear from the endorsement by the conference of the various unification movements, that the principle was meant to legitimize the revision of the political and territorial status quo in certain specific cases.

CONFERENCE OF INDEPENDENT AFRICAN STATES, ACCRA, APRIL 1958

President Nkrumah of Ghana convened this conference as part of his policy of forging close links among African states under his leadership. In addition to the Ghanaian hosts, it was attended by high-level official delegations from the independent African states: Egypt, Ethiopia, Liberia, Libya, Morocco, Tunisia, and Sudan. The record of the discussions was not made public, but it seems certain that boundary questions were among the topics considered, since six of the eight states present had recently been involved in boundary and territorial disputes. The Ghana-Togo problem was then current, as well as Ghana's interest in the unification of the Nzima people, who straddled Ghana's boundary with the Ivory Coast. Two other states, Egypt and the Sudan, had only a few weeks before the conference quarreled over their common boundary, and the Sudan had complained to the United Nations Security Council. King Mohamed V had in February announced Morocco's territorial claims. The Moroccan foreign minister alluded to the problem in his speech at the opening of the conference when he said that "we still pursue our efforts to bring about the unification of our territory." Tunisia was at the time active in pressing its boundary claim against Algeria, which was still under under French control. And, finally, Ethiopia had become increasingly concerned over Somali irredentism.

In a speech closing the conference, President Nkrumah summarized its conclusions:

> Our conference came to the conclusion that in the interests of that Peace which is so essential, we should respect the independence, sovereignty and territorial integrity of one another, and cooperate with each other in all fields of human endeavour. We have decided also that in all matters involving disputes among us, we shall try to settle our differences by direct mediation between the parties concerned, and if such mediation fails, we shall seek the "good offices" of our brother African States in the spirit of the United Nations.[5]

None of the resolutions adopted at the conference referred explicitly to boundary problems.[6] Furthermore, the resolutions on Togo and Cameroon refrained from endorsing unification or boundary changes despite Nkrumah's ambition to annex Togo, and Ghana's support for the Cameroon reunification movement. Nevertheless, two points in the resolutions seemed to delineate a compromise to which all participants could subscribe. First, the resolutions emphasized the determination of the participants "to respect the independence, sovereignty and territorial integrity of one another." This, of course, is a standard formula in conference resolutions, and could not be interpreted as a specific endorsement of the territorial status quo. Second, the participants proclaimed that they would "resort to direct negotiations and if necessary to conciliation or mediation" to settle differences among themselves. This too is standard. But these standard formulations were subject to conflicting interpretations. According to A. K. Barden (who after 1959 served as Nkrumah's principal advisor on African affairs), Liberia had interpreted the resolution as emphasizing respect for the sovereignty and territorial integrity of states. Ghana, on the other hand, believed that the main value of the resolution was in its call for negotiations, conciliation, and mediation to settle differences between states. In other words, Liberia hoped that the pledge to respect territorial integrity could be used to legitimize the territorial status quo, whereas Ghana hoped that the pledge to resort to negotiations, conciliation, or mediation could be used to bring about boundary changes.[7]

THE ALL-AFRICAN PEOPLES CONFERENCE, ACCRA, DECEMBER 1958

The All-African Peoples Conference (AAPC) was, like the AAPSO, ostensibly a nongovernmental body of political parties and organizations. Established in 1958 at Ghanaian initiative, it was apparently intended by Nkrumah to compete with the AAPSO for the allegiance of African radical movements.[8]

The boldest call for boundary revisions was issued by the

first AAPC held in Accra in December 1958. It was included in a series of resolutions entitled "Frontiers, Boundaries and Federations." The resolutions under this title were divided into four parts. The first part proclaimed that "the great mass of African peoples are animated by a desire for unity," and that their "ultimate objective" is a "Commonwealth of Free African States." The second part of this resolution called for the establishment of regional federations and groupings of states. The third part of the resolution is of major concern here and will be reviewed below. The fourth part called for various measures to increase and encourage contact between people of different African territories. The text of the third part of the resolution read:

> Whereas artificial barriers and frontiers drawn by imperialists to divide African peoples operate to the detriment of Africans and should therefore be abolished or adjusted;
>
> Whereas frontiers which cut across ethnic groups or divide peoples of the same stock are unnatural and are not conducive to peace or stability;
>
> Whereas leaders of neighbouring countries should cooperate towards a permanent solution of such problems which accords with the best interests of the people affected and enhances the prospects of realisation of the ideal of a Pan-African Commonwealth of Free States;
>
> Whereas the 20th February, 1959, will be an important date in the history of the Cameroons, when a special session of the United Nations General Assembly will discuss the question of unification and independence of the territory;

Be it resolved and it is hereby resolved by the all All-African Peoples Conference that the Conference:

(a) denounces artificial frontiers drawn by imperialist Powers to divide the peoples of Africa, particularly those which cut across ethnic groups and divide people of the same stock;

(b) calls for the abolition or adjustment of such frontiers at an early date;

(c) calls upon the Independent States of Africa to support permanent solution to this problem founded upon the true wishes of the people;

(d) notes with satisfaction that a special session of the United Nations General Assembly will discuss the question of unification and independence of the Cameroons on the 20th February, 1959.

(e) invites all Africans to observe that date as Cameroons Day.[9]

The resolution raises two broad questions: the first about the meaning of the text itself, and the second about the intentions and purposes behind it.

Was the call for the abolition and adjustment of borders intended as an affirmation of a general principle, or was it directed solely at the problem of the Cameroons, to which the resolution refers in the preamble and in the fourth and fifth subparagraphs? The reference to "this problem" in the third subparagraph casts further doubt on the meaning: was "this problem" the problem of the Cameroons, or the general problem of boundaries? While the text of the subparagraph leaves us in doubt, the context of the resolution as a whole, and the other sections of the resolution, which is after all entitled "Frontiers, Boundaries and Federations," suggest that the call for the revision of boundaries was meant to be a general one.

A second question of interpretation concerns the meaning of the call for the abolition of borders. Whatever this may mean, the implication that the political-territorial division of Africa requires revision is clear. The call for the adjustment of borders is interesting since it seems to suggest that the piecemeal revision of boundaries would help to improve relations among neighboring states. This view runs contrary to the argument subsequently used by advocates of the status quo, who compared the initiation of boundary revisions to the opening of Pandora's box.

There were very few references to boundaries in the public speeches at the conference, an omission which could explain the political background and purpose of the resolution. In summarizing the agenda in his opening speech, Nkrumah said that the delegates would be called upon to discuss "the arbitrary divisions on our Continent with their resultant frontier complexities." These, he said, leave behind to be solved, after independence, heavy "legacies of Irredentism and Tribalism."[10] The only other references to boundary problems in the public speeches were by the delegates from Togoland and Cameroon. The Togolese delegate, representing the Juvento party, referred in his speech to the "legitimate rights" of "the people of Western Togoland" and called for the reunification of Togo. This was an oblique reference to former British Togoland, which had by 1958 already been integrated into the national territory of Ghana. The reunification of Cameroon, of which the Cameroonian delegate spoke, also affected a self-governing African country—Nigeria. It seems likely that a deliberate effort was made to avoid discussion of boundary and territorial problems because it was feared that they would arouse controversy, whereas the conference was supposed to engender solidarity and unity.[11]

Why, then, did the conference adopt this resolution, and why was such a resolution ever formulated? Participants and observers at the conference advanced two interpretations. One was that the resolution was merely an expression of a mood and a sentiment, and it did not reflect any particular issues discussed; nor was it meant to espouse a course of action in a specific situation. The other interpretation held that the resolution was a careful and deliberate formulation which reflected the concern of some of the delegates on particular boundary disputes.

In support of the first interpretation it has been pointed out that the conference was a gathering of representatives of political parties, and not of governments. Delegates were free therefore to express sentiments without paying too much attention to the policies and interests of their governments. As representatives of political parties, the delegates were not burdened with the responsibilities of state office. In addition, the atmosphere at the conference was one of enormous

enthusiasm, and for many of the participants it was a great
emotional experience. In this atmosphere, and under these
circumstances, the exact wording of the resolutions was not
carefully considered.

The other interpretation, that the resolution had been carefully formulated, seems more plausible for several reasons. In
addition to the public plenary meetings, the work of the conference was done by committees that met in private throughout the week of the conference. The thrashing out of issues
and problems took place within these committees. Thus the
resolutions, no doubt, constituted a carefully worded compromise between different viewpoints represented in the
committees. In addition, the conference was carefully managed and guided by its Ghanaian organizers. A leading part in
the management of the conference was taken by George
Padmore and Kojo Botsio, who represented the Convention
Peoples Party (CPP) of Ghana. Padmore was Nkrumah's chief
advisor on African affairs, and Botsio happened to be
Ghana's foreign minister. Their contributions reflected not
only the view of Ghana's governing party, but also the considered opinions of Kwame Nkrumah. Indeed, Nkrumah himself is reported to have dominated the conference from
behind the scenes.[12]

An explanation of the purposes behind the resolution is
offered by W. Scott Thompson in his study of Ghana's foreign policy. According to Thompson, "regionalism," namely
the "amalgamation or federation of territories on a regional
basis," had become a major issue of contention at the time of
the conference. Although Nkrumah continued to believe that
the conference ought to advocate "continental unity," and
viewed "regionalism" as an impediment to the attainment of
this ultimate goal, Padmore as well as other associates and
advisors of Nkrumah did not consider the advocacy of "continental unity" to be politically practical. Thompson commented that "Nkrumah could not, in this period, have over-
ridden such strong opposition to his own *simpliste* ideas.
Instead . . . he made certain that regionalism was specified as
an intermediate policy, and that in the end there would be
one united Africa, in which colonial frontiers would be
redrawn or abolished."[13]   The entire resolution on "Fron-

tiers, Boundaries and Federations" can thus be understood as a compromise between Nkrumah and his advisors.

It is still perplexing, however, that the resolution contained a call for the "adjustment" of frontiers. Nkrumah's vision of continental unity accorded only with the *abolition* of borders; the adjustment of borders carried completely different and indeed even contrary implications. A reasonable guess seems to be that the term "adjustment" was introduced by the opponents of "continental unity," with the purpose of watering down the call for the abolition of borders.

In addition to Nkrumah's own adivsors, the call for continental unity was viewed with misgivings also by some of the other delegations present. Among these, some weight was carried by the delegations from independent states, who, like the Ghanaians, performed a dual role: while formally representing nongovernmental organizations, they in fact acted for their governments. For example the head of the Tunisian delegation and member of the steering committee of the conference was Taeb Slim, who was also the Tunisian ambassador to London. The Ethiopian delegation was led by Getachew Mekasha, a senior official of the Ministry of Foreign Affairs.

If delegations were consulted on the phrasing of the resolutions, as they probably were, most of those from independent states could accept the "abolition or adjustment" phrase since it lent itself to interpretations suitable to their various tastes.[14]   It reflected not only the compromise between Nkrumah and his advisors, but also accorded with Nkrumah's ambitions vis à vis French Togo and the Ivory Coast. Support for border adjustments could be interpreted as supporting Moroccan and Tunisian and Egyptian aspirations. The text was also in accord with Ethiopia's attitude,which countered Somali claims to its territory by the suggestion that the best way to unite the Somalis in a single state would be by their incorporation within Ethiopia.

The resolution, as a compromise, was sufficiently ambiguous to enable each independent African state to interpret it in a way compatible with its policies and interests. Nevertheless, the resolution is chiefly remembered for its denunciation of existing borders, and its call for their abolition or adjustment. In this respect it was a victory for revisionism.

THE SANNIQUELLIE CONFERENCE, 1959

The next major landmark in the debate between the conflicting approaches to Pan-Africanism was the meeting between President Tubman of Liberia, President Touré of Guinea, and Prime Minister Nkrumah of Ghana at Sanniquellie, Liberia, in July 1959. It was called at Liberian initiative. The agenda, proposed by Tubman, contained an item on African unity and another on the Cameroons question.

In his opening speech, President Tubman addressed himself to the controversial question of African unity, without linking the problem of unity with the question of boundaries. In contrast to the Liberian president's speech, President Nkrumah referred to border problems twice in his opening speech, both times in the context of African unity. Nkrumah said that the conference should "examine ways and means of undoing the wrongs inflicted upon Africa by eradicating the artificial divisions and boundaries which are responsible for the balkanization of our continent," and that the "artificial boundaries" gave rise to all sorts of irredentist problems.[15]

Whatever the impact of Nkrumah's other arguments, the claim that unity was necessary because the borders gave rise to irredentist conflicts was unsuitable for the occasion. Liberia had only a few months earlier renounced long-standing territorial claims against Guinea, and the two states had settled their border dispute by accepting the status quo. In any event neither the joint communiqué nor the declaration that emerged from the conference made any reference to boundaries, territorial disputes, or irredentist problems. If anything, the declaration implied the preservation of existing boundaries and territorial structures.[16]

ALL-AFRICAN PEOPLES CONFERENCE, TUNIS, 1960

In view of the blanket endorsement of boundary adjustments by the first AAPC in 1958, it is notable that the second conference did not deal with the general problem of boundaries. Yet, in contrast to the first conference, the second conference did not refrain from pronouncing itself on specific inter-African disputes. Under the leadership of the Ghanaian and Guinean delegations, the conference assumed a distinctly radical character and there was less care and effort to arrive at compromises acceptable to all delegations.

The resolution on Somaliland reflected the radical atmosphere at the conference. The raising of Somali claims provoked a reply from the Ethiopian delegate, Getachew Mekasha (who had represented Ethiopia at the first AAPC in Accra as well). In addition to answering some of the Somali arguments, the Ethiopian delegate criticized the Somalis for using the conference as a "propaganda platform," and disturbing "the atmosphere of brotherhood and unity." He concluded by saying that "petty local questions" should not be brought before the conference, which "has more important things to do," and that such questions should be settled amicably between the parties concerned.[17]

The view that the conference should not become involved in disputes between African states for fear of injuring the atmosphere of solidarity and unity had been brought out on other occasions by a number of states, and seemed often to have been accepted. Yet at this conference the Somali view prevailed, and a resolution was adopted expressing support for the Somali struggle "for independence and unity in order to give birth to a bigger Somaliland."[18]   It was adopted over the strenuous objections of the Ethiopian delegation and without a formal vote, the organizers maintaining that voting might detract from the atmosphere of unanimity.

Another boundary question mentioned in the conference resolutions concerned Algeria. In an apparent response to plans current at the time to retain the Sahara under French rule if Algeria became independent, the conference denounced and condemned the "scheme" to partition Algeria and affirmed "the principle of the indivisibility and integrity of Algerian territory."[19]   The problem of Mauritania came up as well, which was soon to become a lively issue in Africa. A resolution on the French community made special mention of Mauritainia along with Chad, Niger, and the Ivory Coast, as countries whose governments were imposed by "electoral trickery."[20]   Morocco's claim to Mauritania was not brought up and in this the AAPC resolution differed markedly from the resolutions adopted by the Afro-Asian Peoples' Solidarity Organization and Casablanca conferences.

No other boundary questions were raised. The resolution on Cameroon this time refrained from endorsing unification, and there was no resolution at all on the Togolese problem.

AFRO-ASIAN PEOPLES' SOLIDARITY ORGANIZATION, CONAKRY, 1960

The second AAPSO conference was held in April 1960, in Conakry. Some seventy delegations participated, most of them representing radical and left-wing parties and organizations. The radical composition of this conference was reflected in its resolutions, which included reference to three African boundary questions: Cameroon, Somalia, and Mauritania.

One resolution welcomed Cameroon's independence (granted on January 1, 1960), but called for United Nations supervision of the forthcoming plebiscite "for reunification."[21]

The resolution on Somaliland supported "the glorious struggle of the Somali people for their freedom, independence, and unification."[22] By implication, the resolution thus endorsed Somali claims to parts of Ethiopia and Kenya. Unlike the AAPC in Tunis three months earlier, the resolution met with no objections: Ethiopia had refrained from sending a delegation. A delegation from Kenya was present, but apparently decided to ignore the implication of the resolution.

Morocco's claim to Mauritania received an indirect endorsement at Conakry. Both the earlier Accra and Tunis AAPC resolutions had made no reference to Moroccan claims. At the first AAPSO conference in Cairo (1957-1958), a resolution on Morocco had been passed, supporting the return to Morocco of areas still dominated by imperialism. At this AAPSO conference at Conakry, the resolution was entitled "Mauritania." Morocco was not mentioned, and the resolution merely denounced "the existence of the artificial Government imposed upon the people by means of falsified elections."[23] Presumably, this resolution was supported by both the Moroccan delegation to the conference and by the delegates of the Nahda party, which was listed as representing

Mauritania. This party was led by Horma Ould Babana, who had fled from Mauritania following his electoral defeat in 1956, and had settled in Morocco. The fact that Mauritania was listed as having a separate delegation, and that there was no explicit mention of Moroccan claims to that territory, reflected the change in Moroccan representation at the conference. At the first AAPSO conference Morocco had been represented by the Democratic Independence party. At the second conference a prominent part was played by Mehdi Ben Barka who had in 1959 left the Istiqlal to lead a radical faction. Ben Barka had subsequently become critical of the irredentist policy of the Moroccan government, which was strongly advocated by the Istiqlal. The absence of a resolution explicitly supporting Morocco's claim to Mauritania can probably be attributed to Ben Barka's views on the problem.

CONFERENCE OF INDEPENDENT STATES, ADDIS ABABA, 1960

At the conference of independent African states in Addis Ababa in June 1960, the debate between Nkrumah and his opponents about their respective interpretations of Pan-Africanism continued to occupy the center of the stage, even though the heads of state were not physically present. The conference was attended by representatives of Algeria, Cameroon, Ethiopia, Ghana, Guinea, Libya, Liberia, Morocco, Nigeria, Somalia, Sudan, Tunisia, and the United Arab Republic. But this time references to specific boundary disputes by a number of delegates provided the setting.

The Moroccan delegate, Ahmed Taibi Ben Hima, secretary general of the Ministry of Foreign Affairs, accused France of being responsible for the deteriorating relations between Morocco and France because of French positions on the evacuation of troops, the frontiers (an oblique reference to the question of the Moroccan-Algerian border), and Mauritania. He claimed that the "Moroccan character" of Mauritania was solidly established; nevertheless, he said, Morocco was prepared to see the question resolved on the basis of the principle of self-determination.[24] The reference to self-determination is interesting, because Morocco avoided using this argument on most other occasions.

A delegation from Somalia, which was to become independent within a few days after the conference, was also present. At this conference Somalia chose to promote its cause on the basis of a general principle, rather than as a special case. Stating the revisionist argument, the Somali minister of education, Mahamoud Yusuf Aden, said: "We find ourselves facing to-day problems of boundaries all over the continent; these will endanger most our African unity . . . These problems should be treated urgently by the interested States in a friendly and cooperative manner in the African spirit and justice.[25]

The contrary view, that peace and African solidarity would be better served by the preservation of existing boundaries, was expressed by the Liberian secretary of state, J. Rudolph Grimes, who warned that attempts to revise borders might lead to conflict and to outside interference:

> It is quite true that the existing boundaries in Africa were made without ethnic, tribal or economic consideration by the colonial powers. Nevertheless, it is also true that these boundaries have existed over a long period of time and it would be difficult to change them without raising more problems than would be solved by such change. In some cases it may not be possible to change them without ill-will, bitterness and perhaps internecine conflicts, which will do us no good in Africa and perhaps cause irreparable harm.
> The Liberian Government suggests that the African States agree to the principle of generally accepting the present boundaries after the various countries become independent as the boundaries between their respective states.[26]

The Liberian viewpoint must be considered not only in the context of the boundary issues raised in the public speeches, but also in the light of the great debate about the meaning of African unity which continued, mainly in private. Ghana did not in its formal public statements link the advocacy of African unity with the specific border problems raised at the conference. But there is some indication that the link was made in private. Writing about the conference, A. K. Barden, who as director of the Bureau of African Affairs was in charge of Ghana's Pan-African activities, stated that Liberia had struck a new and discordant note: "The acceptance of the Liberian formula means in concrete terms the settlement of existing disputes in favor of Mauritania, Togoland, Ethiopia, and against Morocco, Ghana and Somalia. Far from uniting African countries, the Liberian formula permanently estranged them."[27] The conference did not refer to boundary questions in its resolutions, and no formal stand was taken on these matters.

THE MAURITANIAN QUESTION AT THE UNITED NATIONS, AND THE FORMATION OF THE BRAZZAVILLE AND CASABLANCA GROUPS, 1960-1961

Like other French possessions in Africa, Mauritania had become an autonomous republic within the French community in November 1958. With the announcement that Mauritania would attain complete independence on November 28, 1960, Morocco intensified its efforts to win international support for the claim that Mauritania was part of Morocco, and that it ought not to be accorded recognition as an independent state.[28] The debate over Mauritania was not confined to African conferences: the crucial contest was waged at the United Nations, as the question of Mauritania's membership in the organization and, by implication, of the recognition of its sovereign existence, came to the fore.

The Moroccan challenge to the independence of Mauritania produced another split among the newly independent African states, superimposed upon the steadily deepening divisions over the Congo and Algerian problems. These growing differences prompted a group of French-speaking states to convene a conference in Abidjan (October 24-26, 1960), at which an effort for a joint policy to be pursued at the United Nations and elsewhere would be made. The conference's decision to support Mauritania's admission to the United Nations represented the first of a series of moves by the participating states in support of Mauritania's independence. In trying to assess the factors shaping this decision, great weight should be given to French influence and to the solidarity of the participating states with a sister territory of former French West Africa.[29]

The United Nations discussed Mauritania in two ways. The first was as part of a Moroccan attempt to obtain a General Assembly resolution supporting its claim to the territory, and thus to challenge the validity of Mauritania's approaching independence. The other, in the Security Council, concerned Mauritania's admission to membership in the United Nations.

In the General Assembly, in November 1960, Morocco presented a threefold argument—historical, legal, and anti-imperialist—claiming that Mauritania was an artificial state and that its independence would be fictitious. According to Morocco, France had created Mauritania in order to be able to maintain military bases there and to exploit the country's mineral wealth. Furthermore, in an attempt to ride the wave of strong feelings evoked at that time by Congo's problems, Morocco argued that Mauritania was another Katanga.[30]

The Moroccan claims were supported by the majority of Arab states, India, and the Soviet bloc. But in Africa, Morocco received support only from the United Arab Republic, Sudan, and Libya (members of the Arab League), and from Guinea. Guinea's support of Morocco was based mainly on the anti-imperialist argument, on the conclusion that the 1958 referendum had not been properly held, and that the independence being granted to Mauritania was "sham independence."[31]

The African states supporting Mauritania's independence in the General Assembly debate were those that had met in Abidjan, in addition to the Malagasy Republic and Tunisia. These states claimed that in the 1958 referendum the Mauritanian people had exercised their right to self-determination and chosen to create an autonomous republic. Some of them added that for the sake of peace and solidarity in Africa, the general principle should be established that existing borders ought to be maintained.

The attitudes of the remaining African states were reflected to some extent in the vote in the First Committee on a Libyan motion proposing that the interested parties negotiate a peaceful solution to the problem. The motion was clearly pro-Moroccan, since the implication was that Mauritanian independence, only three days away, would not become effective as scheduled. It was supported by Guinea, Libya, and the United Arab Republic, and opposed by the Central African Republic, Chad, Congo (Brazzaville), Congo (Leopoldville), Dahomey, Gabon, Ivory Coast, Madagascar, Niger, Senegal and Upper Volta (Cameroon did not participate in the vote). Eight other African states abstained: Ethiopia, Ghana, Liberia, Mali, Morocco, Nigeria, Togo, and Tunisia.[32]

The votes cast by the African states suggest the importance of previously formed alignments. The majority of the former French territories supported Mauritania. The United Arab Republic and Libya adhered to the Arab League's policy of supporting Morocco. Togo, which refrained from associating itself with the group of French-speaking states that had met in Abidjan, demonstrated its reserve by abstaining. Several states that had previously expressed views on boundary problems in terms of the general principles involved, also abstained. Thus Ethiopia, Liberia, and Nigeria, which were known for their support of the status quo principle, did not participate in the debate, and abstained from the voting.[33] Ghana, basically revisionist, abstained as well.

Conspicuous for its abstention in the General Assembly vote was Tunisia. On the one hand, Tunisia challenged the validity of the boundary delimited by France between Tunisia and Algeria. In addition to its own grievance against the status quo, Tunisia was bound to Morocco by the ideal of Maghreb solidarity to which it had committed itself. Yet Tunisia supported Mauritania's independence and joined with France in the Security Council in sponsoring Mauritania's admission to the United Nations. The Tunisian delegate explained that "the liberation of a part of the African continent should take precedence over any geographical dispute."[34] However, Mauritania's admission to the United Nations was prevented on that occasion by a Soviet veto in the Security Council.

After the Soviet veto on Mauritania's admission, the states that had met in Abidjan in October, with the Malagasy Republic added, convened again (at Brazzaville, from December 15 to 19, 1960), to consider a joint strategy for the next

stage in the three major contests in which they were engaged—
over the Congo, Algeria, and Mauritania. The greatest measure of agreement existed on the Mauritanian issue. On this,
the final communiqué expressed regret at the Soviet veto,
and invited "all African States anxious for the liberty and
dignity of Africa, and anxious to avoid the cold war on our
continent, to redouble their efforts for the admission of
Mauritania."[35]

If the Mauritanian problem contributed to the crystallization of the Brazzaville grouping, it contributed even more to
the formation of the rival Casablanca group—Ghana, Guinea,
Libya, Mali, Morocco, the United Arab Republic, the Algerian provisional government, and Ceylon—which had held its
conference in Casablanca from January 3 to January 7, 1961.

But while the Brazzaville states agreed on most issues, the
states meeting at Casablanca differed in their ideological
orientation, as well as in their internal and foreign policies.

Morocco convened the conference largely because of the
Mauritanian problem, yet the participants had previously differed in their attitudes toward this very problem. The United
Arab Republic, Libya, and Guinea had sided with Morocco;
Ghana and Mali had, on the other hand, displayed an equivocal attitude—they had abstained from voting in the United
Nations, yet they had recognized Mauritania's independence.
In a telegram announcing Ghana's recognition of Mauritania,
a few weeks after independence, Nkrumah expressed a desire
to establish diplomatic relations.[36] However, it is unlikely
that Morocco would have convened the conference, had it
not been assured in advance of the support of the participants on the Mauritanian question.

Such support Morocco indeed obtained, in the form of a
resolution on Mauritania adopted by the conference. Ghana
and Mali voted for the resolution as part of a general bargain
in which concessions were traded on a number of issues on
which the participants differed, including the Congo and
Israel. Mali's acceptance of the Moroccan thesis on Mauritania probably did not pose much difficulty, as Mali was
itself involved in a border dispute with Mauritania. Ghana's
acceptance was in line with its policy of solidarity with Mali,
which had joined the Ghana-Guinea "union" only the pre-

vious month. Ghana's support can also be understood in the light of Nkrumah's single-minded effort to win acceptance of his Congo policy. This required that Ghana subscribe not only to Arab views on Israel, but also to Morocco's views on Mauritania.

The resolution on Mauritania by the Casablanca conference stated that France had severed from Morocco the southern part of its territory and set up a puppet state. The conference approved "any action taken by Morocco on Mauritania for the restitution of her legitimate rights."[37]

The charter adopted by the conference did not endorse the principle of respect for the territorial integrity of states in general. Instead, it declared the resolve of the signatories to safeguard "the sovereignty and territorial integrity of *our* States."[38] Nothing was said about the revision of borders, but the condemnation of "artificial states," included in the resolution on Mauritania, seems to carry the implication that boundary revisions were desirable, or at least acceptable.

As a sequel to the Casablanca conference, the foreign ministers of the member states (with the exception of Libya and Ceylon), met in Cairo in May 1961, to sign the Protocol of the Casablanca Charter. All the issues discussed in Casablanca in January were mentioned again in a communiqué but with one important omission—Mauritania. Yet the Casablanca position on Mauritania was reiterated at the next regular meeting of the Casablanca powers in June 1962.

For their part, the Brazzaville powers repeated the call for the admission of Mauritania to the United Nations at the Yaoundé (March 1961) and Tananarive (September 1961) conferences, and a similar call came from the Monrovia group in May 1961.[39]

When the United Nations Assemby resumed its fifteenth session in April 1961, the twelve members of the Brazzaville group submitted a draft resolution declaring that Mauritania ought to be admitted to membership, and requesting the Security Council to take note of this view.[40] A Soviet amendment proposed linking the admission of Mauritania with that of Outer Mongolia. The amended resolution was adopted by the General Assembly, with the Casablanca group splitting on this vote: Morocco, the United Arab Republic,

and Guinea voted against the resolution, with Ghana and Mali
abstaining. Two additional African states, Libya and Sudan
(both members of the Arab League), joined the opposition to
Mauritania's admission. All other African states voted in
favor of the resolution.[41]

When the matter was taken up again by the Security
Council in October, the admission of Mauritania was spon-
sored by Liberia and France. The other African member of
the Security Council, the United Arab Republic, was the only
country to cast a vote against Mauritania's admission.[42]
Mauritania's admission was finally confirmed by the General
Assembly in October 1961 by a vote of 68 to 13 with 20
abstentions. This time Mali cast a negative vote, thus joining
Libya, Morocco, Sudan, the United Arab Republic, and
Guinea, who had voted against Mauritania's admission in
April. In explaining his country's position, the representative
of Mali stated that Mali had recognized Mauritania's independence, but he accused the new state of responsibility for
border incidents which, according to the Malian representative, indicated that Mauritania was not a peace-loving state,
and therefore, not eligible for membership. Ghana, the
remaining member of the Casablanca group, abstained in the
vote, as did Congo (Leopoldville). The debate also provided
an occasion for the affirmation of principles. Thus the Ivory
Coast delegate, explaining his support for Mauritania's admission to the United Nations, called for the acceptance of the
territorial status quo in Africa.[43]

INCONSISTENCIES IN THE BOUNDARY PROBLEM

The positions adopted by African states on the boundary and
territorial questions of Congo, Cameroon, and West New
Guinea, which came to the fore simultaneously with the Mauritanian problem, indicate that there was no consistent
approach to the principles of revision or to the maintenance
of the status quo. On the Mauritanian issue the Brazzaville
states supported the status quo, and the Casablanca states
implicitly supported revisionism; their respective policies on
the Congo implied the reverse of these positions.

At first, the independent African states adopted a common

policy on the Congo. At the Leopoldville conference (August 25-31, 1960) they proclaimed the "necessity of maintaining the *unity* and territorial *integrity*" of Congo and condemned secession.[44] The first split in African ranks occurred after the break between Kasavubu and Lumumba, on September 5, 1960. The Brazzaville states adopted a conciliatory attitude toward the secessionist regime of Moise Tshombe in Katanga. In addition to the various forms of diplomatic support by members of the group, notably Congo (Brazzaville) and the Malagasy Republic, their attitude was reflected in conference resolutions. Thus, the Brazzaville conference made no reference to the Congo's territorial integrity. The Monrovia conference in May 1961 (at which the Brazzaville states played an important role), confined itself to calling on all African states "to desist from such activities as the hasty recognition of breakaway regimes." This could be interpreted as directed equally against the recognition of the Gizenga regime in Stanleyville and against the recognition of Katanga's secession. The Brazzaville and Monrovia attitudes contrasted with the specific support by the Casablanca states for Congo's territorial integrity, both in Casablanca in January 1961 and in Cairo in May of the same year.[45]

In fact, neither camp was motivated by any fundamental principles they may have held on boundaries. The antagonism of the Casablanca powers toward Tshombe stemmed from their view that he promoted neocolonialist interests. The Brazzaville group's more tolerant attitude stemmed from President Youlou's antagonism toward the Leopoldville government, the origins of which can probably be traced to Bakongo tribal politics.

Attitudes on the question of Cameroon's unification also deserve notice. Paradoxically, the most persistent supporters of reunification were radical nongovernmental organizations and the Brazzaville states. The radical groups expressed their support at the first AAPSO conference, (December 1957-January 1958) and at the third AAPC in Cairo in March 1961. The later resolution protested against the "division" of the country, and against "frauds" Britain had allegedly perpetrated in the referendum (by which the Northern British

Cameroons had chosen to unite with Nigeria).[46] While the
Casablanca states accepted the results of the referendum, the
Brazzaville states tried to have them declared invalid.

Although the attitudes of the radical organizations and of
the Brazzaville states appeared similar, they stemmed from
different considerations. The support of the radical group for
reunification was a result of their association with the Union
of the Peoples of Cameroon (UPC), outlawed in the Cameroon Republic. The UPC was a fervent advocate of restoring
"Kamerun" to its pre-World War I boundaries. The Brazzaville states were motivated by their solidarity with Cameroon,
a member of the group, which persisted in its claim for
reunification.

Another inconsistency can also be discerned in the attitudes of the Brazzaville states to the question of West New
Guinea (West Irian). This was not an African problem, but it
raised the question of colonial boundaries. Indonesia had
claimed West Irian on the grounds that it had been part of
the Dutch domain, and that it was separated from Indonesia
at the time of independence. The Netherlands, on the other
hand, argued that the people of the territory ought to be permitted to exercise their right of self-determination. When the
question was debated at the United Nations in 1961, the
African states were divided. The radical states supported
Indonesia's claim; the Brazzaville states favored self-determination. The applicability of self-determination was explained
by the delegate from the Central African Republic, who said
that the preservation of the borders of a colonial entity was
justified in some cases, but not where racial and cultural differences existed.[47] This was a surprising argument for an
African state to make, and it was not repeated. The attitude
of the Brazzaville states can perhaps be explained by their
desire to maintain harmonious relations with the Netherlands
at the time of the negotiations over their association with the
European Economic Community. In the same way, the support of the radical states for Indonesia's position came more
from their solidarity with Indonesia's radical orientation, than
from their concern with the principles of boundary questions.[48]

ALL-AFRICAN PEOPLES CONFERENCE, CAIRO, 1961

To the extent that the Cairo conference considered any guiding principles on boundaries, it declared itself against "balkanization as a deliberate political fragmentation of States by creation of artificial entities."[49] Yet this opposition to balkanization was not tantamount to support for the territorial status quo. Rather, inter-African disputes were interpreted according to the ideological position of the parties involved. The conference resolutions reflected the upsurge of radicalism. Thus, Mauritania was viewed as neocolonialist. By implication, in this case, the conference opposed the preservation of colonial borders. The conferences's support for the claim of the Union of the Peoples of Cameroon to reunify the two Cameroons was also implicitly revisionist. On the other hand, by opposing Katanga's secession from Congo and Buganda's separation from Uganda, the conference supported the preservation of the territorial entities established by colonial partition.

A dramatic confrontation at the conference involved Ethiopia. Despite strenuous Ethiopian objections the conference accorded observer status to an Eritrean group advocating the separation of Eritrea from Ethiopia. On the other hand, the conference refrained from supporting Somali claims. When a Somali delegate criticized Ethiopia in his speech the proceedings became tumultuous, as other delegations joined Ethiopia in protesting that the conference should not become a platform for airing inter-African disputes. Despite Somali demands that the conference endorse again the support given to Somali aims by the preceding conference at Tunis, in January 1960, and by the AAPC steering committee in January 1961, the resolutions omitted any mention of the Somali problem.[50] Since Somalia was not identified with the radical orientation in inter-African politics, Ethiopia, which enjoyed considerable prestige in Africa, carried greater weight. Not wishing to offend Ethiopia again, having already done so by admitting the Eritrean separatists to the conference, the conference accepted the Ethiopian viewpoint.

MONROVIA CONFERENCE, 1961

The coalition against the radical Casablanca group was greatly strengthened by the Monrovia Conference, from May 8 to 12, 1961. It was atteneded by twenty states: Liberia, Togo, Ethiopia, Somalia, Sierra Leone, Nigeria, Libya, Tunisia, and the twelve Brazzaville states.

The two major problems on the agenda, Congo and Algeria, prompted much debate, but the harmony necessary for the formation of an anti-Casablanca coalition was threatened by the prospect of disagreements over three territorial problems: Katanga's secession, Cameroon's unification, and the Somali-Ethiopian dispute.

Disagreement on Katanga's secession was successfully avoided by the formula of calling on African states to desist from "the hasty recognition of breakaway regimes in the Republic of the Congo," which could be interpreted as being directed equally against the Gizenga government in Stanleyville and Tshombe's in Elisabethville. Agreement on this formula was facilated by the absence of President Youlou of Congo (Brazzaville), who was suddenly taken ill in Monrovia and thus prevented from advocating Tshombe's case. As for the problem of Cameroon, President Ahidjo accepted the entreaties of his Brazzaville group colleagues not to press the issue, so as not to antagonize Nigeria, whose active membership in the new Monrovia grouping was considered essential.

The Somali problem remained. Somalia first demanded that its dispute with Ethiopia be included in the agenda of the conference. Ethiopia objected, questioning the competence of the conference to discuss the issue. Since Somalia threatened to leave, a compromise was reached whereby specific disputes would not be included on the agenda, but border problems could be discussed under a general heading, "Working Out General Principles for the Settlement of Frontier and Border Disputes which may arise from the Emergence of Independent States."

In view of Somalia's vigorous advocacy of its case, it was impossible for the Monrovia conference to accept the principle of respect for the territorial status quo, which had been proposed by Liberia at the Addis Ababa conference in June

1960. Even a draft resolution recommending the peaceful settlement of disputes and the establishment of a commission that would be attached to the proposed Organization of African and Malagasy States, met with objections from Somalia, who demanded a specific resolution on the Somali-Ethiopian dispute. The compromise agreed upon was that the conference would appeal to Somalia and Ethiopia to renew their efforts for settlement. The Somalis declared themselves satisfied because, in their view, the existence of the dispute had been internationally recognized.[51]

The conference also adopted a resolution on cooperation to achieve unity, listing several principles to govern the relationship between states. Among these principles was "respect for the sovereignty of each State and its inalienable right to existence and development of its personality."[52] There was no mention, either here or elsewhere, of the principle of "respect for the territorial integrity of states," a principle often present in declarations of this nature.

THE CONFERENCE OF THE NONALIGNED, BELGRADE, 1961

The Conference of Nonaligned States which met in Belgrade, September 1-6, 1961, was not a conference of African states only, but attempts were made there to raise the Somali and Mauritanian disputes. The conference also tried to codify norms for interstate conduct.

At the Cairo preparatory conference (June 5-12, 1961), Somalia had suggested that the agenda for the discussion of imperialism and colonialism include the Somali problem. This failed to win support. At the Belgrade conference itself, the Somali president's speech contained a thinly veiled reference to Somali territorial claims:

> While on the subject of unwarranted intervention in the internal affairs of other States may I point out that it would be most unfortunate and inequitable if the legitimate territorial claims of one State against another were to be interpreted as unwarranted intervention and disapproved of on that ground.[53]

In his speech, King Hassan of Morocco mentioned his own
country's claims to Mauritania and to Spanish Sahara. The
king linked the claims to a general anticolonial theme, saying
that colonial infringements on the territorial integrity of
states was a threat to security and peace. He did not, however, mention Morocco's claims from Algeria. As Algeria's
struggle for independence enjoyed warm sympathy among
the participants, raising the claim against Algeria on this
occasion could have boomeranged and harmed Morocco's
own position.[54]

The attempts to raise the Somali and Mauritanian issues
were drowned in silence. The majority of the participants
held that the conference should not concern itself with bilateral matters. Nevertheless, two of the conference's resolutions touched upon boundary problems. Regarding Algeria,
in an apparent reference to suggestions that France retain
control of the Sahara if Algeria attained independence, the
conference expressed support "for the integrity of her
national territory including the Sahara." A more general
theme was struck with reference to the General Assembly's
resolution on decolonization. Expressing support for the
United Nations resolution, the conference said that "the
participating countries respecting scrupulously the territorial
integrity of all states oppose by all means any aims of annexation by other nations."[55]

THE LAGOS CONFERENCE, 1962

A significant aspect of the Lagos meeting of the Monrovia
group (January 25-30, 1962) was the emphasis placed upon
the principle of respect for existing borders. The theme was
introduced by Nnamdi Azikiwe, then governor-general of
Nigeria. After outlining similarities in the principles ennunci-
ated by the Monrovia and Casablanca groups, Azikiwe singled
out one important difference: the conspicuous absence of a
specific declaration by the Casablanca powers recognizing the
right of African states, as at present constituted, to legal
equality, to self-determination, to safety from interference in
their internal affairs, and to the inviolability of their territories from external aggression.[56]

Emphasizing their own position, the Monrovia states affirmed the principle of respect for the territorial status quo in the charter of the Inter-African and Malagasy Organization, adopted at the Lagos conference. Article 3 of the charter affirmed the principles of the organization, among them, "respect for the sovereignty and territorial integrity of each State." Article 5 stated that "each State has the right of defence of its territorial integrity."[57]

Characteristically, upon his return from Lagos the Somali prime minister chose to emphasize that portion of the charter which contained an agreement to establish a Permanent Conciliation Commission (Article 28) to which Somalia's disputes with the neighboring states could be referred for settlement.[58] This may have helped the government domestically since it implied that the Somali case had progressed at the conference. It also served to record the Somali interpretation of the charter as providing a machinery for peaceful change rather than legitimizing the territorial status quo. The majority of the other states had attached greater importance to the status quo.

CONFERENCE OF THE AFRO-ASIAN PEOPLES' SOLIDARITY ORGANIZATION, MOSHI, 1963

The third AAPSO conference, held at Moshi, Tanzania, from February 4 to 11, 1963, was marked by intense rivalry between Russia and China, and hostility between China and India. A few months before the conference, the Sino-Indian border dispute had erupted into a brief war. Much effort had to be invested to prevent these tensions and several other conflicts from disrupting the conference. In their attempt to preserve at least the outward appearance of solidarity, the organizers and the Tanzanian hosts worked hard to prevent quarrels among Asian and African countries from marring the proceedings. Thus, according to one observer, a delegation from French Somaliland "was discouraged from denouncing Ethiopia," and "a Somali argument with Kenya over the NFD was not allowed to be placed on the agenda."[59]

No Ethiopian delegates attended the conference, but the close links between the Tanzanian and Kenyan leaders, and

the presence of a strong Kenyan delegation led by Oginga
Odinga and Tom Mboya prevented the conference from
showing any sympathy for Somali claims against neighboring
states.

The case of French Somaliland was different. That territory
was considered to be under colonial rule, and the conference
adopted a resolution supporting its independence. The resolution actually went further than supporting independence, as
the phrasing implied recognition of the Somali character of
the territory, a contentious issue in the dispute over the territory's future.[60]

Although the conference did not consider the general question of the validity of the borders inherited from the colonial
period, in two of its acts it gave some implied support for
boundary revisions. In its concern to avoid antagonizing
China, the conference refrained from supporting the Indian
thesis concerning the Sino-Indian border dispute, which
rested essentially on the status quo. Instead, the conference
adopted a recommendation (as distinct from a resolution),
expressing the hope that the dispute be settled by negotiations.[61]

A resolution on treaties concluded by colonial powers cast
doubt still further on the validity of existing borders. The
resolution was not aimed at undermining the borders, but
rather at what had come to be called "neocolonialism." Yet
the blanket statement that "agreements or treaties signed
under pressure . . . or, in general, before a truly representative
government was freely elected by the people prior to the
departure of the colonial power, should not be considered as
binding on the liberated peoples," implicitly called into question existing boundaries.[62]

THE FUNCTIONS OF THE CONFERENCES IN
BOUNDARY POLITICS

The conferences concerned themselves with African politics
in a broad sense. Competition for influence among states and
ideological differences over the shaping of Africa's future
were the two central themes. To the extent that the problem
of attitudes toward existing colonial boundaries arose at all,

it was in the context of the debate over conflicting interpretations of Pan-Africanism. The question of principle—whether existing borders ought to be retained or altered, did not arise on its own merit. Neither was the principle linked to the individual border and territorial disputes that were brought before the conferences.

Territorial and boundary questions did not serve as rallying points for any durable alignments. The positions adopted by the participants toward the border and territorial disputes raised at the conferences was determined either by their adherence to previously formed alignments, or by a bargain involving other issues. To be sure, the Mauritanian problem was one of the issues over which the rival Brazzaville and Casablanca blocs were formed. But the solidarity of the Brazzaville states predated the emergence of the Mauritanian problem. On the other hand, Ghana's support for Morocco over Mauritania at Casablanca was part of a bargain involving Congo and other issues, and was not made with reference to any general policy on boundary and territorial questions. Even states that shared a common interest in promoting revisionist principles failed to form an alignment: Morocco and Somalia did not join each other. Similarly, Ghana's support for Moroccan and Somali irredentism was equivocal and short-lived.

It is difficult to assess the value of conference resolutions as propaganda weapons, or their usefulness in the legitimization of claims and policies. Success or failure to obtain a resolution at a conference had some effect on the internal standing of governments and political parties, but whether and how much they helped to encourage the supporters of a cause and to discourage opponents is impossible to assess.

Conferences of states were more cautious in expressing revisionist sentiments than were conferences of political parties. Only Morocco's claim to Mauritania received support at African governmental gatherings, though other claims, as well as the desirability of boundary revisions in general, received some support at AAPC and AAPSO gatherings. In addition, as the number of independent states increased, even AAPC and AAPSO meetings reduced their support of revisionist causes.

The effectiveness of resolutions in legitimizing claims and policies depended upon the prestige and standing of the conferences in the eyes of diverse audiences. In other words, resolutions bearing the imprint of radical states, such as those of the Casablanca conference, and AAPC and AAPSO resolutions, had an impact upon groups and parties favorably predisposed to radical causes, which were interested in the legitimization of revolutionary ideas. On the other hand, forces favoring the status quo regarded radical resolutions as designed to serve selfish or subversive interests, and considered the resolutions supporting the status quo as possessing normative value.

Chapter 4   *Norms and Politics: The Confirmation of the Status Quo*

With the establishment of the Organization of African Unity in May 1963, the style of inter-African relations changed. Now there existed an organization with a very wide African membership which included all the black African states.[1] Although the OAU's pre-eminent status among African organizations was not immediately accepted, its very existence and broad membership gave rise to expectations and hopes.[2] One widely shared hope was that African problems would henceforth be dealt with by an African forum, which would facilitate the handling of problems within the political and normative context of African solidarity.

The desire to tackle African problems in the Pan-African spirit was related not only to the mistrust of external influences common among African statesmen; it stemmed also from deeper reservations toward the politics, norms, and principles of international law current in the western world. Africans hoped that they would set their own norms for the conduct of interstate relations, norms which would derive their validity not from the custom and laws of the older established states, but from African organizations and conferences, in conformity with the ideals of Pan-Africanism. Many of these expectations focused on the Organization of African Unity.[3]

The preceding chapter noted that the conferences and organizations were generally reticent on general principles, but that they frequently adopted positions regarding specific issues. We have also seen how the effect of their resolutions was much impaired by the conspicuously factional character of some of the organizations and conferences.

The OAU did not suffer from the same handicaps. Although not always high, its prestige was nevertheless markedly higher than that of most of the organizations and conferences preceding it. Furthermore, its members assigned to it a norm-creating role. Significantly, the OAU refrained from pronouncing judgment on specific issues and disputes. On the other hand, both in its charter and in subsequent resolutions, the OAU explicitly undertook to formulate general principles and norms.

To be sure, the formulation of principles was prompted by specific state interests. The new states sought to relate their own concerns to general principles, and to give selfish goals the appearance of being in the interests of the African community of states. The strategies of states pursuing territorial claims and states seeking to preserve what they had were asymmetric. In seeking legitimization, revisionist states argued the specific merits of their case and hoped to shape the OAU into an instrument for effecting the particular change they sought. The states on the defensive sought to relate their predicament to more general concerns by arguing that the revision of boundaries would open a Pandora's box of troubles; they worked for the proclamation by the OAU of a general norm calling for the preservation of existing boundaries.[4]

THE ORGANIZATION OF AFRICAN UNITY

The charter. When the Conference of Independent African States met in Addis Ababa, in May 1963, several events served to remind the assembled dignitaries that borders posed pressing and urgent problems. One was the absence of King Hassan of Morocco from the conference, in protest against the participation of Mauritania, which Morocco still claimed as part of its territory. The intrusion of the Somali dispute into conference lobbying and proceedings was another reminder. Since it appeared possible that because of the near universal attendance the resolutions of this conference might be ascribed particular weight, the interested parties campaigned vigorously to obtain support for their cause. Somalia requested the inclusion in the agenda of the preparatory meeting of foreign ministers, held in Addis Ababa, of an item entitled: "General consideration of the question of territorial disputes between neighboring African countries, and the need of establishing effective machinery to examine and settle such territorial disputes."[5] The foreign ministers' conference was also reminded of Somali territorial aspirations in the Somali foreign minister's speech.

At the summit conference itself the Somali president explained the Somali case, arguing that the problem was "unique" because "unlike any other border problem in Africa," the entire length of Somalia's boundaries cut across grazing grounds and divided the people. The speech brought forth a sharp reply from the prime minister of Ethiopia. Characteristically, he dwelt upon the common interest in the preservation of the status quo, saying that many African states would cease to exist if boundaries were redrawn on religious, racial, and linguistic grounds. Therefore, he concluded, "it is in the interest of all Africans now to respect the frontiers drawn on the maps, whether they are good or bad, by the former colonizers."[6]

Kenya, not yet independent, was represented at the conference by a delegation of the Kenya African National Union (KANU). It distributed a memorandum attacking the Somali government's support for the secession of the Somali-inhabited Northern Frontier District (NFD) from Kenya as "following . . . Tshombe's footsteps," as tribalist, and as threatening the territorial integrity of all states.[7]

In addition to the Somali dispute, the Moroccan-Mauritanian dispute was also mentioned in the public debate. In referring to his country's dispute with Morocco, President Ould Daddah of Mauritania declared Mauritania's willingness to establish friendly relations with Morocco, provided Morocco recognized Mauritania's independence and sovereignty (or in other words, abandoned its claim).[8]

Other heads of state also referred in their speeches to the general problem of boundaries. Nkrumah spoke of frontier problems as an argument for a political union on a conti-

nental scale, saying that "only African Unity can heal this
festering sore of boundary disputes between our various
states."[9] The presidents of Mali and the Malagasy Republic,
and the prime minister of Nigeria, on the other hand, argued
that the existing borders should be maintained. In the words
of Modibo Keita, the president of Mali: "we must take Africa
as it is, and we must renounce any territorial claims, if we do
not wish to introduce what we might call black imperialism
in Africa . . . African unity demands of each one of us complete respect for the legacy that we have received from the
colonial system, that is to say; maintenance of the present
frontiers of our respective states."[10]

The advocacy of the status quo by the president of Mali
was particularly interesting in view of the fact that Mali had
itself challenged the boundaries it had inherited at independence, and had claimed certain territories from Mauritania.
The Mali-Mauritanian dispute had been settled only three
months before the conference in an agreement that had satisfied most of Mali's territorial claims.

Despite the attention that the problem of the borders received, no explicit reference to borders was included in the
charter of the OAU adopted at this conference, nor in any of
the conference resolutions.[11] Probably opinions on the subject were too sharply divided. As the participants of the conference regarded the adoption of the charter as their prime
objective, nothing was attempted that could have prevented
its unanimous approval. Nevertheless, some of the provisions
of the charter suggest the general trend of thought about
border problems and territorial claims. The organization as
set up at Addis Ababa is one of sovereign and equal states, a
principle emphasized in Article 3. According to T. O. Elias,
the Nigerian jurist who participated in the drafting of the
charter, the immediate reason for this provision was that a
few of the small states felt misgivings over the intentions of
some large neighbors, especially in matters concerning frontier disputes.[12] The commitment of member states to respect
the sovereignty and territorial integrity of each other is clearly set forth, and emphasized throughout. The preamble affirms the determination to safeguard and consolidate the
independence "as well as the sovereignty and territorial integ-

rity" of member states. The defense of "their sovereignty, their territorial integrity and independence" is listed among the purposes of the organization, as defined in Article 2. And among the principles of the organization in Article 3 is "respect for the sovereignty and territorial integrity of each state."

The 1964 resolution. The second OAU summit conference took place in Cairo in July 1964. In the months preceding this meeting, the OAU had been called upon, under urgent and dramatic circumstances, to intervene in the Algerian-Moroccan war and in the Somali disputes. The OAU seemed to have withstood these initial tests well.* Both disputes were scheduled for further discussion at the Cairo summit meeting. In addition, a new dispute, between Ghana and Upper Volta, was placed on the agenda of the conference. Although not referred to the OAU, a third dispute, between Dahomey and Niger, contributed to the feeling that border disputes had come to plague interstate relations in Africa.

Under the impact of these events, which struck many African leaders as seriously impeding the quest for Pan-African solidarity, an initiative was taken to have the OAU affirm explicitly and more strongly the principle, already embodied in its charter, concerning the preservation of the territorial status quo. When the assembly of Heads of State and Government convened, it had on its agenda the item proposed by Tanzania, entitled "The Study of Ways and Means Which May Help to Avoid New Disputes Among African States."

Why Tanzania took this step is not entirely clear, but several observations can be made. First, Tanzania's elite was very much aware of the Somali problem, because close links existed between Tanzania and Kenya, and because Tanzania contained an articulate Somali community. Second, Tanzania supported the preservation of existing boundaries not because of any general preference for the status quo, but because Tanzanian leaders believed at that time, that "there are more urgent things to do than to redraw them."[13] Third, Emperor Haile Selassie had visited Dar es Salaam in June, several weeks

*For a discussion of OAU's role in the Somali conflicts see Chapter 9, and for the Moroccan-Algerian dispute see Chapter 10.

before the Cairo conference, in the course of a tour which had also taken him to Kenya and Uganda. It is possible that the initiative for a new OAU resolution on boundaries had been discussed during his visit.

The topic proposed by Tanzania was brought up for the consideration of the Assembly of Heads of State and Government without having first gone to the Council of Ministers. This procedure was adopted by its sponsors in order to avoid complications, and to lessen the possibility that the proposal might become bogged down in committees. At the actual conference of Heads of State itself, the atmosphere was certainly influenced by the disputes that had been aired in the Council of Ministers a few days earlier: the Moroccan-Algerian dispute, the Ghana-Upper Volta dispute, and a Somali complaint against the Ethiopian-Kenyan defense treaty. Concern over territorial disputes was also expressed in several of the formal speeches delivered at the public sessions of the Assembly. Prime Minister Kenyatta proclaimed that there was an urgent need to draw up a special charter that would bind the signatories to preserve the territorial status quo. The prime minister of Sierra Leone expressed regret that the charter did not contain an explicit affirmation of the territorial status quo; he suggested that member states enter into agreements with their neighbors defining the borders between them, and that the agreements be based on the principle of the acceptance of the borders as they existed on the date of independence. President Nkrumah said that thus far territorial disputes had been smothered and not settled. He warned that additional disputes were likely to develop, and that the only permanent solution for such problems was through the establishment of a continental union.[14]

The prospect that the item proposed by Tanzania might lead to a resolution affirming the territorial status quo prompted the Somali government to diplomatic activity in an attempt to block such a move. Somali efforts on the eve of the conference had been reflected in a message from President Osman to President Nasser, who was host to the conference. Stating that he was prevented by a government crisis from attending the conference, the Somali president asked Nasser to ensure that legitimate Somali interests not be adversely affected by an attempt to introduce such a resolution. He also warned that the Somali Republic would not consider itself bound by any such resolution.

Subsequently, when the summit convened, the Somali foreign minister warned in his speech that it was dangerous to believe that territorial disputes could be avoided by declarations of high-sounding principles. At a later session, the foreign minister tried to prevent the adoption of the resolution. He protested that it had been added to the agenda at the last moment, and asked that it be deleted. He argued that it would be more appropriate to discuss the question of disputes in connection with the draft protocol of the Commission of Mediation, Conciliation and Arbitration, which the Assembly of Heads of State had before it. Finally, he called the assembly's attention to the text of the agreement reached a few days earlier between the representatives of Somalia, Ethiopia, and Kenya, to delete from the agenda the item concerning the Somalia-Ethiopia and Somalia-Kenya disputes, which included a provision that no action would be taken by any of the three parties that could prejudice future bilateral talks.[15]

The discussion on the Tanzanian proposal took place behind closed doors. Morocco, which had territorial claims of its own, was reported to have expressed reservations about the proposed resolution. Nkrumah argued that the "corollary to the principle of respect for frontiers" should be the activation of the Commission of Mediation, Conciliation and Arbitration.[16] His linking of the two was significant since the commission had been envisaged by some as not merely a peacemaking body, but also as providing machinery for peaceful change.*

The Somali and Moroccan objections and reservations notwithstanding, the resolution enjoyed the overwhelming support of the heads of state present, and was adopted by acclamation. The Somalis commented bitterly that it had all taken only forty minutes. The preamble to the resolution stated that border problems were a factor of dissension, that there

---

*By the end of 1970 no use had been made of the machinery provided by the commission in any of the disputes which had beset African states.

were external maneuvers aimed at dividing African states, and that "the borders of African States, on the date of their independence, constitute a tangible reality."[17] Furthermore, the preamble called attention to paragraph 3 of Article 3 of the charter, which bound member states to respect the sovereignty and territorial integrity of each state. The operative part of the resolution was brief. It reaffirmed "the strict respect" of member states "for the principles laid down in paragraph 3 of Article III of the Charter . . . " And it "solemnly declares that all Member States pledge themselves to respect the borders existing on their achievement of national independence."

The resolution suffered from several weaknesses. One was that Somalia, a state most directly concerned, declared that it did not feel bound by it. This position was proclaimed on a number of occasions: in the speech of the Somali foreign minister to the Assembly of Heads of State and Government before the resolution was adopted and in subsequent statements by him, in a formal communication to the secretary-general of the OAU dated August 1, 1964, and in a resolution of the Somali National Assembly.[18] In addition to the objections made at the Cairo summit Somalia raised some questions of interpretation. It argued, for example, that the resolution was not applicable to its disputes with Ethiopia and Kenya since it had been introduced under an agenda item referring in its title to "new" disputes between African states. Moreover, Nyerere's explanatory remarks that the resolution was intended as a guide for the future and "should not prejudice any discussion already in progress" were interpreted by Somalia as an indication of intent to exempt Somalia's disputes with Ethiopia and Kenya from being affected by the resolution.[19] There was, however, nothing in the text of the resolution to sustain such an interpretation.

Other weaknesses were inherent in the resolution's text. By the resolution, member states pledged themselves "to respect the borders existing on their achievement of national independence." Under this formula, some states, notably Ethiopia, Morocco, and Liberia, could presumably claim territories that had been theirs during their independent existence prior to the colonial partition at the end of the nineteenth century. This was indeed the essence of Moroccan claims. Moreover, there was nothing in the resolution that might help to resolve disputes arising from different interpretations of documents defining the border, as was the case in the Ghana-Upper Volta or Dahomey-Niger disputes.

Finally, the absence of anything in the resolution on the question of self-determination deserves notice. The intent of the resolution was presumably to stabilize the status quo by legitimizing not only existing colonial borders, but also the membership of peoples in states into which they had been "fenced in" by the colonial borders. A logical corollary of the resolution would be that attempts to change the status quo by groups claiming the right of self-determination were to be rejected. Yet the omission of any reference in the resolution to problems of this nature seemed to have left this question open.[20] Nevertheless, when real issues arose, such as claims for self-determination and secession by Biafra and the southern Sudan, the OAU adhered rigidly to the principles of status quo and the inapplicability of self-determination.

CONFERENCE OF THE NONALIGNED, CAIRO, 1964

Held in Cairo from October 5 to 10, 1964, the conference of nonaligned states was the first major gathering of the leaders of these nations since the Belgrade conference in 1961. Fifty-five states participated; twenty-eight of them were African.[21]

The border and territorial disputes in Africa and India's involvement in a territorial dispute with China rendered a discussion of boundaries almost inevitable. However, as any general pronouncements on boundaries were bound to have implications for the interests of several of the participants, the issue aroused some controversy.

Most of the work of the conference was done in committees and through informal consultation, but the debate over the phrasing of the final resolutions was reflected also in the addresses at the plenary sessions. In his speech, on October 7, the Somali president blamed Somalia's strained relations with its neighbors upon the legacy of the colonial borders and proclaimed that the problem would not be solved "until the Somali people, a nation bound by the strongest links of race, tradition, culture, language and religion, are allowed to achieve their unity in the exercise of their right of self-determination.'' Speaking on self-determination, he further warned against adopting double standards whereby ''we follow certain precepts of action for the purpose of ejecting the colonialist powers and yet refuse to follow them when our own conduct is in question.''[22]

The president's speech also referred to the question of military pacts and foreign bases, the role of the United Nations in peacekeeping, and French Somaliland. All these questions were, he felt, related to the Somali dispute with Ethiopia and Kenya. The president's reference to the peacekeeping activities of the United Nations apparently reflected Somalia's desire at that time for some form of international presence along its border with Ethiopia. The same questions were raised again by the Somali delegation in the working sessions of the Political Committee.[23] Somali criticism of military pacts and foreign bases was aimed against the Ethiopia-Kenya defense agreement and against the Ethiopian-American agreement granting the United States the right to maintain a communications base in Ethiopia. On the question of French Somaliland, the Somali delegation was successful in having it specifically referred to in the conference's resolution on the elimination of colonialism: the conference called upon France to enable French Somaliland to attain independence in accordance with the United Nations' 1960 declaration on decolonization.

The phrasing of the resolution on self-determination provoked a debate in the Political Committee which touched indirectly upon the Somali disputes. Two states proposed to qualify the blanket endorsement of the right of self-determination by limiting its application to people under colonial rule. This proposed amendment was strongly opposed by Somalia, which argued that the conference should support the right to self-determination as it was phrased in the United Nations Charter, without qualification. The qualifying amendment was not accepted, and the conference resolution consequently stated that the violation of the right of self-determination and the denial of the exercise of this right were a cause of tension and a source of war.[24]

The draft resolutions that emerged from the committee meetings affirmed respect for the territorial status quo. The participating states pledged themselves "to respect frontiers as they existed when the States gained independence." A similar statement was contained in another resolution, which stated that "the established frontiers of States shall be inviolable." In objecting to the affirmation of the status quo, Somalia was joined by Afghanistan, Cambodia, Morocco, Saudi Arabia, Sudan and Syria. In view of the objections, a subcommittee of the Political Committee, in which both Ethiopia and Somalia participated, was charged with drafting an agreed formula. As no agreement was reached, the matter was referred to the heads of state for decision. In the end, the resolutions embodying the affirmation of the status quo were adopted. In keeping with the practice of the conference, no formal vote was taken. But Somalia entered formal reservations concerning those passages of the resolution containing an affirmation of the status quo.

The objections to the resolution were twofold. First, it was argued that the principle of accepting existing borders contradicted the right of self-determination. The second argument was that the boundaries established by the colonial powers were "unjust," and that "unjust" borders would continue to cause conflicts, the pious resolutions of the conference notwithstanding.[25]

No further changes were introduced in the draft resolutions, perhaps because they were already ambiguous enough.[26] By interpretation, the resolutions could be stretched to accommodate both the revisionist and the status quo viewpoints. The doctrine that only "justice" could secure peace received its due in the section calling for the liberation of dependent territories. The resolution stated that "lasting world peace cannot be realized so long as unjust conditions prevail and peoples under foreign domination continue to be deprived of their fundamental right to freedom, independence and self-determination." The paragraph of the resolution pledging respect for existing boundaries also stated that "nevertheless, parts of territories taken away by occupying powers and converted into autonomous bases for their own benefit at the time of independence must be given back to the country concerned." The qualifications were, of course, vague and lent themselves to contradictory interpretations.

The section concerned with sovereignty and territorial integrity contained a paragraph on "divided nations" which said that "one of the causes of international tension lies in the problem of divided nations." It called for unification by peaceful means. The call for peaceful unification of divided territories was paralleled by a call for a peaceful solution of frontier disputes in general, by way of negotiation, mediation, or arbitration.

The emphasis upon peaceful settlement was probably a pious platitude, yet it tended to favor the revisionist states. The refusal of the states whose boundaries were challenged to negotiate was a source of constant frustration for the states claiming territories from their neighbors. The states being challenged refused to negotiate or submit the dispute to adjudication because this might imply that some revision of the boundaries was acceptable. Such an admission would undermine the principle of the status quo, and thus open to question the legitimacy of the states' territorial possessions. In general, the ambiguity and equivocation of the resolutions adopted by the nonaligned states would seem to have nullified any norm-creating effect they might have had.

FOURTH AAPSO CONFERENCE, WINNEBA, GHANA, 1965

The pressures that prompted the OAU and nonaligned conferences to declare their stand on boundary problems also impelled the fourth AAPSO Conference, in Winneba, Ghana, (May 9-16, 1965), to cope with the subject. The views of the AAPSO on boundary problems in general were embodied in a resolution entitled "Border Conflicts," stating that the conference "condemns the use of force or the threat of the use of force and all forms of intimidation, interference and intervention as a means of imposing settlement of boundary, border and/or territorial disputes between African-Asian nations and strongly recommends the principle of peaceful negotiations as a means to settle the same." The conference strongly "affirms the right of peoples and nations to self-determination."[27]

In contrast to the resolutions of the OAU and nonaligned nations, the AAPSO resolutions did not affirm the status quo. Since China entertained territorial claims against India and the Soviet Union the absence of an endorsement of existing borders can be attributed to a desire to avoid sharpening conflicts within AAPSO, which was beset at the time with difficulties stemming from Sino-Soviet tensions. The call for a peaceful settlement of boundary disputes, and the affirmation of the right to self-determination in this context, again provided the most suitable formula, as it lent itself to different interpretations according to the preferences of the interested parties.

The resolutions on specific issues did not reflect any consistent preference for either the status quo or revisionist principles. On French Somaliland, a revisionist resolution was adopted. It not only condemned French policy but linked the question of French Somaliland to the general issue of Somali unification. The resolution stated that the conference

> Fully supports the right of the Somali territories to self-determination so that these could realize their national aims for freedom and over-all Somali unity.

> It has become doubtlessly clear that it is the wish of all the Somali people to realize their independence and unity and the Conference supports this just objective.[28]

The conference's support for the right to self-determination seems to have been selective. Thus, the revolt in the southern Sudan was not seen as involving this right, but was defined as an imperialist conspiracy for which the United States, Israel, and Zionism were to blame.[29]

Morocco was represented at the conference by the exiled leftist leader, Mehdi ben Barka. Not surprisingly the conference was critical of the Moroccan government. Interestingly enough, among the arguments brought against the Moroccan government in the report of the secretary-general, Youssef el Sebai of Egypt, was the statement that Morocco had brought up "the artificial border dispute" with Algeria "to menace the socialist revolution of the heroic Algerian people led by the great African leader Ahmed Ben Bella."[30] In view of the critical attitude of the conference toward the Moroccan government, it is not surprising that no reference was made this time to the Mauritanian problem.

At this same conference, the AAPSO received an application for membership from the Sanwi Liberation Movement, which had aimed to separate the Sanwi region from the Ivory Coast. Its leaders had established a base of operations in Ghana, the place of the conference. The support of the Ghana government for the Sanwi movement, provided a favorable atmosphere for the Sanwi application. On the other hand, the Ghanaian government's desire to mollify the Ivory Coast and other critics so as to ensure their attendance at the forthcoming OAU summit in Accra dictated caution. In these circumstances the conference chose to evade the question by deciding on further inquiries.[31]

The conference resolutions and its secretary general's report did not reflect any consistent attitude on boundary questions. The conference appears to have been guided in its work by criteria and signposts related to its aim of presenting the image of a united Asian-African camp in confrontation with the West, rather than by reference to the conflicting principles of status quo and revision.

THE EFFECT OF THE RESOLUTIONS: BIAFRA

The defeat of the revisionist position was not as complete at the nonaligned and AAPSO conferences as it was at the OAU. The OAU, however, enjoyed pre-eminent status among African states and, to the extent that states were influenced by the results of conferences, it was the OAU resolutions which mattered. In contrast to other conferences and resolutions that failed to provide guidance on the principles of boundary policies, the OAU charter and its 1964 resolution on boundaries represented definite attempts to codify a norm: that of respect for existing boundaries and maintenance of the territorial status quo.

Any assessment of the effects of the conferences and their

resolutions on state policies must start with the premise that the resolutions themselves were the expression of state policies. Since the overwhelming majority of African states considered the preservation of the territorial status quo to be in their interest, they transformed their tacit agreement to respect existing boundaries into a formal resolution of the OAU. Through the OAU they sought legitimacy for a policy which, on the face of it, was inconsistent with their nationalist ideology, which called for the eradication of the legacies of colonialism; yet the boundaries were certainly one of the most conspicuous inheritances of colonialism. Thus, the resolutions were the result of state policies, and not their cause.

It is possible that once a resolution is adopted, it becomes an independent factor influencing state behavior. It might be argued that the resolutions supporting maintenance of the territorial status quo reinforced the tendency of a majority of the states to adhere to status-quo policies, and served as a hedge against revisionism. To be sure, states have sometimes acted contrary to the status-quo principle promulgated by the OAU. Until 1967, Somalia continued actively to pursue its irredentist policy, and four members of the OAU accorded formal recognition to Biafra. However, these appear to be exceptions. That the general acceptance of the norm may have had *some* effect is suggested by the Biafran case.

Biafra's secession from Nigeria on May 30, 1967 and the outbreak of the war between Biafra and the Nigerian federal government aroused much concern among African states. By August 1967 it appeared that the problem would be raised at the OAU summit conference scheduled to meet in Kinshasa in September. Significantly, Nigeria opposed discussion of the problem, arguing that it was an internal Nigerian affair. Biafra, on the other hand, wanted the question included in the formal agenda, as it expected that the internationalization of the dispute would be to its advantage. When the heads of state convened, it was impossible to disregard the situation and, despite Nigerian objections, the issue was discussed. But, to placate Nigeria, the resolution adopted at Kinshasa solemnly reaffirmed the OAU's "respect for the sovereignty and territorial integrity of member states," reiterated its "con-

demnation of secession," and recognized that the situation
was a Nigerian internal affair. The summit further resolved
"to send a consultative mission of six Heads of State to the
Head of the Federal Government of Nigeria to assure him of
the Assembly's desire for the territorial integrity, unity and
peace of Nigeria."[32]

This did not end the controversy. As the Nigerian government suspected that the consultative mission was going to
attempt mediation, further negotiations with Nigeria were
necessary before the mission could proceed to Lagos. Four of
the six heads of state finally arrived in Lagos on November
23, more than two months after the mission had been formally established. (The four who traveled to Lagos were
Haile Selassie of Ethiopia, President Hamani Diori of Niger,
President Ahmadu Ahidjo of Cameroon, and General Ankrah
of Ghana. President Tubman of Liberia and President Mobutu
of Congo did not go.)

The mission's visit confirmed Nigeria's diplomatic victory
and set the framework for subsequent OAU involvement. The
communiqué issued at the conclusion of the talks reaffirmed
the OAU's condemnation of "all secessionist attempts in
Africa," and called for a solution on the basis of the preservation of Nigeria's unity and territorial integrity. To emphasize
that Nigeria and Biafra did not have equal standing before the
OAU, the mission did not visit Biafra, and delegated General
Ankrah to establish contact with the secessionists.[33]

In the spring of 1968, as the war continued and sympathy
for Biafran suffering mounted, four African states—Tanzania,
Gabon, Ivory Coast and Zambia—recognized Biafra's independence. Explaining Tanzania's decision, President Nyerere
declared: "where boundaries were drawn up without African
consent, they need not be respected."[34]

It seemed at the time as if adherence to the principle of the
status quo had been irreparably shattered, and that additional
states would soon extend formal recognition to Biafra. This
did not happen. On the contrary, the recognition of Biafra by
the four states turned out to have been the exception, as no
additional African government extended recognition. The
resolutions of the OAU summit conferences in 1968 and
1969, as well as the further mediation efforts of the OAU

consultative mission, all confirmed the previous stand of the majority of African states, that the unity and territorial integrity of Nigeria must be preserved. Nigerian and Biafran attitudes toward the OAU were now reversed, and it was Biafra who in December 1969 refused to participate in negotiations under OAU auspices, because it regarded the framework as prejudicial to its case. It was significant and indicative of the OAU's role in the conflict that when Biafra finally surrendered in January 1970, both sides referred to the surrender as representing the acceptance of "the OAU resolution."[35]

It would be wrong to conclude, however, that the norms embodied in the OAU charter and in the 1964 resolution on boundaries prevented widespread recognition of Biafra by African states. All that can be claimed is that they combined with some other factors in preventing some vacillating states from extending recognition. When Biafra seceded there already existed a normative context within which attitudes could be formed. The status-quo norm was available as a previously prepared formula for response. Nigeria's skillful use of this instrument contributed to the final outcome of Biafra's defeat.

Chapter **5** *The Use of Force*

In at least fifteen African boundary disputes force was employed in various forms and to various degrees. By *force* is meant the use of violence, or the threat of violence, to make the adversary change his policy or behavior. It is here assumed that the parties involved regarded the use of force as a means toward the attainment of their political goals. The revisionist side hoped that the use of force would help it to change the status quo; the government defending the status quo expected that by applying force against the revisionist side it would prevent such change. To be sure, the actual outbreak of violence may sometimes have been spontaneous. Yet, since in all cases under review the violence was associated with disputes over the maintenance or revision of the territorial status quo, the assumption that the use of force played a role in the bargaining process seems justified. Since most disputes have not resulted in any alteration of the territorial status quo, it must be assumed that resort to force has not been an effective means to bring about revision of borders in Africa.

CONTROL AND DIRECTION OF ARMED ACTION

To say that force was used by the revisionist side as a means toward the attainment of political goals implies that such force was subject to political direction and control. The direction and control of the use of force is a difficult and complicated task even in orderly states that boast policymaking, command, and control systems. It is more difficult when the states concerned are new and inexperienced, and it is infinitely more complicated when the military organization in question is a decentralized guerrilla movement. On the other hand, even decentralized guerrilla movements have tried to coordinate their activities. The direction and control of use of force is therefore a matter of degree. It will be assumed here that the use of force was subject to a high degree of direction and control if the movement in question explicitly acknowledged a single supreme authority, or if the existence of such control was demonstrated by its ability to switch the military operations on and off. Conversely, a low degree of direction and control can be assumed to have existed in movements in which there was more than one claimant for supreme authority.

The regular armies employed by the revisionist sides were subject to a high degree of direction and control: the Egyptian army in the dispute with Sudan in 1958; the Moroccan army in the 1963 war with Algeria; the Katangese forces (1960-1963); and the Biafran army. On the other hand the Anya-Nya guerrilla movement in the southern Sudan seems to have been a decentralized movement, not subject to an effective single overall command. The Anya-Nya maintained loose links with refugee organizations, but remained independent of them. In Sudan, they operated in small groups, which maintained contact but did not operate under a single command.[1]

Some guerrilla movements did not lag far behind regular armies in the degree of centralized control. The Moroccan Liberation Army (MLA), which waged a guerrilla war in Mauritania, Spanish Sahara, and Ifni, was relatively well organized and subject to a central command. The MLA first appeared in 1955, fighting against French rule in Morocco. After Moroccan independence, the MLA initially refused to submit to government control. By early 1957, the Istiqlal, which stood in the forefront of Moroccan irredentism, obtained predominant influence among the southern elements of the MLA. At the same time, since the MLA acknowledged the supreme authority of the king, the palace too was able to establish its influence. Thus, at the time of the MLA's operations in Mauritania, Spanish Sahara, and Ifni, during 1957-1958, it was under centralized but extragovernmental control, with the government having influence over the MLA but unable to control it.[2]

Official disclaimers notwithstanding, the Somali government has apparently been able to establish considerable control over the Somali *shifta** (guerrilla) movements in Ethiopia and Kenya. Yet the situation was not uniform. At first the shifta in Ethiopia operated without any central command: the Somali government exercised influence over their operations, but was unable to control them. The risks of such a situation became apparent in January and February 1964, when shifta activities provoked large-scale operations by the Ethiopian army which spilled over into the Somali Republic. A Somali minister was reported to have commented about these developments by saying: "One wonders if this republic is run from inside or out."[3]

After the formation in July 1964 of a new Somali government headed by Abdirazaq Haji Hussein, efforts were made to establish control over the Ethiopian shifta. That these efforts bore some results became evident in the autumn of 1967, when the subsidence of shifta operations was timed to coincide with Somalia's new policy of reducing tension.

From the outset the shifta operations in Kenya were apparently subject to a high degree of control. Captured shifta have told their interrogators about command and supply channels; according to these prisoners there was even a shifta command structure, with responsibility divided territorially by districts.[4] Even if their descriptions were inaccurate, the ability of the Somali government to control operations can be deduced from the way in which shifta activity began on a large scale in November 1963 and subsided with the Somali government's initiative to reduce tensions in September 1967.

The Eritreans, also, have boasted of the existence of a cen-

---

*There is controversy concerning the term *shifta*. To the Ethiopians the term denotes bandits and outlaws. For this reason, the Somalis object to its use to describe Somalis fighting against the Ethiopian and Kenyan governments. Nevertheless, it has come to be widely used. Its use here is not intended in any derogatory sense.

tralized command.[5] But it is difficult to verify whether such a command structure actually existed, and how effectively it controlled shifta in the field.

But how are control and direction exercised? The discipline through which the armed forces of states are directed and controlled has a twofold basis: the voluntary acceptance of an authority that is considered legitimate; and the authority's capacity to exercise coercion, with that coercion being viewed as legitimate.

The direction and control of all guerrilla forces in Africa were based upon similar foundations. Guerrilla fighters usually regarded as legitimate those leaders whose authority they accepted, and, to a large measure, their acceptance of such authority was voluntary. This fact illustrates the essence of insurgency: the rejection of the authority of the government of the country and a denial of its legitimacy, coupled with the transfer of allegiance to some other authority, which is considered legitimate. Such legitimacy is based either on a cause, such as a nationalist or separatist ideology, or upon traditional links of tribal allegiance, or both.

Like most political attitudes in Africa, insurgency as well as loyalty to the government was usually not the attitude of atomized individuals, but of the societies to which they belonged. Thus, a close association between guerrilla movements and tribal groups often existed. Collective tribal participation in insurgency or in progovernment forces is illustrated by the case of the Reguibat, who roam the deserts of northern Mauritania, Spanish Sahara, and southern Morocco. At first they joined the MLA, and the MLA's 1957 operations relied upon them. In a speech at M'Hamid on February 25, 1958, King Mohamed V, publicly espousing irredentism for the first time, specifically appealed to the Reguibat to support the Moroccan cause. This was to no avail. They switched sides and in a colorful ceremony in April 1958 "rallied" to the Mauritanian side. Their formal *ralliement* was accompanied by the turning of their guns against the Moroccans.[6]

Among the Somali shifta operating against Kenya, clans seemed to serve to identify different military units. Thus, a defector told the Kenyan authorities that "he was responsible for issuing arms and ammunition to the Murille shifta" in the Bula Hawa camp.[7]

Why do some tribes or clans support insurgency while others, members of the same nation, remain loyal to the government? One explanation is that antecedent, specific, political, economic, and social interests and alignments express themselves in the new terms of rejection or acceptance of the government and of the state. Thus it is significant that the Marehan and other tribes, who straddle the border between Somalia's southern region and Ethiopia, and depend for their livelihood on water and grazing in Ethiopian territory, have been particularly prone to insurgent activity. On the other hand, the Ogaden Somalis in Ethiopia, who have been favored by the Ethiopian authorities in matters of access to wells and grazing, and have benefited from small-scale development projects, were involved in shifta activities to a much lesser extent. In Kenya, the Ogaden around Garissa have generally refused to cooperate with the shifta, while some of their traditional rivals, who were linked with kinsmen across the Somali border, have been the mainstay of shifta activities in Kenya.

Besides antecedent interests and alignments, the attitudes of influential individuals are important in determining tribal or clan policies. Traditional leaders had, of course, much influence on tribal alignments. For example, in Mauritania the pro-Moroccan forces greatly benefited from the adherence to their cause of Mohamed Fall Ould Oumeir, the emir of Trarza, one of the four leading religious authorities in Mauritania.

Other individuals, whose achievements in administration or government formed the basis of their influence, also swayed members of their clans to join the insurgency. In such cases there was sometimes a conflict between competing leaders with different qualifications. An interesting illustration is from the Ogaden Somalis in Ethiopia, who, as mentioned, tended to identify their interests with Ethiopia. The traditional chiefs, who were receiving government salaries, were among the advocates of this course. Their policy was challenged by Mukhtal Dahir, an Ogaden tribesman who had risen in the ranks of the Ethiopian provincial administration to become a district commissioner. He defected in 1962 and began organizing a shifta movement. But opinions among tribesmen were divided. The division was carried further by some of the educated youth, who endeavored to establish an independent position. They claimed that they identified with the Somali nationalist cause, but that the circumstances were inopportune for an insurgent movement.[8]

There are other examples of insurgent leaders with achievements in modern life and affairs. Some shifta officers in Kenya had held Kenya government posts. Isaya Mukirane, leader of the Ruwenzururu movement in Uganda, was a former school teacher and member of the Toro Legislative Assembly. Among the southern Sudanese leaders there were former noncommissioned officers from the Equatoria corps of the Sudanese army, as well as administrative officers, politicians, and clergymen. Bernardino Mau, who led the attempt to capture the town of Wau in January 1964, was the son of a Dinka chief and had served with the Equatoria corps. Father Saturnino, killed in January 1967, had been a Catholic clergyman and member of the Sudanese parliament.[9]

The coercive means that contribute to the ability of a guerrilla leader to exercise direction and control differ of course from the means available to a government in imposing discipline upon its armed forces. One method is terrorism, which is applied sometimes against those who reject authority, or who wish to establish their independence from hitherto accepted authority. Such punitive measures, if successful, have the double effect of eliminating opposition and intimidating followers.

A more common form of direction was control over supplies. Weapons, and often other supplies, had to be obtained from external sources. The distribution or withholding of supplies could thus become a means to enforce discipline. Supplemented by training, it also served as an instrument to direct the activities of the movement and determine its tactics. Thus, when in 1966 the Somali shifta in Kenya began to lay plastic antivehicle mines, this new tactic did not stem from the decision of a commander in the field. It required a high-level policy decision, the procurement of the mines in Egypt, and training in sabotage techniques.

The policies of Somali governments toward the shifta operating in Ethiopia exemplify the importance of supplies in the
attempt to control guerrilla operations. Until 1964 Abdirashid Ali Shermarke's government provided encouragement
and support to almost any group requesting assistance. It
refused to recognize the supremacy of any one leader, and
when approached by Mukhtal Dahir with a proposal to recognize his group as the "Provisional Government of the Somali
Western Territories," the Somali government turned him
down. This was done in part because of doubts about Mukhtal Dahir's ability to command the undivided support of
Somalis in Ethiopia. But the rejection of the scheme
stemmed also from the government's apparent belief that it
would be able to influence the shifta most by preventing the
emergence of an overall authority, and by maintaining direct
contact with individual leaders. The government of Abdirazaq Haji Hussein, which came into power in 1964, modified
this policy, and exercised much greater selectivity in supporting specific groups.[10] Through the control over supplies the
Somali government gradually succeeded in establishing a high
degree of control over the shifta, and in coordinating their
war with government policies.

In the case of the southern Sudan's Anya-Nya, no effective
central authority existed. The Sudan African National Union
(SANU), which was for a time the principal political organization of the southern Sudan, and operated from exile in
Uganda, played a leading part in the initiation of the Anya-
Nya insurgent movement in 1962. But SANU politicians soon
receded into the background, while leadership of the movement was assumed by the fighters in the field, many of whom
were former Sudanese army personnel. The absence of a
central command can be explained by a number of factors:
difficult communications, tribal rivalries, and the divisions
within SANU between moderates and radicals, which finally
split the movement. Following the split, SANU in 1965 appealed to the Anya-Nya for a cease-fire. But by this time
SANU had lost any influence it had had, and its rival, the
Azania Liberation Front (ALF), assumed the role of the
political wing of the separatist movement.

Probably the most important reason for the absence of a

central command was the ability of the small Anya-Nya groups to operate in almost complete independence of external support. They gained this ability largely by capturing weapons and supplies which were destined for the *simba* insurgents in Congo. Whatever limited influence exiled political leaders had on the Anya-Nya came from their occasional role as agents for procuring weapons. They also helped to establish contact with the Congolese army, which at one time supplied the Anya-Nya with weapons in return for the Anya-Nya's assistance in fighting the *simba* rebels.[11]

With the suppression of the rebellion in Congo, Congolese sources of weapons began to dry up. Consequently, the importance and influence of weapons' procurement organizations began once more to increase. But by 1967 the Anya-Nya leaders assumed this role, as well as other political roles, including foreign affairs, while the influence of the exiled political leaders declined further.

To be sure, the coercion accompanying attempts to establish a central authority did not necessarily involve threats or the application of sanctions. Often the relationship between the supreme authority and components of the insurgent forces was one of negotiating and bargaining, rather than command relations. But the significant point is that there was a central authority, which was accepted as such, and whose influence upon the insurgent movement was paramount. It employed the forces at its disposal with the purpose of attaining political objectives.

OBJECTIVES

The objectives of the side defending the status quo have been relatively clear. The defending side, always a government, employed force with the purpose of thwarting or destroying the revisionist party, thus eliminating the challenge.

Not being privy to the secrets of revisionist movements, we cannot know their goals with certainty. Therefore, we shall propose a model, classifying the possible goals of movements that employed force to change the status quo. But the attempt to assess such goals entails several difficulties.

One major difficulty stems from the vagueness that has

characterized the aspirations of some revisionist movements, a vagueness often due to the unsophisticated nature of the movements. The Targui rebellion in Mali in 1963-1964 is an example. It is not clear whether the rebels wished merely to secede from Mali and to be left alone, whether they wanted to be incorporated into one of the neighboring states, or whether they hoped that the Touareg from neighboring territories would join them in setting up a Targui state. Similarly unclear were the aims of the Ruwenzururu movement of the Baamba and Bakonjo peoples in Uganda in 1962-1963. Did they want merely to be separated from Toro and to form a separate district within Uganda, or did they wish to secede from Uganda?

In other cases, goals were deliberately phrased in vague terms. Defining goals in this way can serve to unite factions of a revisionist movement that differ over the ultimate goals. In the case of the southern Sudan, in 1960, the then foremost political leaders, William Deng and Joseph Oduho, declared that the goals of the South were termination of its servitude to the North, and recognition of its right to self-determination.[12] They did not define precisely what they meant by self-determination. But in 1964-1965 the movement split over conflicting interpretations of this very goal: some leaders were ready to accept federal status for the South, others insisted upon secession.

The stillborn insurrection in British Togoland in 1957 also encompassed different attitudes. Although there was probably wide agreement on the immediate tactical objective of reversing the integration of British Togoland into Ghana, there were different views concerning the ultimate goal: while some continued to hope for Ewe unification, others aspired to Togoland unification. And, according to an account of the Ruwenzururu movement by Tom Stacey, the British journalist, that movement split in 1963. One faction was prepared to accept a Uganda government proposal to separate the area from Toro and place it under direct administration by the central government. But an irreconcilable faction, headed by veteran leader Isaya Mukirane, refused and continued to fight. The insurgency in Chad in 1965-1967 is another example of vagueness, because different goals were pursued by different leaders. This was partly a movement by eastern and northern Moslems to overthrow a government dominated by southern Christians, and in part it was inspired by separatist sentiments that had particularly deep roots in the Wadai Province, on the Sudanese border.*

A distinction should also be made between the ultimate goals of a particular movement and the immediate objectives of using force. Indeed, it is probable that the more sophisticated the leadership, the greater the ability to distinguish between immediate objectives and ultimate goals, as well as among the various means employed to attain them.

A final difficulty in trying to assess objectives derives from the changes they often undergo. The factors causing change are many, important among them being the course of the armed struggle itself.

Despite the difficulties in defining the objectives of force, we shall assume six general categories of goals toward which the use of force has been directed.

The most common category is the somewhat unsophisticated expectation that force yields concessions. In many cases there was probably no specific planning or calculation of the kind of force to be applied or the kinds of concessions to be expected. Most of the insurrections being considered were based on some vague expectation of concessions, unlimited. But some also aimed at specific concessions, or intermediary limited objectives. Unlimited concessions shall be allocated to one category; specific limited concessions to a second category.

A third possible kind of objective is to establish a fait accompli of boundary revision or secession. The fourth category includes the objective of attracting international intervention. This was usually not a primary objective but more often a fallback position, in the event the adversary refused to grant concessions. Border disputes that are symptoms of a primary conflict of greater importance comprise the fifth category. In such situations, force along the border is applied

---

*This is not to be confused with the "Front de libération nationale Tchadienne" (FROLINAT), the rebel movement which developed in the northern provinces after 1967, and which aims at the overthrow of the existing government, rather than secession.

mainly toward obtaining concessions in the primary conflict, rather than toward boundary revisions.

While all these objectives are related to values that the revisionist side would hope to extract from the adversary, there is a corollary objective common to almost all cases of insurgent action: to arouse the populace, stimulate its political consciousness, and induce its mobilization in support of the insurgency. Thus, political mobilization will be considered a sixth objective.

MEANS

It is an easier task to classify the different forms of force. They can be encompassed in three main categories: (1) riots; (2) terrorist and guerrilla acts, carried out by irregular forces; and (3) troop movements and frontal fighting, in which regular armies are engaged. Let us consider some examples of the use of force and discuss them in relation to the objectives toward which the use of force was directed.

Riots as part of a campaign for the revision of boundaries have not been common. Undoubtedly, riots could contain an important element of spontaneous anger, but to the extent that they are aimed at attaining political objectives, their object would be to extract concessions from the government. Concessions could be expected on the assumption that the riots were embarrassing to the authorities, since they drew the attention of public opinion and of foreign governments, an attention which may in a sense constitute pressure on the government concerned to do something to calm the situation.

The concessions hoped for could be general and unspecified. Even if specific demands were made, such as the demand of the Djibouti Somalis for "total independence" in the riots of August 26 and 27, 1966 during President de Gaulle's visit, the organizers may actually have been aiming at more limited, intermediary objectives. In Djibouti, their aim was probably the replacement of the Ali Aref government by another in which Somali nationalists would carry greater influence.[13]

The Somali riot at Isiolo in Kenya in August 1962 is another example of a riot aimed at a limited political objective. It was designed to block the integration of the region into Kenya. The riot erupted when Somalis broke up a rally of the Kenya African National Union. Subsequently, the scheduled visit of the Kenya Regional and Constituency Delimitation Commission, which would have implied that Isiolo was in Kenya, was postponed. A Somali leader, Abdirashid Khalif, stated the political objective of the riot: "We have several times informed the local administration that in view of the people's strong feelings for reunion with the Somali Republic, they will not tolerate hostile elements canvassing policies opposed to the principle of reunion."[14]

Terror has sometimes been used to intimidate persons wielding influence or authority. If a person in office is murdered, the victim's successor can be expected to be more attentive to the wishes of the terrorist movement. The murder by Somalis of the Boran Galla chief Galma Dida in June 1963 is an example. The chief had reportedly shifted from a pro-Somali to a pro-Kenyan position a short time before his death. Killed with him was the district commissioner of Isiolo, Daudi Dabasso Waweru, whose commitment to Kenya could have influenced his wavering tribesmen in the Marsabit region of northern Kenya. Another example is the attempt on the life of Ali Aref, the president of the governing council (equivalent of prime minister), in the Afar and Issa territory. The murder of William Deng, leader of the SANU faction which had returned to Sudan and agreed to cooperate with the Sudan government, is a further example. An example from Mauritania is the assassination of Abdellahi ould Obid, member of the National Assembly and mayor of Atar, in November 1960.[15]

Sometimes terror was applied against groups, as distinct from terror against individuals. Insurgent movements used this method as a means to elicit cooperation from the group, and to induce it to resist government policies. An example is the shifta attack on the Abdalla clan of the Ogaden Somalis in Kenya in punishment for their declaration of loyalty to the Kenya authorities.[16] Governments have also been known to resort to similar methods.

It is often an aim of guerrilla warfare to extract unspecified, general concessions. Examples include the actions by
Morocco and Mali against Mauritania, by the Touareg in Mali
against the government, by the Somalis against Ethiopia and
Kenya, by the Eritrean separatists against Ethiopia, by the
Southern Negroes in the Sudan against the Arab-dominated
government, by Arabs and Moslems in Chad against the government dominated by the Negro and Christian Sara people,
and by the Bakonjo and Baamba tribesmen in Uganda against
both the regional and central governments.

Some of these movements may have hoped that the guerrilla operations would eliminate government authority from
the territory in question, leaving a new situation of de facto
secession. Some of the southern Sudanese leaders apparently
entertained such a hope. Somali leaders may have had similar
hopes in 1963 with regard to the NFD. It is also possible that
the Touaregs of Mali believed that they could assert de facto
independence from Mali.

Several movements expected that in the event of failure to
create a fait accompli or obtain concessions, their guerrilla
operations would at least bring about international intervention in the dispute. By intervention I do not mean the extension of material aid to the revisionist movement, but rather,
the term refers here to the application of diplomatic pressures by third parties upon the side of the status quo in an
attempt to induce it to grant concessions to the revisionists.

The abortive insurrection in British Togoland in 1957 is
one example. The organizers apparently hoped that the eruption of violence would lead to United Nations intervention
which would lead it to reconsider the integration of British
Togoland with Ghana, sanctioned by the United Nations only
a few months before.[17] Some of the Eritrean separatists seem
also to have hoped to arouse international interest, which
would press the Ethiopian government to grant concessions.
Their expectation of international interest was directed
mainly at the United Nations, because the federal relationship between Ethiopia and Eritrea had been devised under its
auspices.

A different form of international intervention was sought

by the Somalis in 1964. After fighting between Somali and Ethiopian troops had erupted, the Somalis appealed to the United Nations Security Council, and subsequently to the Organization of African Unity, seeking to establish some form of international presence along the border.[18] This would have benefited the Somalis in at least two ways. If an international force were posted along the border to separate the regular armies of the two sides, it would have shielded Somalia from possible retaliation by Ethiopian forces against shifta activity. An international presence in the disputed territory would also have had the effect of diluting somewhat the Ethiopian claim to sovereignty and exclusive jurisdiction over the Somali-inhabited territory. It would imply international recognition of the fact that this was a disputed territory in which the international community might be called upon to play a role.

A different scenario of international intervention was apparently hoped for by some southern Sudanese leaders. They expected that the flight of refugees to neighboring countries would help to awaken international concern. Furthermore, William Deng, at that time secretary-general of the Sudan African National Union, and some of his associates, in 1962 hoped that by launching guerrilla raids into the southern Sudan from bases across the frontier, they might involve the Sudanese government in a conflict with its neighbors "and that the resulting UN intervention would provide the opportunity for securing the plesbiscite."[19]

Regular armies, too, have been used in pursuit of several objectives. An example of the pursuit of limited, specific concessions can be taken from the Moroccan-Algerian war of 1963. One of the Moroccan objectives was to induce Algeria to negotiate the boundary question. Morocco pressed for this at the cease-fire negotiations at Bamako, and in the end obtained Algeria's agreement that the problem be examined by an OAU commission.[20]

Regular armies were employed also to create faits accomplis, which have intrinsic value, of course, but can also be used as bargaining counters in negotiations. One of the Moroccan objectives in the 1963 war with Algeria might have been to alter the existing de facto border in Morocco's favor. But this advantage, which Morocco obtained in the fighting, was traded at Bamako for Algerian agreement to have the problem examined by a commission of the OAU. Regular troops were also used by Katanga and by Biafra in their struggles to secede from Congo and from Nigeria respectively. In both cases, the aim of the military operations was to establish the fait accompli of secession.

Egypt's occupation in 1958 of territories it claimed from Sudan may also have been aimed, at least in part, toward the creation of a fait accompli. Yet if it is assumed that the territorial dispute was not the primary cause of Egyptian-Sudanese tensions, but merely a symptom of a conflict stemming from other causes, then the use of troops may have been intended in part to exert pressure on Sudan to soften its position on issues other than the territorial question. The other issues included the difficult negotiations over the revision of the 1929 Nile waters agreement, and over the compensation Sudan claimed for the expected flooding of the Wadi-Halfa region, which would result from the construction of the Aswan dam.

EXAMINING THE EFFECTIVENESS OF FORCE

The most common objective of insurgent movements and revisionist states has been to weaken the resolve of the governments defending the status quo and to obtain concessions. The hope of extracting concessions has been based on the assumption that military conflict might impose upon the adversary political strains and economic burdens that it is unwilling or unable to bear.[21]

The cost of financing military operations makes up a major element of the economic burden. The cost to the government of defending the status quo can be regarded as high when compared with the relatively low cost of sustaining a guerrilla campaign. The dislocations caused by the fighting place an additional burden upon the government and may carry the political corollary of rendering the government unpopular, because it is forced to levy new taxes, or is prevented from fulfilling development promises. Additional political costs to the government include the embarrassment and loss of face which it suffers when a section of the population rejects its legitimacy. Casualties may lead to a weakening of morale and may inspire opposition to the government. If fighting the insurrection requires foreign assistance, criticism of the government's international orientation and dependence on foreign powers is likely to rise. The brutality of violence may expose the government to external pressures.

A government that finds itself in such a quandary may hope that counterpressure would induce the revisionist side to desist. The logic of the government's strategy is similar to that of the rebels'. The government hopes that successive defeats will weaken the insurgents and reduce both their will and capacity to continue. In addition, counterterrorism and administrative measures directed at the insurgents' social base may reduce aid for the insurgents and perhaps induce the population to withhold its support from them. In addition, of course, governments may hope to eliminate the challenge by destroying the insurgents.

In most cases the revisionist side has failed to attain its objectives. In only two instances can the granting of concessions be attributed—and then in part only—to military pressure from the revisionist side. In the Mauritania-Mali border agreement of February 1963, Mauritania conceded some Malian claims. The Mauritanian concessions can in part be attributed to guerrilla operations in the Eastern Hodh region of Mauritania. These guerrilla operations were believed to have received assistance from Mali, and it is reasonable to assume that they impressed Mauritania with the possibility of Malian-Moroccan cooperation aimed at the partition of Mauritania. The Mauritanian concessions to Mali appear to have been granted with the aim of breaking up the Mali-Moroccan front. The second example of concessions comes from the brief Algerian-Moroccan border war in 1963. Morocco could claim that one of the outcomes of the war was Algeria's agreement at Bamako that an OAU commission examine the border dispute and submit recommendations for a settlement. Actually, Algeria did not promise anything new, since it had already conceded the need for negotiations on the boundary in its unfulfilled promise of July 1961 to enter into negotiations. Algeria's renewed promise can be explained by its relative weakness in October 1963, when in addition to Moroccan pressure, it had to cope with the domestic Kabylia rebellion. Furthermore, the Algerian promise to negotiate had been vague, and Algeria continued to interpret it as a promise to negotiate about the precise delimitation and demarcation of the de facto boundary, and not, as the Moroccans would have liked to see it, as a promise to negotiate about the substance of the Moroccan territorial claims.[22]

In general, coercion through the use of force was not effective in extracting concessions, and the question must be asked whether the implicit expectations of the cost-calculus were well-founded. To be sure, the costs to the government of fighting insurgents can be considerable, and can impose a heavy economic burden on the state. Yet, often the burden carried by the government was offset by external aid. In some cases (notably Mauritania and Kenya), an external power carried the major part of the burden, and greatly eased the immediate pressures under which the African governments operated.

Among the political pressures that weigh upon governments can be included the embarrassment and loss of face resulting from the rejection of a government's legitimacy by a section of the population. It is interesting, however, that such embarrassment and loss of face did not prod governments toward making concessions, but rather propelled them in the opposite direction, of exerting themselves to suppress the insurrection.

The Targui rebellion in Mali is an illustration. Mali undertook to suppress the rebellion despite the high cost and economic burden imposed by the operations. The Mali government could have refrained from attempting to integrate the Touareg into the country's economic and political life. The fact that the government decided to suppress the rebellion, and to proceed with the integration of the Touareg, can be explained by its deep commitment to political mobilization for nation-building, which had to encompass all parts of the country and all tribes within Mali's boundaries.[23]

The growth of internal political opposition is often stimulated by governments' dependence on foreign powers. The needs of fighting insurgents and warding off irredentist pressure can greatly contribute to the creation of such dependence since governments may require external assistance in the conflict. Illustrating such situations are Togo, Dahomey, and Gabon, which maintain close links to France; Kenya, which maintains close ties with Britain and the United States; and Somalia, which has become dependent on assistance from the Soviet Union. Yet criticism of the government by the political opposition has usually been directed at its international orientation, and not at its resistance to the revisionist challenge. Indeed, it is probable that the opposition groups would have followed similar policies had they been in power, since resistance to territorial claims or secession is often a basic interest of the state, and not only of the government that happens to be in power.

If fighting secessionism becomes a major preoccupation of the government, it may have political consequences on the domestic scene. In Sudan, for example, the fighting against the southern insurrection contributed greatly to the creation and perpetuation of political instability. Among the indirect consequences of the rebellion in the south were the military coup in 1958, the revolution which deposed the military regime in 1964, and the 1969 coup d'etat. Yet it is significant that although each regime was critical of its predecessor's policy toward the soutern rebellion, all governments continued with the efforts to suppress southern secessionism.

There are two major reasons why the combined economic, social, and political impact of military pressure has failed to induce the status-quo side to grant concessions. The states concerned have been relatively invulnerable to guerrilla activity in remote areas or to military conflict along the frontiers. The relatively unintegrated character of most African states has served to cushion and diminish the impact of such war. The effect of the war varies, of course, with the country and with the locus of the insurrection. Secessionist attempts by important revenue-producing areas such as Katanga or Biafra were bound to have serious consequences for Congo and Nigeria. On the other hand, the Targui uprising in Mali, or the Somali insurrections in Ethiopia and Northern Kenya, took place in areas which were not intimately bound up with the

economic life of the country, and their economic impact was
therefore much more limited. The same can be said about the
social or political effects of insurrections in areas which were
relatively remote and not integrated into the life of the country. Thus the undeveloped condition of the state accords it a
measure of immunity against the military and social pressure
of insurrections.

In addition, the pressures of insurgency have usually failed
to extract concessions because of the perception by status
quo governments of the choices they face. Such governments
have preferred to continue to bear the costs indefinitely, no
matter how heavy. They have been willing to bear the cost,
including their dependence on external assistance, because
they believed that the alternative of concessions was likely to
lead to the disintegration of their states.

How effective was the use of force in bringing about international intervention favorable to the revisionist side? In the
case of British Togoland, the international community failed
to intervene, mainly because the attempted uprising was so
quickly and effectively crushed. But even had Ghana failed to
suppress the rebellion so quickly and so effectively, it is
highly unlikely that the United Nations would have retracted
its previous approval of British Togoland's integration into
Ghana since such action would have been interpreted by the
anticolonialist bloc as a retrograde step running counter to
the process of decolonization.

Somalia's attempt to obtain international intervention in its
dispute with Ethiopia in 1964 developed in two stages. Somalia first appealed to the United Nations Security Council.
But this appeal was thwarted by those African states who
preferred to have the dispute handled by the Organization of
African Unity. Reluctant to become involved in this controversy, non-African states supported the view that the matter
should first be referred to the OAU. At the OAU conferences
there was at first some support for the proposal that a neutral
African force be placed between the Somalis and the Ethiopians, either as a patrol, or as observers. But Ethiopia objected,
arguing that the root of the problem was Somali irredentism
and that boundary clashes would cease if Somalia stopped

pursuing its territorial claims. Since the pursuit of such irredentist claims ran contrary to the norms that the majority
of African states wished to establish, the Ethiopian argument
produced an impact. In any event, since Ethiopia rejected the
interposition of a third party, nothing could have been done.

In the case of the southern Sudan a form of international
intervention did take place. The massive flight of refugees
into neighboring territories, and the fact that neighboring
territories were used as bases for the Anya-Nya operations,
resulted in tensions between these states and Sudan, and
inevitably led to international intervention in the conflict.
Contrary to the expectation of the southern Sudanese separatists, however, the intervention tended to favor the cause of
the Sudanese government. Uganda imposed restrictions on
the activities of the southern Sudanese on its territory, and
exerted pressure on them to attend a conference which the
Sudanese government convened in Khartoum in March 1965.
Uganda and several other African states attended as observers, although the conference was ostensibly a gathering of
Sudanese parties discussing internal matters. At the conference, Uganda's influence was directed mainly at the southern
insurgents in an attempt to induce them to accept the north-
erners' proposals for a settlement. The position of Uganda
and other African states that adopted a similar stand may
have stemmed in part from their commitment to the principle that the integrity of African states, within the boundaries
established upon their emergence to independence, must be
preserved. But probably a more important factor was their
concern not to be drawn into a conflict with Sudan, and their
belief that pressure on their part was likely to be more effective against the insurgents, than against the government.[24]

Biafra too was successful in attracting intervention, but
politically, it rebounded to its disadvantage. The intervention
of the OAU at first appeared to be embarrassing to the Nigerian federal government. But soon Nigeria succeeded in trans-
forming the OAU's involvement into an instrument for the
defense of its territorial integrity. Biafra, too, was successful
in arousing the sympathy of public opinion in many countries to the suffering of its civilian population. But such sympathy failed to produce effective political pressure on the
Nigerian government to compromise with the secessionists.

In general the results of international intervention were not favorable to the revisionist side. Although, logically, the very fact of intervention may tend to undermine the status-quo position, the interests of the intervening states may accord with those of the status-quo party.

How successful were the attempts to establish faits accomplis by the resort to force? Three such attempts were crushed: Katanga's attempt to secede from the Congo was defeated by the superior combination of United Nations and Congolese forces; the Targui rebellion in Mali was suppressed by the Malian army; and Biafra's secession from Nigeria was terminated by the victory of the army of the federal government. If the Somalis of the Northern Frontier District hoped that they would be able to establish de facto secession, then their attempt may be counted as another case of failure. At this time, only the outcome of the insurrection in the southern Sudan remains undecided.*

A fait accompli depends entirely upon the military capabilities of the parties. The obvious reason for the failure of revisionist movements to establish such a situation was their relative military weakness compared to the forces available to the government defending the status quo.

One of the goals of the appeal to force has been the mobilization of the population for greater support for the cause. Yet such an appeal to force tends to stimulate mobilization on both sides of the dispute. The outbreak of shifta attacks in northern Kenya raised the political temperature among Kenya Somalis; at the same time, it aroused the Kenya elites, who had hitherto been indifferent, to demand that the Kenya government adopt firm measures to cope with the situation. The Moroccan-Algerian war in October 1963 was used by both governments to rally support at a critical moment when they were challenged by domestic opponents.[25]

The use of force has usually not been an effective instrument for bringing about boundary revision. The pressures generated by guerrilla and military activities failed to produce

*It was reported in February 1972, as this book went to print, that agreement has been reached between the Sudan government and insurgent leaders for ending the guerrilla war, and for granting the southern provinces regional autonomy.

concessions from the status-quo side. External interventions, when they occurred, tended to favor the government defending the status quo. And the relative military weakness of the revisionist movements was not sufficient to produce faits accomplis.

SOME FACTORS INFLUENCING THE USE OF FORCE

The incidence of the resort to force has been relatively high in comparison to the overall number of boundary and territorial disputes. This can be accounted for, in part, by the emotions generated by separatism and irredentism. A further partial explanation may lie in a traditional background of violence in the relations between the disputants. A tradition of conflict exists between Moslem Somalis and Christian Ethiopians, as well as between the Moslems of Eritrea and the Christian Ethiopians. Traditional animosities form a partial background to the conflict between the Negro south and the Arab north in Sudan and to a lesser extent in Chad. The Bakonjo in Uganda rose against their Toro rulers in 1919, as they did again in 1962. Tribesmen from the opposite sides of the Mali-Mauritania border also have a long tradition of conflict. Several of the populations involved in these disputes have practiced raiding and violence as part of their traditional way of life. This is the case not only with the Somalis, but also with some of the nomads, who have been involved in boundary fighting and insurgent movements in Chad, Mali, Mauritania and Eritrea.

Accidental, or politically uncontrolled outbreaks of violence, on a small scale, may also have contributed to the use of force. The Moroccan-Algerian war was stimulated by clashes between the two sides as they tried to occupy positions evacuated by the French. Ethiopian-Somali fighting early in 1964 was at least in part the outgrowth of clashes between shifta and Ethiopian troops. The Targui rebellion in Mali started as a result of Malian attempts to impose the government's authority upon the tribesmen. Biafra's secession from Nigeria was in some respects the direct consequence of Ibo massacres in the north.

On the level of rational calculation, a false perception of

the adversary played an important part in inducing the revisionist side to take action. In a number of cases the revisionist side believed that the adversary's state was near disintegration. Such were some Katangan images of the Congolese state and assessments of their relative strengths in 1960. Biafrans expected in 1967 that their example would be emulated by other people and regions, which would likewise claim the rights of self-determination and secession. Somalis spoke of Ethiopia as if it were on verge of disintegration, and expected that Kenya would be preoccupied with intertribal strife after independence.

Conversely, abstinence from use of force was probably in some cases influenced by the estimate that the adversary, or his protectors, possessed superior military strength. Thus Ghana's military restraint in its disputes with Togo, the Ivory Coast, and Upper Volta, despite its actual superiority, may have been induced in part by the possibility of French intervention on the side of its former colonies. According to some accounts, when Dahomey and Niger were nearing a clash in 1963, they were both deterred from embarking upon hostilities by French warnings and by actual measures taken by French personnel on both sides to prevent such a fratricidal clash.

JUSTIFICATIONS FOR THE USE OF FORCE

Most African governments, and some revisionist movements, claim to be devoted to the principle of Pan-African solidarity. How then, can the use of force against Africans be justified?

Two levels of justification should be distinguished: the popular-traditional level, which is entirely domestic, and the modern-political level, which involves a domestic audience which has adopted the values of modern political life, as well as the external audience of elites in other African states.

At the popular-traditional level, the internal propaganda of governments sometimes justified policies by arguments appealing to the traditional spheres of life. In some situations, such arguments are not in short supply. In the Somali, Eritrean, and Sudanese disputes religious and historical arguments were used. Somali communiques reporting fighting with "Kikuyu" and "Amhara" troops carried connotations of ethnic antagonisms. In Katanga, animosities between the Baluba and Lunda are known to have been an important factor in fanning the flames of conflict. Ethnic animosities were also a major factor in the Biafra-Nigeria conflict. The Bakonjo-Toro dispute in Uganda seems to have been argued to a very large extent in traditional tribal terms. As for the Targui rebellion in Mali, the Touareg are known for their racialist disdain of Negroes, with whom they identified the Mali state.[26]

While effective in some situations, such justifications are essentially at variance with the ideology belittling tribal and other differences among Africans and advocating Pan-African solidarity. Turning to the sphere of modern politics, there is a tendency to attune arguments and justifications to prevailing political ideologies. To get around the contradiction between Pan-Africanism and the resort to force against fellow Africans, two kinds of arguments have been used: the anticolonialist and the antineocolonialist.

According to the first, boundary and territorial disputes among Africans are legacies of colonialism. The people resort to arms in order to right a wrong inflicted by colonialism. The Moroccan Liberation Army fought against the French in Mauritania and along the Algerian frontier (only after 1960 and 1962 respectively, did the question of conflict with African brothers arise). Britain, France, Italy, and Ethiopia were accused of having unjustly and arbitrarily divided the Somali territories. France, Britain, and Germany were accused of dividing the Ewe, and of having partitioned Togo and Cameroon. The northern Sudanese blamed the south's separatism on Britain's policies of "divide and rule," whereas the southerners attributed to the northern Arabs colonialist policies of exploitation and oppression.

The anticolonial argument, however, can only be used for a limited time. The colonialists can be blamed for the origins of the problem, but the existence of an African government that persists in perpetuating a situation created by the colonialists cannot be ignored for long. Since the a priori assumption has been that fellow Africans are brothers and anticolonialists, in such cases the blame is shifted to the regime, which is accused of being a servant of the colonialists. An insurrection can then be justified by the argument that the African government concerned was not a truly nationalist government. Thus, Morocco depicted the Mauritanian government as a neocolonialist puppet; Somalia has on occasions referred to the Kenyan government in similar terms; the Eritrean secessionists have accused Ethiopia of serving neocolonialism; Biafra accused Nigeria of serving British imperialism.[27] Only seldom were African states themselves accused of evil motives: both Ghana and Ethiopia were charged with pursuing policies of "black imperialism." In other words, they were not accused of being dupes, but rather, of having adopted the evil ways of the imperialist powers.

In some respects, justifications for the use of force by the revisionists, and of the repressive measures of the governments, have amounted to a contest about "who is a better anticolonialist." In this contest, the status-quo forces seek not to lag behind. Thus, some governments defending the status quo have accused their revisionist adversaries of serving neocolonialism. Another Pan-Africanist argument has maintained that the revisionists were sowing tribalism and disunity. According to this argument secessionism was motivated by tribalism and was running counter to Pan-African ideals. The two evils of colonialism and tribalism were sometimes linked when certain policies of the former colonial administration could be cited as having encouraged tribal or separatist sentiments. Thus Ethiopia has argued that the idea of "Greater Somalia" was an imperialist scheme, originally devised by Britain after World War II. Italian encouragement of Somali raids on Ethiopian posts in the 1920s, and British support for the Somali Youth League (which subsequently became the government party in Somalia), were mentioned by Ethiopia as evidence of colonialist responsibility for the problem. Kenyan leaders have charged that the British-imposed restrictions on contacts between the Northern Frontier District and the rest of Kenya hindered the integration of the Somalis with their Kenyan brethren, and these were to blame for the Somalis' feeling of separateness. The Sudan government has charged the southern secessionists with serving imperialism and Zionism. It also attributed southern secessionism to the policies of the British administrators who fostered the separateness of the south. Mali has accused the Touareg of being an instrument of French neocolonialism, and blamed the origins of the problem upon the favoritism which the French colonial administration allegedly had shown to the Touareg. Algeria has accused Morocco of serving French and American imperialism. Charges that the revisionist side was serving neocolonialism were made also by Congo against Katanga and by Nigeria against Biafra.

Thus, although Pan-African ideology is probably a factor inhibiting the resort to force in inter-African relations, ample arguments can be mobilized to justify the resort to force and to render it consistent with the values and norms of Pan-African ideology.*

*To the extent that *legal* justifications were used, the defenders of the status quo were able to avail themselves of arguments with a Pan-African flavor. In defense of their policies they cited the OAU charter and the OAU resolution affirming respect for existing boundaries. On the other hand, the arguments of the revisionist side were not specifically African in character. They referred to the right of self-determination as embodied in the United Nations charter, as well as to other arguments of international law.

Chapter **6** *The Roles of Friends and Allies*

States involved in disputes seek friends and allies for support and assistance. This has also been true for the parties involved in border disputes, whether states or other groups. The support sought, and sometimes received, has included military, economic, and diplomatic assistance. The relationships which evolved have been formal on occasion, embodied in a treaty; but more often there existed only a tacit agreement to collaborate. Support has been durable and continuous in some cases, and merely transient in others.

The associations formed by six sets of parties involved in border and territorial disputes will be reviewed here, followed by an examination of some of the patterns and effects of these associations. The disputes included: (1) Morocco-Mauritania; (2) Mali-Mauritania and the Targui insurrection in Mali; (3) Morocco-Algeria; (4) Somalia-Ethiopia and Somalia-Kenya; (5) The north-south conflict in Sudan; and (6) Ghana's disputes with neighboring countries.

CASES

1. *The Moroccan-Mauritanian dispute.* When Morocco became independent in 1956 a number of issues with France remained outstanding, among them the questions of Mauritanian independence and of the frontier with Algeria. Morocco accorded priority to the Mauritanian claim for independence, which appeared more urgent because of the rapid

strides toward independence being made by the French African territories in general. It was also considered that the question of the Moroccan-Algerian border would complicate Moroccan relations with the Algerian National Liberation Front (FLN).

The first task Morocco set for itself was to prevent Mauritania's accession to self-government and later to independence. When it became clear that neither could be prevented, Morocco attempted to isolate Mauritania politically and block its admission to the United Nations. Morocco's diplomatic efforts at international conferences as well as its military actions were reviewed earlier; here the search for support for these policies will be examined.

Morocco was able to form a very valuable relationship, for its own purposes, with opposition groups in Mauritania. Of these, the most important was the Nahda party, established in 1958 and banned in 1960. Though the party adopted pro-Moroccan positions for a number of reasons, in their attempts to win a following opposition leaders commonly played upon the Moors' racial feelings, arguing that President Ould Daddah's course of independence for Mauritania was bound to result in subservience to Negro Africa. As for the Moroccan government, the existence of pro-Moroccan opposition groups helped both to lend credibility to the Moroccan claim, and to provide Morocco with an organizational base for attempts to undermine Mauritania's independence. By 1963, however, these groups had ceased to be an important factor, having been eliminated by a combination of repression and Ould Daddah's adroit policies.[1]

For international support on the Mauritanian question, Morocco turned first to its Maghreb sisters and then to the other Arab states. Both habit and an estimate of common interest suggested this choice. These states had supported the Moroccan independence movement. Furthermore, France was then their common enemy: Morocco regarded France as its adversary in Mauritania; the Algerian FLN was locked in a struggle for independence from France; Tunisia had clashed with France over a series of issues, among them its southern border with French-held Algeria; and Egypt was on bad terms with France because of the Suez War and Egyptian support for the FLN. In addition to the common enemy, these states also had a common Islamic-Arab culture. The three Maghreb countries had even more in common culturally, and also shared the heritage of French rule. Finally, they shared common ideologies: the Maghreb leaders were committed to the idea of Maghreb solidarity, whereas antiimperialism served as another link to the Arab world and beyond.

One of the earliest expressions of Tunisian and Algerian support for the Moroccan claim to Mauritania appeared in the resolutions of the conference of the Maghreb's principal nationalist parties, which met in Tangier in April 1958. Tunisia was represented at the conference by the government party, the Neo-Destour; Algeria by the FLN, and Morocco by the Istiqlal. The main concerns of the conference were the struggle in Algeria and the future of the Maghreb. But one of the resolutions expressed the conference's "active solidarity with the Mauritanian people's struggle for liberation."[2]

In his search for Arab support, King Mohamed V in 1960 visited six Arab states: the United Arab Republic, Saudi Arabia, Jordan, Kuwait, Iraq, and Lebanon. On each occasion, a joint communiqué endorsed the Moroccan position on Mauritania. Furthermore, the Arab League conference in Shtora, Lebanon, in August 1960, adopted a resolution committing the Arab states "to support Moroccan efforts to recover Mauritania, which is an integral part of its national territory." A Mauritanian attempt to counteract Moroccan influence failed, as a Mauritanian delegation which sought to visit Arab states in October 1960 was refused entry. Indonesia, Moslem though not Arab, also expressed support for the Moroccan claim.[3]

The Moroccan struggle to prevent Mauritania's admission to the United Nations, and the formation of the Casablanca bloc, have already been discussed earlier (see Chapter 3). Here, only a little needs to be added about the conduct of three states: Tunisia and the Soviet Union, which deserted Morocco, and Mali, which became an active ally.

Tunisia's desertion of Morocco was striking because it joined France in co-sponsoring Mauritania's admission to the United Nations in December 1960. This act illustrated the estrangement that had occurred between the two states.

Resentment was reciprocal, as Tunisia felt that Morocco had failed to support it in its dispute with France over the Algerian boundary.

The Soviet Union's support for Morocco at the United Nations in 1960 reflected a temporary convergence of interests. By blocking Mauritania's admission in that year the Soviet Union earned Morocco's gratitude, and at the same time gained a bargaining position for itself, which it subsequently used to achieve the admission of Mongolia. An arms aid agreement, concluded in 1960, was another aspect of Soviet support. Morocco may have derived some consolation for the withdrawal (in 1961) of the Soviet veto blocking Mauritania's admission to the United Nations, by the arrival of Soviet arms during 1961 and 1962. The visits to Morocco of Leonid Brezhnev in February 1961 and of Anastas Mikoyan in January 1962, were further indications of the favorable climate of Moroccan-Soviet relations.

The benefits of this relationship to Morocco were several. One was the strengthening of the Moroccan army. Morocco also expected that improved relations with the Soviet Union would carry the political advantage of making France and the United States (both with bases in Morocco) more amenable to Moroccan views. Domestically, the Soviet aid agreement helped the Moroccan government as it served to blunt some of the criticism of the leftist opposition. As for the Soviet Union, it hoped that the military aid it extended would help loosen Morocco's ties with the West.

Among Morocco's Casablanca partners, Mali deserves special mention. Mali's policy of active support for Morocco on the Mauritanian issue stemmed, of course, from Mali's own dispute with Mauritania. The closeness of Moroccan-Malian cooperation was reflected by Mali's granting permission for Moroccan-aided terrorists to use Malian territory as their base of operations against Mauritania. The alliance lasted until the conclusion of the Mali-Mauritania border agreement in 1963, when Mali withdrew its active support of the Moroccan claim, since its interest in collaboration with Morocco had ceased.

Whereas Morocco's supporters were anti-French and radical, Mauritania's were at first pro-French and conservative.

That Mauritania in 1961 reinforced its links with France was not surprising. Such action followed as an extension of the colonial bonds with France. French investments in the development of Mauritania's mineral resources had broadened both the scope and the intensity of Franco-Mauritanian relations. Mauritania's lack of trained personnel also tended to increase its dependence on France. On top of this, Moroccan hostility drove Mauritania into the French embrace.

From 1957 until about 1963, Mauritania's most urgent concerns were internal security and external defense. France provided both. The successful fight of 1957-1958 against the Moroccan Liberation Army was carried on by the French army, while internal security was in the hands of French personnel. After Mauritania became independent in November 1960, the French role was placed on a new basis, enunciated in the Franco-Mauritanian agreements of June 19, 1961, several of which dealt with defense and military assistance. The defense treaty was the most important of these. Several of the provisions, defining the principles and framework of defense cooperation, are of special interest here.

Article I of the defense treaty stated that France and Mauritania would "lend each other aid and assistance to prepare and assure their defense." Article II affirmed that Mauritania was responsible for its internal and external defense. It provided, in addition, that Mauritania "may request the French Republic for assistance, according to the conditions defined by special agreements." The treaty also provided for the formation of a joint defense committee, and French assistance for the establishment of the Mauritanian armed forces. By Article V each party undertook "to render the other all facilities and all aid necessary for defense."[4]

Like all defense agreements between France and its former colonies, the treaty was interpreted as containing a French guarantee of Mauritania's sovereignty and territorial integrity.[5] Yet in fact the French commitment as embodied in the published text of the agreement was vague and contained no explicit mention of a guarantee. All that the agreement said was that Mauritania *may* ask for French assistance, but it refrained from committing France to grant the assistance so requested. The "special agreements" referred to in Article II were not published. There may have been a secret French commitment to come to Mauritania's assistance if so requested. The deterrent value of a guarantee kept secret is smaller than of a guarantee made public. But, perhaps, a formal public guarantee was deemed unnecessary; the stationing of French troops in Mauritania, their active participation in antiguerrilla and antiterrorist operations, and French assistance in the establishment of the Mauritanian army and police, were perhaps considered sufficient indications of the measure of French commitment.[6]

The benefits derived from the agreements were of course not onesided. The agreements served two major French interests. One was to safeguard France's predominant position in Mauritania. The second was related to the Algerian war, because of which France considered it particularly advantageous to retain bases and forces in Mauritania.

The close association with France was, not doubt, embarrassing to the Mauritanian leaders; it seemed to lend substance to Moroccan accusations that Mauritania was a "neo-colonialist puppet." The Brazzaville group's support for Mauritania helped somewhat to alleviate this embarrassment. Yet Mauritania still felt uncomfortable and, soon after independence, President Ould Daddah began making efforts to broaden Mauritania's international contacts and to overcome the hostility of Arab and radical states. In addition to Mauritania's desire to diminish international support for the Moroccan claim, domestic politics also dictated such a course. The Moorish majority in Mauritania felt attracted to the Arab world and sought to reduce Mauritania's dependence upon its black African neighbors in the south. The policy of expanding international contacts helped to blunt opposition attacks on the government for its estrangement from the Arab world and its close association with negro Africa.[7]

In pursuit of such a policy, Ould Daddah expressed Mauritania's solidarity with the Arab struggle against Israel. He also declared support for Algeria's struggle for independence, opposed French nuclear tests in the Sahara, and stated that French military bases in Mauritania were only temporary.[8] Partial success was indicated by the state visit made by President Ould Daddah to Ghana in January 1962, and to Guinea in October 1963. The United Arab Republic modified its attitude slowly, but steadily, as a result of its growing disagreements with Morocco, as well as the dissolution of the Casablanca bloc. Formal recognition of Mauritania by the United Arab Republic was announced in October 1964.[9] A further shift to a more radical posture began in the second half of 1964: it was marked by the establishment of diplomatic relations with most communist countries, including China and North Korea. Another gesture was Mauritania's withdrawal in July 1965 from OCAM.*

2. Mali-Mauritania and the Targui insurrection. The close relationship with Morocco served Mali well in two respects. On the one hand, it constituted pressure on Mauritania that was designed to bring about a favorable settlement of their border dispute. On the other hand, the alliance served as an insurance for Mali that in case Mauritania disintegrated, Morocco would be favorably disposed to Mali's receiving a share of the spoils. As events turned out, Mali obtained considerable concessions from Mauritania in the settlement of their border dispute. It is highly probable that the factors influencing Mauritania's generosity were its concern over the Mali-Moroccan alliance and its hope to disrupt this alliance by a settlement with Mali. This indeed happened. From the Malian point of view, the alliance with Morocco had successfully served its purpose and was allowed to fall apart.

In the second problem Mali faced, that of Targui separatism, Mali received help from Algeria. Algerian cooperation was essential for the success of Malian operations against the Touareg, because, whenever threatened by Malian forces, the rebels were able to escape across the border into Algeria. The Algerians, for their part, were willing to act against the Touareg in punishment for their help to France during the war.

Even before the outbreak of the Targui rebellion, Mali and

*OCAM (Organisation Commune Africaine et Malgache) was established by the former UAM (Union Africaine et Malgache) members at the Nouakchott conference in February 1965 for the purpose of promoting economic and functional cooperation. In fact, it acquired a political character as the inheritor of the UAM, which had been dissolved following the establishment of the OAU.

Algeria had in 1962 concluded an agreement for joint supervision of their border. The agreement was not satisfactorily implemented, reportedly because of obstructionism by Colonel Mohamed Chaabani, who was in charge of the area and opposed to the Ben Bella regime. Toward the end of 1963 cooperation between Mali and Algeria improved. President Ben Bella granted Mali the right to pursue rebels across the Algerian border. There were no joint operations, but on several occasions the Algerians captured rebel leaders who had crossed the border and handed them over to the Malian authorities. The cooperation between Mali and Algeria was subsequently reinforced by a border agreement concluded in July 1964, and by the visit of Mali's president to Algeria in August.[10]

3. *The Moroccan-Algerian dispute.* Morocco had much greater difficulty obtaining support for its claim against Algeria than for its Mauritanian claim. When the Moroccan-Algerian war erupted in the autumn of 1963, Algeria could still draw on the wide international sympathy it had won during the struggle for independence. On the other hand several of Morocco's former friends deserted it; many remained neutral; and a few tried to mediate the dispute. The position of the United Arab Republic was somewhat exceptional; it was one of the states that had offered to mediate while at the same time coming to Algeria's assistance with supplies and military advisors.[11]

The policies of the great powers toward the Moroccan-Algerian conflict differed substantially from their attitudes to the Moroccan-Mauritanian dispute. Unlike the Moroccan-Mauritanian dispute, at the outset of which the communist states supported the Moroccan thesis while the West recognized Mauritania's sovereignty, both the United States and the Soviet Union formally adhered to neutrality and refrained from taking positions on the merits of this dispute. The West was irritated by Algeria's flirting with the communist world but anxious not to strain relations any further. On the other hand, the communist states accepted the official Algerian view that the war was a western attempt to intervene in Algeria in support of the Kabylia revolt. Yet they did not blame Morocco, but the West.[12]

China too adopted a neutral stand, and gave expression to it when Premier Chou En-Lai visited both Algeria and Morocco a mere two months after the start of the war. The joint Chinese-Algerian communiqué, issued on December 27, 1963, at the end of Chou's visit, declared China's support for "the African countries in their efforts to settle their disputes through peaceful consultation." The joint communiqué issued at the conclusion of the Chinese leader's visit to Morocco reaffirmed that the two states endorsed the principle of settling "questions between Asian and African countries left over by history" through peaceful means, and "in the spirit of justice and equity."[13]

Yet, in the practical terms of military and economic support, Soviet policy clearly favored Algeria and United States policy favored Morocco. The military and economic strength of the two states became dependent on the two great powers. In the arms race that developed, the Soviet Union and the United States have, from time to time, been asked to lend additional assistance. These patterns of support notwithstanding, Algeria has continued to receive some assistance from western countries, whereas Morocco has continued to receive some aid from the Soviet Union. Although Morocco would have liked to have depicted Algeria as aligned with the communist camp, and Algeria would have liked to depict Morocco as an imperialist agent, both countries wanted to appear nonaligned in the cold war, and both the great powers supporting them wanted to remain nonaligned in the local conflict.[14]

4. *The Somali-Ethiopian and Somali-Kenyan disputes.*   Somalia's search for political support was at a disadvantage, since most states formally professed respect for the territorial integrity of others. Yet, although Somalia's claims were not officially endorsed by any state, Somalia drew encouragement from the sympathy of several.

One was Egypt. Long before Somalia's independence, Egypt had expressed sympathy for a greater Somalia. Encouragement for Somali separatists in Ethiopia and Kenya was broadcast by Cairo radio in its Somali-language programs. Egyptian support was also extended at international confer-

ences and through the AAPSO secretariat, located in Cairo.
After independence, Egyptian support was reconfirmed by
the extension of military aid. Although Egypt was subsequently replaced by the Soviet Union as a major source of
Somalia's military supplies, Egypt continued to supply arms
to the Somali Republic, some of which reached the shifta in
Ethiopia and Kenya.[15]

But Somalia's expectations of Egyptian diplomatic support
were not fully realized, and in view of Egypt's aid and expressions of sympathy, the omission of official public endorsement of Somalia's territorial claims was conspicuous and
disappointing for the Somalis. Furthermore, Egypt did not
help Somalia in its attempt to raise the Somali problem at the
Conference of Nonaligned Nations in Belgrade, in 1961, and
failed to extend the support which the Somalis expected at
other occasions and conferences as well.

Egypt's sympathy was reciprocated by Somalia's diplomatic support for Egypt and its identification with Arab
causes, notably with respect to Israel. But Egypt too had its
share of disappointments in that Somalia refrained from
adopting the Arabic script for the Somali language and declined invitations to join the Arab League. Egypt was also
irritated by Somalia's initial support, in 1965 and 1966, for
the idea of an Islamic alliance and by the Somali president's
visit to West Germany at the very time that the United Arab
Republic had severed diplomatic relations in retaliation for
the establishment of relations between Germany and Israel.

Other occasional strains in Somali-Egyptian relations were
caused by the murder of the Egyptian member of the United
Nations Advisory Council in Mogadishu in 1957, Somali
irritation at what they regarded as high-handed Egyptian
behavior, and friction in their commercial relations.

Despite these strains, Somali-Egyptian cooperation persisted because it brought benefits to both sides. It was valuable to Somalia both for the resources made available by
Egyptian aid and for the occasional diplomatic support. By
supporting Somalia, Egypt acquired a leverage for applying
influence on Ethiopia and on Kenya. This Egyptian policy
was a contemporary expression of a historic Egyptian interest
in the upper reaches of the Nile and the regions controling
the river's sources.

Public justification of the collaboration was expressed in both traditional and anticolonial terms. The bonds of the common Islamic religion served as one justification and, in fact, provided the association with Egypt with a wide popular base. The modern political justification described the relationship as being directed against both colonialism and neocolonialism. Ethiopian and Kenyan rule over Somali populations was depicted in radio broadcasts as "colonialism," and Egyptian-Somali collaboration was described as aimed against western and neocolonialist influences in the region.

Somalia also established close relations with Sudan. Here, too, Islam was a common bond, reinforced by personal connections established by Somalis from former British Somaliland who had attended Gordon College and other Sudanese schools. Although relations were close during the period of military rule, which lasted until 1964, the Sudanese government maintained neutrality toward the disputes between Somalia and its neighbors.

Following the overthrow of the military regime in October 1964, Sudanese policy changed. The Sudanese government did not come out openly in support of Somali irredentist aspirations. But on various occasions prominent political leaders expressed their sympathy for the Somali cause. The new Somali-Sudanese relationship was reflected also in the exchange of high-level governmental delegations, including visits to Mogadishu by the Sudanese prime minister, minister of defense, and chief of staff. The visits led, in April 1967, to reports that a defense agreement between the two governments was being considered.[16]

The warmth displayed by Sudan toward Somalia can be explained in the context of post-1964 Sudanese policy toward Ethiopia. Beginning in 1964, Sudanese-Ethiopian relations had deteriorated because of Sudanese support for the Eritrean guerrillas and Ethiopian assistance to the southern Sudan separatists. The attitude that "my enemy's enemy is my friend" was undoubtedly an important factor in cementing Somali-Sudanese collaboration. Yet there was a logical contradiction in Sudan's sympathy for Somali irredentism. With respect to Somalia, Sudan supported the thesis that the principle of self-determination was applicable to populations that formed part of African independent states. At the same time, Sudan denied the applicability of self-determination to the Negro population of the Southern Sudan. Apparently the inconsistency did not harm either policy.

Somalia's search for support was much less successful in black Africa. At the time of independence, Somalia had very few African links and Somali identification with African causes was relatively recent. Soon after Somalia's independence African states divided into moderate and radical blocs. Somalia first chose to associate itself with the moderates, and participated in the Monrovia Conference in May 1961. Somalia obtained only minimal satisfaction at that conference.

In a way it is surprising that Somalia did not join the Casablanca group. Somalia's revisionist goals fit better with the mood of Casablanca and with the resolutions adopted there, than with Monrovia. In particular, it would have been reasonable to expect Somalia and Morocco to cooperate in attacking colonial-imposed boundaries, and in demanding their revision. But politics are not shaped by the logically consistent application of abstract principles.

The lack of cooperation between Somalia and Morocco can be traced to the invitation extended to Mokhtar Ould Daddah to attend Somalia's independence celebrations on July 1, 1960. This was not intended to be a political gesture, as he was invited along with other leaders of the emerging states of former French West Africa. However, Somalia's subsequent support for Mauritania at the United Nations, and its participation at the Monrovia conference, were calculated political decisions. A conclusive explanation of this policy course cannot be made, but it will probably not be far off the mark to attribute the policy to the strong western influences which prevailed in Mogadishu at that time.

When the Moroccan-Algerian dispute erupted, Somalia's strong sympathy for Algeria, which had developed during Algeria's independence struggle, prevented Somalia from supporting Morocco. There was, however, some similarity in the positions Somalia and Morocco adopted at the OAU Council of Ministers and summit meetings in 1964. During the discussion of the Somali-Ethiopian dispute at the extraordinary session of the Council of Ministers in Dar es Salaam, Morocco objected to a proposal whereby the parties to the dispute would explicitly renounce appeal to any organization other than the OAU. Both Morocco and Somalia seemed to prefer United Nations intervention in their dispute to the OAU's handling of the matter. At the summit conference in Cairo, in July 1964, Morocco objected to the resolution on boundaries. On these occasions Somalia and Morocco found themselves adopting similar positions, each for its own reasons. To the extent that this resulted in any cooperation between them, it was ad hoc and strictly limited.

Soon after the Monrovia conference a marked change in Somalia's orientation began, with a gradual but steady drift toward radicalism. One expression of this new policy was the visit paid by President Aden Abdulla Osman to Ghana in October 1961. At the conclusion of the visit Presidents Osman and Nkrumah issued a joint communiqué expressing their views on a number of subjects, including boundaries:

> The two Presidents, while expressing the view that a political union between the independent African States would automatically make these obsolete, and feeling that these problems provided a strong case for the early achievement of a political union between the independent African States, recognized the imperative need to remove the existing frontiers artifically demarcated by the colonialists without respect for ethnic, cultural or economic links.
>
> President Nkrumah and President Osman were of the view that this objective could be achieved by adherence to the principle of self-determination.[17]

The communiqué should not be considered an expression of Ghanaian support for Somali territorial claims. In fact, Ghana never explicitly supported Somali aspirations. The wording of the communiqué can be explained as an expression of Ghana's strong commitment to radical Pan-Africanism and to the reshaping of the map of Africa. Ghana's own irredentist claims with respect to Togoland and the Ivory Coast also probably influenced the Ghanaian position. The measure of Ghanaian support for Somalia can perhaps be gauged by

the summarized version of the communiqué published in the
Accra *Daily Graphic.* The item was headlined "Somali Boys
to Study in Ghana Schools." With respect to the boundaries,
the *Daily Graphic* reported only that the two leaders expressed the view that political union between African states
would automatically make boundaries obsolete.[18]

Did the applicability of parts of Ghana's official ideology
to Somalia's irredentist policy provide a sufficient basis for
an alliance between the two states? On several occasions their
policies converged, suggesting the possibility of collaboration.
At the sessions of the OAU Council of Ministers in Dar es
Salaam and Lagos, in February 1964, Ghana strongly supported the Somali request that observers be placed along the
Somali-Ethiopian border. Subsequently, Ghana helped Somalia in the debate in the Council of Ministers in July 1964, in
Cairo, concerning the Somali complaint against the Kenyan-
Ethiopian defense treaty. In the discussion by the heads of
state of the resolution on boundaries in Cairo in July 1964,
President Nkrumah argued that the "corollary to the principle of respect for frontiers" should be that the Commission
of Mediation, Conciliation, and Arbitration of the OAU be
activated.[19]

On the whole, cooperation between Ghana and Somalia was
intermittent and marred by strains and disagreements. Somalia rejected a Ghanaian attempt to recruit its support for the
Casablanca group. In the spring of 1962, Somalia requested
that Ghana recall its ambassador in Mogadishu. A further
blow to Ghana was Somalia's opposition to President Nkrumah's proposal at the 1965 OAU summit for the establishment of an executive council for the OAU. Yet there remained an underlying sympathy between Somalia and Nkrumah's Ghana. Its final symbolic manifestation was a formal
expression of "dismay" at the coup that deposed Nkrumah,
whom the Somali foreign minister described on this occasion
as the "Messiah of African Freedom." Somalia also delayed
its recognition of the new government.[20]

Tanzania was another African state that attracted Somali
diplomatic efforts. The cultivation of good relations with
Tanzania was important to Somalia for two reasons: first,
Somalia hoped that through Tanzania some influence might

be exerted to modify the adamant Kenyan opposition to
Somali claims; and second, Somalia was interested in becoming associated with some of the activities of the East
African Common Services Organization, and hoped that good
relations with Tanzania might help to overcome Kenyan
objections to such an association. Somali-Tanzanian contacts
began as early as 1960, when Julius Nyerere attended Somalia's independence celebrations in Mogadishu. After Tanzania
(until 1964 called Tanganyika) attained independence, Somalia opened an embassy in Dar es Salaam—one of the very few
foreign embassies maintained by Somalia.

Tanzania remained, however, unfavorably disposed toward
Somali irredentism for two main reasons. One was ideological: the concern that boundary claims would be detrimental
to African solidarity. The second was historical and practical:
the great sympathy for Kenya, stemming from the close
association which had developed among the three East African territories. The educated Tanzanians—politicians and civil
servants in particular—tended to identify with Kenya on the
Somali question. As one high ranking official commented
with some heat (and much exaggeration) in 1963: "Soon the
Somalis of Arusha and Tanga will also want to join Greater
Somalia."[21]

In the crisis of 1964, and in subsequent OAU debates,
Tanzania played an active diplomatic role, usually supporting
Kenya, Ethiopia, and the territorial status quo. The crowning
act of this diplomacy was President Nyerere's sponsorship at
the summit conference of the resolution pledging states to
respect existing borders.

A modification of Tanzania's attitude became noticeable in
1965. Diplomatic support for Kenya gave way to a new posture of neutrality. The most important expression of this new
policy was President Nyerere's acceptance of a Somali proposal that he mediate between Somalia and Kenya, and the
invitation he extended to the Somali president to pay a state
visit to Tanzania. The mediation failed, but President Osman's state visit was marked by a Somali-Tanzanian agreement to enter into closer relations. President Nyerere's return
visit to Somalia, in August 1966, was another indication of
Tanzania's dissociation from Kenya.[22]

Somalia's success in cultivating relations with Tanzania was limited. Unlike Sudanese leaders, Tanzanian personalities did not make statements supporting Somali claims. Yet Somalia's success in Tanzania helped to relieve Somalia's isolation.

How can the modification of Tanzania's attitude from support of Kenya to neutrality be explained? A partial explanation is provided by the gradual estrangement between the Kenyan and Tanzanian governments. This estrangement was reflected in the failure of the East African states to federate in 1964; its reasons were mainly economic and ideological and unrelated to the Somali problem. Once Kenya and Tanzania began to draw apart, Tanzanian identification with Kenya faded and a policy of neutrality toward the dispute seemed to be better attuned to the new style of Tanzanian-Kenyan relations. On the other hand, the rapprochement between Somalia and Tanzania was facilitated by the radical mood of both the Somali and Tanzanian governments.

In their international policies the Somalis have sought to identify their cause with the plight of other "divided nations." While in the cases of Korea and Vietnam this line has led the Somalis to sympathize with the communist side, it is interesting to note that Somalia referred to the theme of self-determination and reunification in its relations with West Germany. This was probably done in the hope that it would make the Somali cause popular in West Germany. The Germans reciprocated and they too referred to the theme of unification, as a problem common to both countries. But no significant political results ensued from these mutual attentions.[23]

Ethiopia too searched for political support. Ethiopia's foreign policy was also much influenced by its dispute with Somalia, In addition, Ethiopia's external relations were affected by a somewhat similar concern over Eritrean separatism, and the nation's responses to these two challenges were related.

Ethiopia's African diplomacy was directed toward several mutually supporting goals. One was the enhancement of Ethiopia's prestige and standing in Africa in general. A second was the acceptance by the majority of African states of the principle of respect for existing boundaries. A third goal was to dissuade any potential ally of Somalia or of the Eritrean separatists from extending them aid.[24]

Ethiopia was not wholly successful in preventing the Eritrean and Somali separatists from obtaining aid, but this failure should not be attributed to a shortcoming of Ethiopian diplomacy but to the circumstances that rendered this goal difficult. Ethiopia was more successful in its pursuit of two other goals. The location of the OAU headquarters in Addis Ababa reflected Ethiopia's prestige among the African states; and Ethiopia's diplomacy played an important role in preparing the ground for the OAU resolution on borders. It is probable that Ethiopia's involvement as mediator in the Algerian-Moroccan dispute was in part motivated by the Ethiopian desire to help establish precedents and principles for the treatment of territorial disputes. It would, however, be unfair to argue that Haile Selassie offered his services as mediator solely for this purpose. The emperor became involved in the mediation efforts both in his personal capacity, and as representative of the OAU provisional secretariat.*

Of particular importance in Ethiopia's diplomacy were its relations with Kenya, Uganda, Tanzania, Egypt, and Sudan. Ethiopia and Kenya faced a common enemy in Somali irredentism, and this led them, naturally, to ally with each other. The initiative was taken by Ethiopia, which began cultivating relations with the nationalist leadership of the East African states before they attained independence.[25] In 1962 Ethiopia joined the Pan-African Freedom Movement for East, Central and Southern Africa (PAFMECSA), the common organization of nationalist movements, which served as a vehicle for the strengthening of those relations.

In June 1963, several months before Kenya's independence, Kenya and Ethiopia concluded a defense agreement.[26] The agreement came into force formally after Kenya's independence in December 1963 and provided for mutual assistance in defense, Ethiopian aid in the training of Kenya's armed forces, and regular consultation between the

---

*Ethiopia was responsible for the provisional secretariat of the OAU until July 1964, when the Heads of State Conference appointed Diallo Telli, Guinea's Permanent Representative to the United Nations, as Administrative Secretary General of the organization.

responsible ministers and military authorities of the two states. Presumably some cooperation in intelligence and operations against Somali guerrillas were also established, but each state retained exclusive responsibility for activities on its side of the border.

As part of Ethiopia's diplomatic drive, in June 1964 the emperor paid state visits to Kenya, Tanzania, and Uganda. The official communiqués on the talks he held with Kenyan and Ugandan leaders (though not the communiqué concluding the visit to Tanzania), specifically referred to boundary questions. The communiqué on the talks between the emperor and the prime minister of Uganda stated that the two leaders "agreed that claims by African States against each other adversely affect the interests of African Unity and Progress. They therefore affirmed that all boundaries existing at the date of Independence of each State should not be changed."[27]

In relations with Egypt, the task for Ethiopian diplomacy was to bring about a cessation of Egyptian support for the guerrilla movements, or at least to prevent an open endorsement by Egypt of Somali and Eritrean separatism. Ethiopia hoped that it could minimize hostile Egyptian action by creating and maintaining an atmosphere of cordiality and friendship. To this end on his trips abroad the emperor paid periodic visits to Cairo.

Particular attention was paid by Ethiopia to Sudan. Their relations were always somewhat delicate because of Sudanese sympathy for the Eritrean and the Somali secessionists, and because of the assistance the Eritrean shiftas received from Sudan. Ethiopia also suspected that sympathy for the Eritrean secessionists was motivated by Sudan's desire to annex parts of Eritrea (when the future of Eritrea was considered after World War II, Britain had proposed to partition Eritrea between Ethiopia and Sudan). A border dispute between the two countries also complicated their relations. However, during the military regime of General Abboud, Sudanese assistance to the shifta was minimal, and the Sudan government tried to maintain good relations with Ethiopia. Sudan's attitude was undoubtedly influenced by concern that if relations between the two states were unfriendly, Ethiopia might become an important source of support for the rebels in the south. Thus, both governments' policies were influenced by complementary fears and tacit quid pro quos. The degree of mutual confidence attained between them during General Abboud's regime was reflected by Ethiopia's consent that Sudan mediate between Ethiopia and Somalia in 1964.

Following the overthrow of the military regime in October 1964 Sudan's policy changed and support for the Eritrean shifta increased. As was to be expected, Ethiopia, on its part, reciprocated by adopting a more sympathetic attitude toward the southern Sudan rebels. Relations deteriorated and, in these circumstances, the border dispute also assumed importance.

Attempts to restore confidence and to improve relations between the two governments led to an agreement, signed July 28, 1965, whereby the two states pledged themselves to prevent actions within their jurisdictions which were harmful to the other. In addition, a joint ministerial consultative committee was established to consider problems arising between the two states.[28] Yet despite this agreement and subsequent high-level visits, friction and mutual recriminations continued. Confidence was not reestablished, and each side believed that the other was aiding its enemies.

Among non-African states, France held a special place in Ethiopia's external relations. Historically, this stemmed from France's role at the end of the nineteenth century in helping Ethiopia to preserve its independence against Italian attempts to establish dominance, and from the franchise held by a French company for the Addis Ababa-Djibouti railroad line. The significance of Djibouti for Ethiopia and the Somali claim to this French-held port, placed relations with France among Ethiopia's most important concerns.

Here Ethiopian policy faced a dilemma. Ethiopian and French interests converged in their desire to prevent Somalia's claim to French Somaliland from being generally recognized and, in the longer run, to frustrate the Somali efforts to annex Djibouti. However, Ethiopia's commitment to anti-colonialism, and its own aspirations toward Djibouti made it difficult for Ethiopia to cooperate with France. Furthermore Ethiopia was constrained to act with great caution in advancing its own claim to Djibouti lest it arouse French hostility. For the record, Ethiopia periodically reiterated its own claims to French Somaliland but refrained from initiating any action designed to dislodge the French. Furthermore, at international gatherings Ethiopia sought to keep African demands for decolonization in French Somaliland at a low key. In this, Ethiopia was assisted by several of the French-speaking African states.

A critical period for Franco-Ethiopian relations began in August 1966, when the riots in Djibouti provoked President de Gaulle into declaring that the territory could obtain independence if a majority voted for such a step in a referendum. For a while it was unclear whether the French decision to hold a referendum signified a renunciation of French interest in the territory, or whether France would attempt to influence the vote in order to secure continued control over French Somaliland. This uncertainty and the unrest in the territory prompted Ethiopia to take a stronger anti-colonial stand, and to declare most emphatically its own interest in the territory.[29] The result of the referendum, in which the majority voted for continued association with France, relieved the immediate crisis. But, since undercurrents of unrest persisted, Ethiopia remained faced with the almost incompatible tasks of maintaining an irreconcilable anticolonial image, building up a following among the population of the Afar and Issa Territory (as French Somaliland came to be called), and, at the same time, preserving its friendship and mutual trust with France.

Kenya's search for political support in the Somali question dates back to 1963, when Kenya emerged to independence under the shadow of the Somali problem: Kenyan leaders were then greatly worried about the Somali challenge and the growing unrest among the Somali population in northern Kenya. Thus, at the time of independence Kenya's most pressing concerns were of a military and security nature. Nevertheless, Kenya, too, played an active role in the diplomatic struggle over the OAU resolution on boundaries. Although a relative latecomer to the councils of independent states, Kenya's position was enhanced by the prestige President Kenyatta enjoyed as a founding member of Pan-African groups in London in the 1930s and 1940s.

The Kenyan case initially met with much sympathy in Tanzania and Uganda. An early indication of Ugandan and Tanzanian support for Kenya was the announcement in 1963 that the three countries would cooperate in defense matters. Whatever intentions for defense cooperation the three East African states had were, however, disrupted by the army mutinies which took place in all three territories in January 1964, and which were suppressed with the help of British troops. Subsequently Tanzania decided to cut its military ties with Britain, while Kenya's defense connections with Britain remained very close. These differences of policy rendered defense cooperation between the three states much more difficult and their original intention was not implemented.

Initially, Kenya also received political support from its sister East African states. Tanzania's attitudes were discussed above. As for Uganda, it provided more active diplomatic assistance to Kenya than did Tanzania. Following the publication of Kenya's constitution in March 1963, which indicated that the Northern Frontier District would not be separated from Kenya (and before Kenya attained full independence), the Uganda prime minister, Milton Obote, initiated an exchange of correspondence with the Somali prime minister, Abdirashid Ali Shermarke. In his letter, dated March 25, 1963, Obote explained that as a member of the East African Common Services Organization Uganda was concerned with Kenya-Somali relations. He criticized Somalia's call on Britain to separate the Northern Frontier District from Kenya before independence, noting that the independence struggle was directed against just this kind of arbitrary imperial action. Obote further stated that such questions should be discussed between African states only after they had attained full independence. Although Obote's arguments favored the Kenyan position, it is interesting to note that he did not take a stand on the merits of the particular dispute, nor concern himself with the principles of maintaining colonial borders or revising them. (Subsequently Obote did express himself about the principles involved, in the joint communique issued by him and the Ethiopian emperor in June 1964). The

Somali prime minister's reply, dated April 14, 1963, stated
that Obote was not guided by accurate knowledge of the
situation. Somalia supported the right of the people in the
Northern Frontier District to self-determination, and the
colonial power which had created the unfortunate situation
there should accept responsibility for solving it, rather than
leaving it to poison relations between African states.[30]

Like Tanzania's, Uganda's initial support for Kenya can be
attributed in large measure to a habit of solidarity which had
developed among the three East African states before independence. But Uganda, more than Tanzania, also had good
reason to support the principles of respect for existing
boundaries and the preservation of the territorial integrity of
states. Uganda, too, was threatened by lingering separatist
sentiment in Buganda, and by the Ruwenzururu movement.

After 1964 active Ugandan support for Kenya subsided.
Uganda did not develop relations with Somalia, as Tanzania
had done, but assumed a detached posture. Although not as
active in mediation as Tanzania, Uganda nevertheless took
some part in mediation efforts, and President Obote was one
of the observers present at the Somali-Kenyan conference in
Arusha in October 1967.

All three states, Somalia, Ethiopia, and Kenya, involved in
disputes they regarded as vital, made special efforts to obtain
large-scale military assistance. Their desire to acquire modern
equipment on easy terms, as well as additional economic
support to sustain their military efforts, led them to seek the
support of the great powers. Such efforts entailed the danger
of becoming entangled in Cold War rivalries.

Somalia's initial western orientation in the early 1960s was
reflected in the aid Somalia received from Italy, Britain, and
the United States. Western support was limited to the provision of economic and military aid and did not entail support
of Somali irredentist claims. In 1961 Somalia began to develop its relations with the communist countries. This was
done not only to obtain more aid, but also to prod the West
into showing greater sympathy for Somali aspirations. The
first important result of this policy was the agreement with
the Soviet Union whereby Somalia was to receive Soviet
credits amounting to fifty-two million dollars. This credit

represented the largest amount of aid per capita any African country was then receiving, with the exception of Liberia. Agreements were also signed with other communist countries, including China.

But the most important step in Somalia's cultivation of close relations with the communist world was its decision, in 1963, to accept a Soviet offer of military assistance. Somalia had first appealed to the West for help in expanding its military forces. As a result, the United States, Italy, and West Germany made a joint offer of ten million dollars. Somalia declined the western proposal, however, in preference for a Soviet offer of credits amounting to 32 million dollars, which were to enable Somalia to expand its forces to about 20,000 men, and greatly to strengthen the airforce as well.

As for Ethiopia, its historical experience of striving to preserve its independence in the face of the scramble for Africa, led that country to a policy of diversifying its external associations in order to avoid being dependent for its security on any one nation or bloc. In accordance with this principle Ethiopia sought and received military aid from many countries, while, at the same time, remaining suspicious of all its friends.

Ethiopia's suspicions of Britain and the United States were intensified in early 1959, after Britain's offer of help to the Somalis in arranging for the unification of British and Italian Somaliland after independence. Ethiopia interpreted this as encouragement to Somali nationalism. British and American efforts to allay Ethiopian objections caused friction, and heightened Ethiopian suspicions.[31] It was perhaps symptomatic that the emperor paid his first visit to the Soviet Union in the summer of 1959. On this occasion an agreement was concluded whereby the Soviet Union agreed to furnish Ethiopia with aid amounting to $100 million. The political by-products of the aid agreement were a warning to the West to pay heed to Ethiopian views on the Somali question, and an indication to the Soviet Union that a neutral position toward the dispute might be advantageous.

Occasional friction between Ethiopia and the United States notwithstanding, Ethiopia received considerable military assistance from the United States. American military aid to Ethiopia began long before the Somali problem became seri-

ous, and was initiated under the general American policy of
constructing a network of defense alliances. Part of the
American aid was considered to be in compensation for Ethiopian agreement to the maintenance of an American communications base on Ethiopian territory. Between 1953 and
1965 American military aid amounted to nearly eighty-one
million dollars in grants and included equipment and training.

In accordance, however, with Ethiopia's general policy
concerning its external aid agreements, Ethiopia has not
relied exclusively upon the United States. Ethiopia has received assistance from Sweden for the air force, from Norway
and Britain for the navy, from Israel for the air and land
forces, from India for the military academy, and from West
Germany for a mobile gendarmerie.[32]

Kenya believed at the time of independence that it faced
urgent military and security problems. Government worries
about security stemmed from the fear that the country might
simultaneously face a threat from the Somali separatists and
from elements in the population whose resentment against
British domination and land alienation had long been suppressed. The dimensions of the Somali threat were unclear,
but Kenyan leaders expected a full-scale insurrection in the
north, and feared possible harassment from the Somali Republic across the border. In these circumstances, among the
first steps of the newly established Kenyan government was
the conclusion of defense agreements with Britain and Ethiopia.

The negotiations with Britain on the defense agreement
began before Kenya's independence and were concluded in
June 1964. Under the terms of this agreement Kenya received a grant in the amount of 3.5 million pounds consisting
of arms and equipment, vehicles, and aircraft. Britain also
promised assistance for the establishment of a Kenyan navy
and for the training of Kenya's armed forces. The agreement
further provided for the transfer of British military assets in
Kenya to the Kenya government. But of perhaps greatest
immediate importance was Britain's agreement to lend support for the antiguerrilla operations in the north. This support consisted of escort units, engineers who built roads, and

logistical and technical support, including air transport. Furthermore, in 1966 there were still over three hundred British officers and noncommissioned officers on secondment to the Kenyan armed forces. Thus it would be difficult to exaggerate the vital role of British assistance in Kenya's antiguerrilla war in the north.[33]

While furnishing aid, the great powers endeavored to maintain a neutral position with respect to the dispute. From time to time, as the occasion warranted, they issued general statements which were sometimes interpreted by one of the sides as implying support for its point of view and, by its adversary, as proof of the great power's partiality. While seeking to reap the benefits of the feelings of gratitude that their policies engendered, the great powers nevertheless declined to commit themselves, and sought to maintain open lines to both sides in the conflict.

The western powers were assumed by Somalia to be siding with Ethiopia and Kenya. Ethiopia was not altogether satisfied with the degree of western support and retained its suspicions. But even Ethiopia was undoubtedly pleased by the implied American support reflected in the joint communiqué issued by President Kennedy and the emperor on October 2, 1963, at the conclusion of the emperor's visit to the United States. The communiqué stated: "The Emperor and the President also endorsed the principle of the Charter of the Organization of African Unity which called for respect of the sovereignty and territorial integrity of each state and for its inalienable right to independent existence."[34]

The Soviet Union's policy of neutrality was stated publicly in February 1964, following the Somali-Ethiopian border clashes, when the Soviet Union sent Deputy Foreign Minister Jacob Malik to Addis Ababa and to Mogadishu and offered mediation. On the same occasion Khrushchev sent identical messages to the emperor of Ethiopia and the president of Somalia: the Soviet leader expressed the view that there could be no territorial dispute which would require recourse to force and called for a cease-fire and peaceful settlement.[35]

Yet, Soviet expressions of neutrality notwithstanding, the Somalis regarded the Soviet Union as their ally and were immensely grateful to the Soviets, especially for their military assistance. The author was struck during his visit to Mogadishu in November 1965 by how frequently Somalis referred with pride to Soviet military aid. In contrast, they spoke only reluctantly, and with embarrassment, of American food aid, which was helping to stave off starvation in the interior. According to the rumor circulating in Mogadishu concerning the terms of Soviet military aid, the Soviet negotiators requested that the weapons to be furnished by Russia were not to be used against Somalia's neighbors. But, according to the same story, they did not request the insertion of such a provision in the formal agreement, since "the Russians do not attach any strings to their aid." Whether this version of the aid agreement is true or not, it was widely believed in Somalia and taken as another indication of Soviet sympathy for Somali aspirations.

For the same reason, Ethiopia and Kenya regarded the Soviet Union with suspicion. The fact that the shiftas were usually armed with weapons made in communist countries sharpened this suspicion. The Ethiopian response was to seek reassurances through personal contacts between the emperor and Soviet leaders. But Ethiopian expressions of concern at Soviet arms deliveries to Somalia did not result in any modification of Soviet policy.

At the time of independence, Kenya's relations with the major communist powers were relatively good, but they grew progressively worse over the years. This worsening of relations stemmed primarily from Soviet and Chinese support for the opposition to President Kenyatta, led by former Vice-President Oginga Odinga. Soviet arms shipments to Somalia and suspicion of Chinese assistance to the Somali guerrillas, were only secondary factors contributing to this gradual worsening of relations. Unlike Ethiopia, Kenya's concern over Russian and Chinese assistance to the Somalis did not result in attempts to improve relations with these two powers. Russian and Chinese assistance to the internal political opposition apparently precluded such a course.[36]

Ethiopia's concern over Chinese attempts to win Somali friendship may have contributed to the modification of Ethiopia's policy on China. One expression of the change was Ethiopia's voting at the United Nations on the question of

Chinese admission to membership. Until 1958 Ethiopia voted against China's admission; in 1959 it abstained; and since 1960 Ethiopia has voted for China's admission. Although no diplomatic relations were established, the emperor invited Chou En-lai to visit Ethiopia during his African tour in February 1964.

However, like the Soviet Union, China too has refrained from endorsing Somali territorial claims. Premier Chou En-lai's statements on the occasion of his visits to Ethiopia and Somalia, in February 1964, exemplify China's adroit diplomacy. It was bad luck which made the Chinese premier's visits take place when the Somali-Ethiopian crisis resulting from the clashes along the borders was at its peak. Thus, there was no way to avoid reference to the excited atmosphere in which the Chinese premier found himself. But, both in Ethiopia and in Somalia, Chou emphasized China's neutrality and urged the two states to solve their dispute peacefully.

Naturally, the emphasis varied, attuned to please the hosts. The joint communiqué issued at the conclusion of the visit to Ethiopia said that the emperor and the premier "stressed that nations should refrain from interference in the internal affairs of others and declared their continued support for the territorial integrity and sovereign equality for all states."[37] The joint communiqué issued in Somalia declared, among other points, that the existence of foreign bases in Africa and Asia constituted a threat to international peace. China had made the same point many times before but, to the Somalis, the reference to foreign bases meant an implied criticism of Ethiopia.

Although offered several opportunities to express his support for the Somali cause, Chou declined. At a press conference in Mogadishu on February 3, Chou was asked by a Somali correspondent about China's attitude on the Somali-Ethiopian dispute. According to the official Chinese version, the premier answered:

> disputes among African countries should best be settled in accordance with the Charter unanimously adopted by the Summit Conference of African Countries. President Osman said at the banquet this evening that he stood for a

fair and reasonable settlement of the border dispute between Somalia and Ethiopia through peaceful negotiations. Emperor Haile Selassie I of Ethiopia has repeatedly
indicated to me that he was willing to hold negotiations
any time for the peaceful settlement of the border dispute . . . China's attitude towards disputes among African
countries is that of non-involvement but it appeals to the
countries concerned to settle their disputes peacefully.[38]

Somalia renewed its efforts to obtain Chinese endorsement
of its claims during President Osman's visit to Peking in July
1965. In a speech in Peking President Osman denounced the
boundaries based on "illegal" treaties made by the colonial
powers, an argument which China itself was using with reference to its disputes with India and the Soviet Union. President Osman also depicted Somalia's plight as a divided nation. In an official publication describing the visit, the Somali
Ministry of Information said that both China and Somalia
"are divided nations seeking re-unifications through the principle of self-determination."[39] Yet Somali statements failed
to evoke a response from China.

The reluctance of the great powers to align themselves by
public declaration with a party in the dispute should not be
misleading. The crucial and most important aspect of the
involvement of the great powers in the dispute was their
military aid. The acts of the great powers carried greater
significance than their words, and had important effects on
the conflict.

The effects of this aid were several. It tended to strengthen
the self-confidence of the disputants. It also increased the
danger that if the disputes erupted into open conflict, they
would be fought at a higher level of violence and might lead
to more active great power involvement. But, undoubtedly,
the most important effect of the external military aid was the
increase in the capacity of each party to pursue the conflict
by force. On the one hand it enabled the Somali government
to sustain the shifta movement; on the other, it greatly enhanced the capacity of Ethiopia and Kenya to wage antishifta
operations.

The involvement of the great powers was, of course, related

to their global interests and to the Cold War. Nominally, the aid furnished was without strings and the association with great powers did not detract from the devotion of the recipients to nonalignment. Yet the Somali-Russian aid agreement helped to introduce Soviet influence where it had previously not existed and established Soviet presence at the southern entrance into the Red Sea and the shores of the Indian Ocean. Similarly, American and British aid to Ethiopia and Kenya enabled the United States and Britain, respectively, to retain a measure of influence in these two countries. In addition to the considerations of world politics, British aid to Kenya was probably also motivated by Britain's concern for British investments there, and for the future of British settlers who chose to remain in Kenya after independence.

Yet, if we accept the premise that the great powers took advantage of the local conflict to try to promote their own influence in the region, then, in that context, it appears that they acted with relative restraint. It was probably their desire to maintain a neutral position and to avoid commiting themselves exclusively to one side, lest they burn all bridges with other states, which imposed this restraint upon them. Thanks to this reluctance of the powers to commit themselves, the boundary conflict did not become a live Cold War issue, as some other African conflicts (notably in Congo), had become.

5. The Sudanese Conflict. East African alignments have been influenced to a considerable extent by the Sudanese conflict. The separatists in the southern Sudan hoped to receive assistance from the governments of the neighboring territories, mainly Uganda, Congo, and Ethiopia, and to a lesser extent from Kenya and Tanzania. They expected two kinds of aid: the acquiescence of these governments to the establishment on their territory of bases for the Anya Nya and some assistance in the equipping of the guerrillas with necessary supplies and weapons; and political support as well, resulting in international intervention on their behalf.

The guerrilla movement did indeed receive intermittent help from the neighboring countries. This aid was not wholly reliable, since the attitudes of the Ugandan, Congolese, and

Ethiopian authorities varied from time to time. But on the whole, despite occasional restrictions, the neighboring governments have not prevented the southern Sudanese from acquiring supplies through their respective territories. No reliable information is available about the sources of these supplies. The Sudan government has alleged that the southern separatists have received aid from Ethiopia, Israel, and philanthropic and church organizations in Western Europe.[40]

The hopes of the southern Sudanese for active political assistance were totally disappointed. The struggle enjoyed wide sympathy in the neighboring countries and especially among northern Ugandans, whose kinsmen were among the separatists. Nevertheless, none of the neighboring territories, nor any other African state, was willing to commit itself publicly in support of the southern Sudanese, nor to press the matter on their behalf at international gatherings.

Thus, although the southern Sudanese were not mistaken in their assessment of the sympathetic feelings of the neighboring territories, they were mistaken in their expectation that sympathy would be translated into unequivocal support. Concern over possible reprisals by the Sudanese army, fear of possible Sudanese aid to separatist movements or subversive groups in their own territories, and commitment to the principle of the territorial status quo, resulted in a fluctuation of policy between assistance to the rebels and pressure on them to cease their activities and accept the Sudan government's terms.

Sudan's foreign relations in general were naturally much influenced by the conflict in the south, and the sympathy, sometimes active, which some of its neighbors showed to the separatists. This was an important factor contributing to the Somali-Sudanese entente. It was also closely related with Eritrean separatism, since Ethiopian assistance to the southern Sudanese was sometimes used to press Sudan to cease its support for the Eritreans, and vice versa. Similarly, Congolese aid to the southern Sudanese was related to Sudan's support of the *simba* rebels in the Congo. Yet despite occasional friction with Ethiopia and Uganda, and to a lesser extent with Congo (Kinshasa), Kenya, and Tanzania, Sudanese relations with these states have had the appearance of normality. Moreover,

Sudan has been a regular participant at East African Summit meetings.

Until 1967 Sudan had relied on Western countries (mainly Britain, and to a lesser extent West Germany and the United States) for military assistance. In 1967 Sudan concluded a military aid agreement with the Soviet Union. The agreement signified not only an anti-Western gesture but also a new drive for rearmament and expansion of the armed forces. Sudan turned to the Soviet Union for military aid because of internal political developments, and not because of its search for support against the southern separatists. But military needs provided an additional stimulus. Also, the close relationship established with Egypt and Libya after the 1969 coup and the rise of General Jafar Numeiry stemmed from ideological affinities rather than from a search for allies in the southern war. In this case, too, Egypt's willingness to provide military aid (southerners have alleged that the Egyptian air force was taking part in operations), strengthened the ideological friendship by providing the additional bond of a Sudanese military interest in the relations.[41]

6. *The Ghana-Togo and Ghana-Ivory Coast disputes.*
Ghana's border disputes with its three neighbors were matters of secondary importance in Ghana's foreign policy. The primary place was reserved for the pursuit of Nkrumah's conception of Pan-Africanism and its corollaries—establishment of Ghana's leadership in Africa and influence in the non-aligned world. Ghana's territorial ambitions were, along with other foreign policy goals, subservient to these primary aims.

The call for the removal of colonial boundaries in Africa was an important theme in Nkrumah's Pan-Africanism. Until 1961, Ghana recommended two approaches: continental unity, which would make the boundaries obsolete; and piecemeal revision when boundaries interfered with ethnic or other traditional links between African peoples. However, when Ghana came to realize that advocating piecemeal revision would hurt its image among other African states by imputing to it expansionist ambitions, it discontinued advocating such revision. After 1961 Ghana restricted itself to the argument that continental unity would bring about the abolition of borders. Thus, while Nkrumah's Pan-African and revisionist ideology was probably influenced by Ghanaian concern over the territorial dispute with Togo and Nkrumah's support for Nzima unification, subsequently the policy as well as the ideology of territorial revisionism were played down, in order to protect the fundamental tenets of Ghana's Pan-African ideology from the imputation of selfish Ghanaian motives.

The only serious territorial dispute that Ghana was involved in was with Togo. Its effect on Ghana's foreign policy was less than its impact on Togo. Nevertheless, it stimulated Ghanaian initiatives for an understanding with Dahomey. The geopolitical fact of Togo being sandwiched between Ghana and Dahomey made the Ghana-Dahomey association almost natural, conforming to the Kautilyan, or checkerboard, pattern of forming alliances with one's neighbor's neighbor.[42]

Another circumstance suggesting that Ghana's and Dahomey's interests might converge was the occasional friction between Togo and Dahomey. This friction originated in the competition between Togo and Dahomey over the location of French-financed development projects. In addition, an undercurrent of political mistrust existed between Togo and Dahomey, stemming from the ambition of some Togolese to extend the Ewe unification scheme in order to incorporate part of Dahomey. The claim to Dahomey was merely a brief episode in the history of the Ewe unification movement in the 1950s. But the suspicions it created lingered on.[43] Other factors favoring the establishment of close relations between Ghana and Dahomey included the ideological attraction to Ghana felt by some of Dahomey's leaders, and the presence in Ghana of some 150,000 Dahomeyans.

The major attempts at collaboration between Ghana and Dahomey consisted of a trade agreement between them in the summer of 1961, the hope of Dahomeyan leaders that Ghana might be included in a proposed Benin Union, and the Dahomeyan attempt to mediate between Ghana and Togo in 1962. A dramatic episode in the Ghanaian-Dahomeyan collaboration was the urgent consultation between Ghana and Dahomey on the day of President Sylvanus Olympio's assassination. On that occasion the two states exchanged mutual promises that neither of them would intervene in Togo.[44]

While Ghana's border disputes with three neighbors did not have an important impact on its foreign relations and, conversely, the disputes were not much influenced by Ghana's alliance policy, Togo's external relations were determined mainly by fear of Ghana. It is doubtful whether Togo ever faced a real military threat from Ghana, and Togolese fears in this respect were apparently caused more by concern over Ghanaian attempts at subversion than by a prospect of Ghanaian military action to achieve annexation. Nonetheless, Togolese fears of Ghana were genuine.

These fears led Olympio, whose reputation as a nationalist leader had been built on opposition to French policies, to reconsider his attitude toward France. Within days of his electoral victory in 1958, Olympio began making statements about his desire to cooperate with France. As relations with Ghana deteriorated further, Olympio declared shortly before independence that, in view of Nkrumah's expansionist designs, Togo would consider some form of a pact with France.[45]   And indeed, merely six days after Togo attained independence, it entered into a defense agreement with France by an exchange of letters dated May 3 and 28, 1960. The same policy of relying primarily on France was continued by the new regime headed by Nicholas Grunitzky, which came into power after the assassination of President Olympio in January 1963. A new defense agreement (along with other agreements on cooperation), was concluded between Togo and France on July 10, 1963. It was believed that the defense agreements included a French guarantee of Togo's independence and territorial integrity, but this was not confirmed officially.[46]

Togo's African policies have gradually changed from deliberate isolation to expanding cooperation. Initially, under Olympio, isolationism was an important feature in Togo's policies. Togo did not attend the conference of African states in Addis Ababa in June 1960, and refused to join either of the rival Brazzaville and Casablanca groups. Only in 1963, after President Grunitzky acceded to power, did Togo join the Afro-Malagasy Union (UAM), to which most former French territories belonged.

In view of the antagonism to Ghana which Togo shared with the Ivory Coast, it could have been expected that the two states would enter into a close relationship, either directly or through the framework of the Entente Council. But, here too, Togo was a reluctant joiner. Repeated attempts by the entente states to establish a closer relationship with Togo were rebuffed. Only in 1965 did Togo begin to participate in some of the Entente Council meetings, while still refraining from joining the council formally. Togo finally became a member in June 1966.[47]

The most important result of Togo's dispute with Ghana upon Togolese alliances was Togo's close association with France. This had not been as predictable as in the case of the other former French territories. In contrast to the majority of the leaders of the former French territories, whose attitudes virtually assured the continuation of close links between their states and France, Olympio's background predisposed Togo to an estrangement from France. There were probably several factors that influenced Olympio to change his attitude, but the dispute with Ghana, seen by the Togolese as a threat to Togo's territorial integrity and independence, was undoubtedly the most important.

The bad relations which existed between Nkrumah's Ghana and its two other neighbors, Ivory Coast and Upper Volta, can be attributed only in part to the border disputes between them. Ideological differences accounted for the fundamental antagonism between Ghana and these two states, as well as the rivalry between Nkrumah and Félix Houphouët-Boigny, president of the Ivory Coast. These were also the main factors which shaped the associations and alignments of the states concerned. The border disputes were probably only a minor influence in those developments.[48]

Ghana's association with Guinea and Mali was to a large extent motivated by ideological affinity, but the geopolitical fact that Guinea and Mali border on the Ivory Coast and the Upper Volta suggests again the Kautilyan pattern of alliances. Another point to be noted is that, among its other purposes, the Entente Council served to encircle Ghana by friends and allies of the Ivory Coast. Togo's association with the Entente Council in 1965 tightened this encirclement. It is also probable that Ghana's claim to Ivory Coast territory contributed to the Ivory Coast's interest in a defense treaty with France. It is difficult to separate this influence from other factors shaping the attitudes of the Ivory Coast to France. The willingness of the Ivory Coast leadership to rely primarily on French assistance for development and to establish very close relations with France stemmed from political and economic attitudes and past associations completely unrelated to and independent from the border dispute with Ghana. The defense treaty with France would have been concluded even if Ghana had made no territorial claims on the Ivory Coast. But the existence of such claims was a further argument in favor of the defense treaty and for the close relationship with France. Like the other defense agreements, the published text of this agreement makes no mention of a French guarantee. But in this case as well, the existence of such a guarantee has been widely assumed.[49]

The Ivory Coast's defense agreement with France is not a bilateral treaty, like the Franco-Mauritanian and Franco-Togolese agreements. It is a quadrilateral treaty between France, Ivory Coast, Dahomey, and Niger. Conspicuous by its absence is Upper Volta, which, along with the three other African signatories of the treaty, is a member of the Entente Council. Upper Volta declined to join its entente partners in the defense treaty with France, and it is interesting that its border dispute with Ghana (1963-1966) did not cause Upper Volta to reconsider this policy. Probably Upper Volta's concern over alleged Ghanaian territorial ambitions was not as great as the Voltaic complaint to the OAU in 1964 had suggested.

PATTERNS AND EFFECTS

One way to classify the relationships among these nations is according to the *nature of the parties* involved (examples in parentheses):
  1. Secessionist movement—secessionist movement (Ethiopian Somalis-Eritrean Liberation Front)
  2. Secessionist movement—neighboring African state (Sanwi-Ghana; Eritrean Liberation Front-Sudan; southern Sudanese-Ethiopia)

3. Secessionist movement—non-neighboring African
   state (Biafra-Gabon, Tanzania)
4. Threatened status-quo state—neighboring threatened
   status-quo state (Ethiopia-Kenya)
5. Threatened state—its neighbor's neighbor (Kautilyan
   pattern) (Somalia-Sudan)
6. Revisionist African state—revisionist African state
   (Somalia-Ghana)
7. Secessionist movement—non-African state (Eritrean
   Liberation Front-Syria)
8. African state—non-African state (Somalia-Soviet Union;
   Mauritania-France)

Another way to classify the relationships is by the *kinds of
benefits* derived from the association by the party involved in
the border dispute—or by the functions of the association.
Here, a distinction can be drawn between military aid and
other forms of defense support on the one hand, and political
benefits on the other. Military aid and defense support were
often *vital* in enabling the party in the dispute to persevere in
its policies, while political assistance was usually of *secondary*
importance. Revisionist movements depended for their capacity to operate upon the benevolence of a neighboring state.
Yet the primary and principal sources for vital military aid
and defense support were non-African powers. Inter-African
alignments were the main source for political assistance,
although collaboration with non-African powers also had
political uses.[50]

The associations between revisionist movements and neighboring states can be distinguished according to the motives of
the parties and the benefits they derived. In some such associations, the neighboring state was involved because it itself
claimed the territory in question, and the parties, namely the
revisionist movement and the neighboring state which supported it, fully identified with each other. In such cases, the
relationship was often one of *vital sustenance* to the revisionists.

The Somali case and the association between some Mauritanian groups and Morocco, are the obvious examples of such
a high degree of identification. Both sides derived benefits
from their relationship and their policies were interdepen-

dent. In the Somali case, the Somali Republic sustained the secessionist movements and, if it were not for the Somali government's initiatives and support, the secessionist movements would not have emerged, or would have ended soon after their inception. In return, the existence of insurrections in Ethiopia and in Kenya helped to sustain Somalia's irredentist claim and, if it were not for the shiftas, Somalia's claims could not have been kept alive. The Moroccan case further illustrates the interdependence. After the Nahda party, and other pro-Moroccan groups in Mauritania were suppressed, the Moroccan claim to Mauritania lost momentum.

An example of a different kind of interdependence, and of a much lower degree of identification, was the collaboration between the Sanwi secessionists in the Ivory Coast and Ghana. Nkrumah, and perhaps other leaders and groups in Ghana, coveted the Sanwi region of the Ivory Coast. The Sanwis were somewhat ambivalent about their goals: they referred to the kinship links with the population on the Ghana side of the border, but did not claim union with Ghana. Rather they spoke of an unrealistic aim of separatism and independence for their region. In May 1959 a Sanwi government-in-exile was established in Ghana, and in general the Sanwis benefited from their association with Ghana by being able to operate from a friendly base contiguous to the Sanwi district in the Ivory Coast. In addition they apparently received some financial support from Ghana. Ghana gained from this association an intrument for embarrassing Houphouët-Boigny's regime, and a live example to confirm Nkrumah's argument that the boundaries between African states divided brothers and needed to be revised or abolished.[51]

There have also been several cases of collaboration between separatist movements and contiguous states that did not pursue irredentist policy. The links between Sudan and the insurgents in Eritrea and in Chad, or between Uganda and the southern Sudanese, are examples. Sudanese leaders may have entertained vague aspirations for annexing parts of Eritrea, but they were not committed to irredentism and did not identify with the Eritrean separatists in the same way that Somalia was committed to and identified with Somali

secessionism. Similarly, the existence of irredentist sentiments among some Sudanese groups vis-à-vis portions of
Chad has not led to an official identification with Chad insurgents. And, despite the fact that people have for decades
been discussing the advantages of uniting southern Sudan
with Uganda, there is no irredentist Ugandan claim for southern Sudan. Ethiopia and the Congo, which have also aided
the southern Sudan separatists, did not claim territory from
the Sudan either.

   The benefits derived by secessionist or unification movements from such associations were often vital. Refugees
found asylum with kinsmen in the neighboring state. The
provision of weapons and other supplies for insurgent movements usually depended on the good will and sympathy of
the contiguous state. Furthermore, bases for the training and
organization of guerrillas often enjoyed the sanctuary of the
neighboring state. The bases for the movements' political
activity and their link with the outside world were also provided by the neighboring state. Thus, the capacity of such
movements to sustain themselves depended greatly on
whether they enjoyed the sympathy of a contiguous state
and whether that state enabled them to operate within its
territory. The vital necessity for support from a contiguous
state is exemplified by the quick liquidation of the attempted
insurrection in British Togoland in 1957, and the defeat of
Biafra. The French authorities in Togo were unsympathetic
to the Togo unification movement, and did not extend assistance to the insurgents in British Togoland. Cameroon was
neutral in the Biafran-Nigerian conflict, and did not permit
its territory to be used for supplying Biafra. The failure of
these movements can thus be attributed in large measure to
the unavailability of support from a contiguous territory.

   The state that aided insurgents in the neighboring territory
exposed itself, of course, to certain liabilities. Therefore, if
that state did not claim the territory, why did it become
involved? In many cases it simply could not remain aloof and
indifferent since kinsmen of its citizens were involved. Even
when the related frontier population was not in a position to
press the government to extend aid to their brethren, the
state could be drawn into involvement simply because the

conflict was taking place along its frontiers. It would have been extremely difficult, if not impossible, for governments to prevent border populations from extending shelter and comfort to kinsmen from across the line. Also, the instinct of governments to opt for the course that appears politically least hazardous for their own survival in power often influenced them to offer sympathy or assistance, even when they did not claim the territory in question.

The shelter and assistance provided by northern Ugandans to their kinsmen from Sudan is an example. On the one hand, the Ugandan government was eager to placate Sudanese anger, and therefore, from time to time, it imposed restrictions on southern Sudan leaders in Kampala. On the other hand, unable to act against its own political supporters in the north, the Uganda government refrained from enforcing legislation passed in December 1964 making it an offense to harbor refugees without official permission.

Governments that did not claim territory for themselves became involved also because by helping the secessionists they hoped to exert pressure on the government of the state concerned. The goal of such pressure was often to induce the neighboring government to stop its support to rebels in one's own territory. This is exemplified by Sudanese-Ethiopian and Sudanese-Congolese (Kinshasa) relations.

Sources of economic and military assistance provided another kind of association that was vital to the party involved in the border dispute. These sources were usually non-African states, since only they had the capacity to extend aid of the needed quality and comparative magnitude.[52] Such associations were vital because they increased the African state's capacity for military action—both offensive and defensive. It is possible that military assistance agreements had an indirect effect on the will and resolve of the disputing parties to maintain uncompromising positions—in some cases helping states to preserve their territorial integrity and refuse concessions, and in others helping states to persist in their territorial claims. But although it is possible that military assistance encouraged uncompromising policies, this does not mean that specific relationships of aid should be blamed for prolonging disputes. In almost all cases, military aid was available from several alternative sources. Had the aid not been supplied by one power, another would have stepped in to fill the gap.

Nevertheless, there were a few instances of military support provided by African partners: Kenya-Ethiopia, and the United Arab Republic with Somalia, Algeria, and Nigeria. The aid granted by Mali to pro-Moroccan insurgents in Mauritania, and by Algeria to Mali's action against the Touareg are further examples. Moreover, members of the Union Africaine et Malgache were linked by a joint defense pact, concluded at Tananarive in September 1961. But in none of these cases did the military aid received from an African state play a vital role in enabling the party involved in a border or territorial dispute to sustain its policy.

The significance of the military aid agreements between France and certain African states lies not only in the material assistance furnished, but also in the guarantees believed to have been provided. It is uncertain whether the military aid agreements actually contained a formal French guarantee of the territorial integrity of the African partner, yet, it is an important political fact that the treaties were assumed to contain guarantees. This assumption could conceivably have performed a deterrent function. Since neither Morocco, nor Ghana, nor any other African adversary of the states assumed to be covered by a French guarantee had a substantial military capability, the assumption of a French guarantee probably had no important effect on deterring overt external aggression. However, the assumption of a French guarantee no doubt exercised a general restraining and moderating influence on the dynamics of internal dissension and the propensity of revisionist adversaries to intervene. This restraining and moderating influence undoubtedly helped to stabilize the status quo.

The military associations between African parties to border disputes and non-African powers were not of equal value to both sides. To the African party the military and economic aid was vital. In many cases, had it not been for this aid, the African party would not have been capable of persevering in its policies, or would have been forced to reduce its activity and to adopt more conciliatory policies. On the other hand, for the non-African party, the association was merely one of the means it was employing in pursuit of the preservation or expansion of its influence.

Secondary or political benefits were derived mainly from associations with African states. The support received by the party involved in the border dispute from its African partner was often only indirect or tacit, as African states sought to remain formally neutral. In such cases, support was expressed through quiet diplomatic collaboration.

There have also been a number of cases of African states expressing direct and explicit support for parties involved in disputes. Such was the case with the Casablanca and Brazzaville blocs, which explicitly aligned themselves with the respective adversaries in the Moroccan-Mauritanian dispute. The support of the United Arab Republic for Algeria in the Moroccan-Algerian war of 1963 is another example. In the Katangan and Biafran disputes, explicit support was extended by many states to Congo and to Nigeria in their struggles to preserve the status quo, whereas Biafra's independence was formally recognized by four states.

A common form of political assistance was the coalition formed for the expression of majority consensus in favor of the status quo. These expressions of consensus contributed to the creation of an atmosphere and to the codification of the norm that existing borders must be respected. This may have had some effect on the course of individual disputes, hindering the revisionist forces and reinforcing the status-quo cause.

Political assistance was also valuable to those aiming at a revision of the status quo by helping them to overcome their political isolation in Africa, and lending them some ideological respectability. To be sure, this was not always the case. Since Malagasy's devotion to Pan-Africanism had been suspect, its indirect support for Katanga did not promote the acceptance of Katanga by other African states. But the radicals' support for the Moroccan claim to Mauritania, and the recognition extended to Biafra by four African states, lent considerable ideological respectability to those two revisionist positions.

Beyond this, bilateral political collaboration only had the intangible and limited effect of encouraging one side and damaging the morale of its adversary. Even the momentous decision of four states to recognize Biafra had very little, if any, influence on the destiny of the Biafran independence movement.

One exception to the general ineffectiveness of such alliances was the Moroccan-Malian alliance on Mauritania. To be sure, the alliance was not purely political. It also had a military aspect, since Mali facilitated the operation of anti-Mauritanian guerrillas. However, the Moroccan-Malian combination had an important influence on President Ould Daddah's decision to neutralize Mali by settling the border dispute with it, even at the price of considerable concessions.

As with the military links it is interesting to speculate why states associated themselves politically with partners involved in border and territorial disputes. In this connection it is useful to distinguish between Kautilyan allies, namely with a neighbor's neighbor, and other more distant partners. The Kautilyan pattern was motivated mainly by a convergence of interests, with both parties seeking to exert pressure, albeit for different reasons, on their common neighbor. But collaboration with more distant states could also serve to exert pressure on a common adversary. An example is the United Arab Republic's support for Somalia. Somalia and the United Arab Republic are far removed, and the United Arab Republic is not contiguous to Ethiopia or Kenya. But its support for Somalia served as a reminder to Ethiopia of its capacity to cause difficulties for Ethiopia, a reminder which enabled the United Arab Republic to influence Ethiopian policies. Similarly, support for the secessionists may have been used as a lever by the United Arab Republic in its dealings with Kenya and Chad.

Not all states have continent-wide interests and ambitions. Often, political support extended by one party to another lacked tangible benefits, except perhaps the satisfaction of what appeared to be moral or ideological requirements. It would certainly be difficult to explain Tanzania's or Zambia's recognition of Biafra in other terms.

THE CHOICE OF PARTNERS

Obviously, the concerned parties believed it in their mutual interest to support each other, yet, to attribute the action of a state solely to its interest can be merely a rationalization. If we assume that states' actions are guided by their conceptions of interest, then anything that states do is done because the interest of the state required it.

To avoid such unhelpful rationalizations, we shall assume that the conception of interest contains an implicit calculus of utilities, or values. These values can be classified according to two main categories. One category is essentially political and includes such key political concepts as power, influence, and bargaining. The second category can be termed cultural and, in addition to other culture traits, includes habit and ideology.

Sometimes the political interest appears very clear and the choice of the partner therefore obvious. The alliance between Ethiopia and Kenya stemmed almost naturally and necessarily from the fact that both states were threatened by Somali irredentism. Somalia's collaboration with Sudan can also be seen as a consequence of Sudanese-Ethiopian friction. Since both Somalia and Sudan wished to exert pressure on Ethiopia, association between them naturally suggested itself. The collaboration between Morocco and Mali on the Mauritanian issue can be explained in a similar way.

Choices of partners by separatist, secessionist, or unification movements were largely determined by geography. Their need for a sanctuary, for supplies, and for convenient communications rendered the association with a neighboring state particularly advantageous. Often the geographic choice was reinforced by cultural or kinship ties. When neither political interests nor geographic considerations carried decisive weight, "cultural" values seem to have been an important influence upon the choice of the partners. The cultural factors can be divided into several categories: indigenous, including religion; colonial links with the former master; a European culture shared with other societies which had been subject to the same colonial rule; habit, including political habits, and routine or set responses; and ideology.

Common indigenous culture influenced the formation of many associations. Kinship links were an important factor in many cases. A common religion, especially Islam, was also an important influence, reinforcing other determinants. Examples of religious links influencing the growth of political collaboration are the support which Somalia and the Eritrean separatists derived from the Arab world, and which the southern Sudanese and Biafrans received from Catholic organizations.

The habit of relying on the former colonial master also affected the pattern. Kenya's defense treaty with Britain and the defense treaties between former French colonies and France are examples. When these countires had to choose between accepting the aid offered by the departing colonial power, or turning to other sources, the easiest and most natural choice was to accept the offer of the former colonial masters.

Colonial rule also created bonds among countries that had been subject to the same European power. In addition to the shared culture, many personal links and friendships were formed between leaders from different territories. Such personal ties influenced the policies of the former French territories, for example, which formed the Brazzaville group and extended their support to Mauritania. The sympathy of East African states for Kenya can also be attributed to this kind of association. An example of the influence of personal connections is Nnamdi Azikiwe's tour of East and Central Africa in March 1968. Azikiwe's personal prestige and his reputation as a zealous fighter for African causes, both particularly high in English-speaking Africa, added weight to his arguments on behalf of Biafra, and thus played a role in the Tanzanian and Zambian decisions to recognize Biafra.

Political habits have influenced the pattern in a few instances. Tanzania's and Uganda's support for Kenya, and the support extended by the French-speaking states to Mauritania, are among the cases in which the habit of political association led to support over border disputes.

Common ideology has often been mentioned as one of the factors contributing to the attraction between states, and disposing them toward collaboration with each other. The United Arab Republic's identification with Algeria and its support for Algeria in the conflict with Morocco in 1963 were influenced by the radical ideology shared by the two countries, and also perhaps by the sympathy for Algeria, developed during Algeria's struggle for independence. Most of the participants in the Casablanca group were motivated by a radical ideology. Algeria's appeal to the Soviet Union for military assistance can also be attributed in large measure to ideological attraction.

A discussion of political and cultural determinants of interest goes some way toward explaining the associations of support and collaboration formed over border disputes. Numerous additional factors, as well as fortuitous circumstances, contributed to the process, but must remain outside the scope of this discussion.

JUSTIFYING COLLABORATION WITH PAN-AFRICAN IDEOLOGY

The question of justification arises because associations, both between African states and between African states and external powers, have frequently been described as inconsistent with Pan-African ideology. The formation of blocs or groupings between African states has been criticized on the ground that they inhibited the development of African solidarity, and were contrary to the charter of the Organization of African Unity. This argument was used by Somalia in criticizing the Ethiopian-Kenyan defense treaty before the OAU Council of Ministers.[53] Associations between African states and non-African powers have sometimes been criticized as inconsistent with nonalignment. Such ties could also be criticized for impinging upon the desire to insulate African disputes from world conflicts and the Cold War, and to solve local disputes within an African framework. Obviously any assistance received from non-African powers by parties involved in border and territorial disputes tends to weave into the dispute strands of world politics, instead of keeping it clear from non-African influences.

Although some governments sometimes took care to justify their associations as consistent with ideology, it is interesting to note that, on the whole, they were not much concerned with such justification. Nevertheless, those states receiving aid from Western powers usually felt a greater need to justify their acts than those which received assistance from communist countries. This was necessary because Africans often believed that a defense treaty with a Western country and acceptance of military assistance from it served the neocolonial purpose of preserving existing relationships of dependence between Africa and the West. Kenya is interesting in this respect. Strong anti-British feelings in Kenya made it particularly embarrassing for the government to have entered into a defense treaty with Great Britain. But, as has already been pointed out, the reality of the Somali threat and of the guerrilla war in the north, coupled with Soviet support for the Somalis, helped the government in justifying its policy.

It seems that the defense alliances between France and some of the French-speaking African countries were less embarrassing to the African governments concerned than similar relationships between former British colonies and the United Kingdom. Several explanations for this difference have been suggested. Ali Mazrui has argued that this is because the alliance with France did not compromise nonalignment:

> if French military aid is for internal security in an African country against, say, mutineers, or the aid is for "defense" in very general terms without reference to any cold war strategy, then non-alignment is not an issue at all. Admittedly, France is a member of the Western alliance. But France can have relations with her former colonies as France and not as a member of the Western bloc.[54]

C. T. Thorne, Jr. attributed this to a strong commitment to French culture, the influence of President de Gaulle, and the size and extent of French assistance:

> A main reason has been that France has done so much to meet the needs of those countries. This has reduced the temptation, strong in so many other African states, to pursue a policy of diversification, since there has been reason to doubt that any other outside country, or combination of countries, would be prepared to take on French commitments in economic and military aid, trade, technical assistance, and the educational and cultural field.[55]

Both Mazrui and Thorne have contributed to an understanding of the policies of maintaining links with France, but it would seem that the attitudes of the leadership and the general atmosphere which made continued close association with France possible should be attributed to the policy of "assimilation" practiced by France in the colonial period. It helped create among the elite an image of France which was distinct and separate from their experience with French colonial rule. It was a France with which many members of the elite identified. Thus, the postindependence association with France was not only possible, but "natural," and did not require justification.

Military aid from the communist countries seems to have posed the least problems of justification. Such aid was seen by many as reflecting a policy of diversification of sources of aid, thus breaking the pattern of dependence on the former colonial master. Links with communist countries were also regarded as symbols of protest against the West. We do not know whether fewer strings were really attached to Soviet military aid than to Western assistance, since "strings" are seldom displayed in public. But, as evidenced in the Somali case, it was *believed* to be free of strings. Thus, the acceptance of Soviet military assistance was more easily justified as consistent with Pan-African ideals than was Western aid.

AFRICAN AND GLOBAL ALIGNMENTS

Boundary and territorial disputes have had a lesser impact on inter-African politics than have some other issues. The competition for continental leadership and the Congo problem have had a much greater influence on the shaping of African alignments than the border and territorial disputes. To be sure, on some occasions, such disputes contributed to the shaping of alignments. The Mauritanian problem, for example, was a factor in the coalescence of the rival Brazzaville and Casablanca groups, but it was only one factor among several and, compared to the importance attached to other issues, it was of secondary interest to most states except, of course, Morocco and Mauritania themselves.

Among the "non-effects," it should be noted that no alignment of revisionists vs. advocates of the status quo has emerged. The question of principle did not become a rallying issue. Neither was there any distinct correlation between radicalism and revisionism, or conservatism and advocacy of the status quo. Revisionist Somalia did not identify with radical coalitions, while Algeria, which advocated the preservation of the territorial status quo, prided itself on being in the forefront of radicalism.

Similarly, there has been no consistent pattern of correlation between territorial revisionism and links with communist countries, or advocacy of status quo and association with the West. The Soviet Union has provided military assistance to revisionist Somalia, as well as to Algeria and Nigeria, who have sought to preserve the status quo. The United States has helped both revisionist Morocco and status-quo Ethiopia. Usually both superpowers adopted a neutral position on border disputes. Among the exceptions were the Katangan secession, which was opposed by both the United States and the Soviet Union, the Moroccan claim to Mauritania, which was temporarily supported by the Russians, and the Biafran attempt to secede from Nigeria, which was condemned by the Soviet Union.

This record contrasts with the popular assumption that the West supports the status quo while the Soviet Union follows revisionist policies. This may be so if "status quo" is taken to mean the predominance of Western *influence* in Africa. But this has not been the case with respect to the *territorial* status quo.[56] Even China, when addressing itself to the general problem of African borders has declared itself in favor of respect for the territorial integrity of states and the peaceful settlement of disputes.

The clue to the policies of the major world powers should not be sought in their views on abstract principles, nor in their attitudes on territorial and boundary arrangements in Africa in general, but rather in the links between African states and the outside world. The West has sought to preserve the status quo of its predominant influence in Africa, whereas the communist states have pursued a revisionist policy of undermining Western predominance, and establishing links between themselves and the African states. "Status quo" and "revisionism" in political ties between African states and the outside world should not be confused with status quo and revisionism with reference to African territorial disputes and boundaries. The two are not identical.

Competition has led the rival great powers to try to maintain an open door to all governments; hence their emphasis on neutrality. In addition to verbal assertions of neutrality, they often entered into aid agreements with both states in a dispute. The Russians offered credits to Ethiopia and made approaches to Kenya, while supplying arms to Somalia. Morocco has been a beneficiary of Soviet aid, although not of the same kind and scope as Algeria. While Ghana maintained close ties with the Soviet Union, Togo, too, was offered Soviet aid. The United States has followed similar policies of seeking to establish or maintain influence on both sides of various border and territorial disputes. The United States has assisted and equipped the Somali police (which includes semimilitary units for frontier duty), while being a major source of military aid to Ethiopia.[57]

The desire to gain influence placed the great powers in a position where their protestations of friendship were tested on issues that mattered. Therefore they could not avoid providing important assistance which has had a profound effect on the course of the disputes. The attitudes of the parties involved toward the great powers have been shaped accordingly. Both the Somalis and their adversaries judged the Soviet Union not by its formal declarations or its ideas on the principles involved, but by the function performed by Soviet aid. The aid of great powers to other states involved in the disputes was assessed according to the function and effect on the course of the dispute. Therefore, the protestations of neutrality were often unconvincing. Nevertheless, the policy of neutrality can be regarded as successful, since it enabled the great powers to retain access to the adversaries of their protegés. Nonalignment can work both ways.

Chapter **7** *Negotiations and Their Results*

The term *negotiations* can be used in several different ways and the process of negotiations may take different forms. The term will be used here to denote discussions between the adversaries through which each side tries to modify the position of the other party. Negotiations are another instrument of policy, and part of a bargaining process that includes conference diplomacy, force, and the enlistment of support by friends and allies.[1]

THE OUTCOME

Four kinds of results can be distinguished:
1. Negotiations that failed. Includes those between revisionist government and colonial power—Morocco-France; Tunisia-France; Somalia-Britain; and between secessionist movement and government—southern Sudan-Sudan government; Biafra-Nigerian federal government. (See Appendix, p. 289, no. 24)
2. Negotiations leading to disengagement. Egypt-Sudan; Congo (Brazzaville)-Gabon; Dahomey-Niger; Ghana-Togo; the Somali disputes.
3. Negotiations leading to compromise agreements on boundary revisions: Mali-Mauritania; Ethiopia-Kenya.
4. Negotiations leading to agreements recognizing the status quo. Liberia-Guinea; Liberia-Ivory Coast; Tunisia-Algeria; Morocco-Algeria; Morocco-Mauritania.

The first category includes negotiations that failed and thus did not produce a reconciliation. Category 2 contains cases in which disengagement and détente took place but no agreements were reached on the substance of the boundary or territorial dispute; the parties agreed, however, either explicitly or tacitly, to discontinue their quarrel and to institute normal relations. Since the status quo remained in effect, disengagement and détente actually necessitated a concession on the part of the revisionists and a decision to suspend the active pursuit of the revisionist claim. Category 3 comprises those negotiations that produced a compromise agreement on boundary revision, in the sense that the revisionist side did not attain all its claims. Formal agreements confirming the status quo, category 4, differ from other results in which the status quo remained intact by being explicit contractual confirmations of the status quo.[2]

The classification of negotiations by outcome is necessarily qualified by time. None of the results can be regarded as final, since the disputes that appear to have been resolved may be revived, and disputes which appear intractable may one day be resolved. The categorization of outcomes is nevertheless useful because it helps to distinguish among processes and the factors that affect them.

Numerous factors influenced the course of negotiations and their outcome. It is difficult to analyze the impact of the various factors because they are interrelated and thus influence each other. Nevertheless, it is useful to list them here as if they were isolated. The factors can be divided into four major categories: those pertaining to the perception and definition of the issue in dispute; environmental factors; personal or idiosyncratic factors; and procedural factors.

1. The *perceptions* and *definitions* of the parties as to the issue had foremost influence upon negotiations. Border and territorial disputes were sometimes considered to involve "core values" associated with the "national self." In such cases each party to the dispute believed its image of the future to be incompatible with the image held by the adversary. Such a definition of the issue was often accompanied by the assumption that the dispute could not be solved by compromise, since any concession would impair the integrity of the national "self" and undermine the party's identity. Conversely, when the issue was not considered to involve "core

values" and to impair the "national self," the situation was entirely different, and the negotiations bore a different style.[3]

2. The main *environmental* factors were of three kinds. One consisted of the background factors that shaped the capabilities of the party and its capacity to fight or to negotiate: these included the party's resources, both internal and external. Of particular importance were political structure and public opinion, since they significantly determined the government's freedom of action in negotiations.

A second aspect of the environment was the international system. Negotiations were influenced by the policies of third parties, and in particular by alliances or associations to which the parties to the dispute belonged. International organizations also affected the negotiations, since they provided a place to meet, offered procedures for the settlement of disputes, and served to codify norms of behavior.

Ideology, a third aspect of the environment, influenced the attitudes of the actors. By affecting images and perceptions of the "self," of the adversary, and of the environment, it also influenced negotiations.

3. The third group of factors was *personal.* In many situations personality traits, emotions, suspicions, or other attributes of the individuals involved influenced matters to a very great extent. Perceptions of the adversary were also related, of course, to personalities. Rapport among negotiators, their facility of communication, or the feelings of confidence or suspicion toward each other they evoked were also important. So were the political talents and negotiating skills of the main actors.

4. Among the *procedural* factors which influenced negotiations were the tactics employed, the level of negotiations, and the intermediaries, if any.

The role of force in the bargaining process is probably the most important problem in shaping tactics. The application of force, and the mere threat of force, have often influenced the course of negotiations. Yet it is difficult to assess under what circumstances the threat or application of force inhibited negotiations, as Boulding has suggested might be the case, and under what circumstances the parties were stimulated to modify their terms, their priorities, and their goals.[4]

Negotiations by subordinate officials normally moved with greater difficulty than negotiations at the summit, since governmental leaders had greater freedom of maneuver than their subordinates. On the other hand, negotiations between subordinate officials were essential to clear the way for progress by the heads of governments. And, of course, failure at the summit was a greater obstacle to the resumption of talks than a deadlock at the subordinate level.

A distinction can be made between different kinds of intermediaries: an international organization, a government, or a statesman in his personal capacity. Ultimately the intermediary was always a person, and therefore, his personal qualities influenced the process. But if he acted on behalf of an international organization, the character and prestige of the organization usually affected the negotiations. Another distinction can be made between different roles played by the intermediary. In some cases, the intermediary merely provided a *place* to meet. In others, the intermediary provided an institutional and procedural framework for discussion. Conferences or committees of the Organization of African Unity are the obvious examples. In still other cases, the intermediary may play an active role as conciliator or mediator.

A crucial question in any analysis of the negotiations is what induced *changes* in policies. Some changes were affected by the adversary, as he influenced the course of the conflict. A stalemate or the high cost of protracting the conflict sometimes induced a reassessment of policies, or even of goals. Other changes were unrelated to the adversary, but followed from the environment, domestic or international. More often changes of policies were the result of changes in government or of the advent of new personalities.

CHOICE OF NEGOTIATING PARTNER

In several cases the revisionist side had to decide with whom to negotiate. It faced the alternative possibilities of presenting its claims to the colonial power still ruling the territory in question, or of presenting them to the indigenous nationalist movement.

Liberia adopted one approach to this problem. For many decades after the delimitation of Liberian borders with neighboring French and British possessions, Liberia entertained territorial claims, arguing that Britain and France had encroached upon Liberian territory. In 1958, in an effort to negotiate a rectification of its boundaries with the French territories of Guinea and the Ivory Coast, Liberia made new approaches to France. The timing of this renewed approach to France was probably influenced by the assessment that the French territories in Africa had embarked upon the road to independence, although in early 1958 this independence still appeared to be far away.

In October 1958, after Guinea's accession to independence and the Ivory Coast's attainment of autonomy within the French community, Liberia decided to drop its claims. When President Sékou Touré visited Monrovia in November 1958 President Tubman told him that Liberia renounced all territorial claims to Guinean territory. Liberia's renunciation of its claims was reaffirmed on the occasion of President Tubman's visit to Guinea in May 1960. At the close of the visit it was announced that the two leaders "agreed upon a solution for the boundary dispute that had existed between France and Liberia up to the time when France transferred that territory to the Republic of Guinea."[5] Subsequently, after the Ivory Coast became fully independent, President Tubman sent a mission to Abidjan with a similar message. The renunciation of Liberian claims against the Ivory Coast was reaffirmed by President Tubman when the Ivory Coast President, Houphouët-Boigny, visited Monrovia in November 1961.

How is the Liberian approach to be explained? Ideological and Pan-African considerations can probably be eliminated. From the general style and character of Liberian policies it does not appear that Liberia was much moved by ideological considerations. Neither does it seem that the Liberian decision to abandon its claims stemmed from an assessment that the bargaining prospects looked unfavorable. To be sure, the Ivory Coast was closely linked with France, but since Liberia considered it worthwhile to press its claims even while France exercised sovereignty, it is unlikely that it decided to abandon the claims because of the prospect of French support for an independent Ivory Coast. Guinea, the other territory in question, was isolated after it broke with France and could not count on the effective support of any major power. Thus, the bargaining prospects did not worsen in the autumn of 1958, and Liberia's decision cannot be explained in these terms.

What had changed with the independence of the two countries was the environment. Both the internal stability of the new states and their foreign policies were viewed as uncertain. Such changes in the environment probably led to the consideration that an unsettled boundary might induce counterclaims, based on ethnic grounds. Liberia's internal political structure and the tensions between the Americo-Liberians and the indigenous tribes rendered Liberia particularly vulnerable to irredentism and separatism. Therefore, it seemed much wiser to stabilize the new status quo than to undermine it.

A different approach was displayed by Tanzania, which objected to the way the boundary with Nyasaland had been drawn on the Tanzanian side of Lake Nyasa. However, in a statement in the Tanzanian parliament (then still called Tanganika), on June 11, 1962, Prime Minister Rashidi Kawawa said that Tanzania could not contemplate entering into negotiations with the government of the Federation of Rhodesia and Nyasaland (regarded as a racist white-settler regime), or the British government, for an alteration of the boundaries of Nyasaland. If there were to be negotiations on this question, they would have to be with the government of Nyasaland itself and would have to await Nyasaland's independence.[6]

It is possible that the Tanganyikan decision was influenced by an assessment that Britain was unlikely to alter the Nyasaland border shortly before the colony's independence. However, in view of the marked ideological flavor of Tanganyikan policies, it is reasonable to assume that the decision was much influenced by Nyerere's commitment to Pan-Africanism, and by a reluctance to negotiate with Britain on matters that affected inter-African relations.

Ideology could also be used to support the opposite approach of negotiating with the colonial government. Since the colonial power was responsible for delimiting the unjust border, it was logical to appeal to it to correct the injustice. This was the argument advanced by Morocco, Tunisia, and Somalia. By their appeal to the colonial power, however, the three states exposed themselves to charges of seeking to strike a bargain with the colonialists at the expense of fellow-Africans. The three states concerned were not insensitive to such an argument. They justified their policy as being consistent with African solidarity by reasoning that it was their desire to begin their relations with the neighboring country with a clean slate, and that the colonial power should be called upon to put right the injustice which it had perpetrated.

There were also other reasons why Morocco, Tunisia, and Somalia chose to negotiate over their claims with the colonial power. Sovereignty over the territory in question was still exercised by the colonial power. Thus the colonial power had the capacity to satisfy the claims, whereas the nationalist leaders in the neighboring territory were unable to do so. Furthermore, the three states concerned probably assessed the moment of decolonization as more fluid than the situation which would come immediately thereafter, and considered it propitious for altering the status quo.

Yet in the Moroccan case it is doubtful whether its negotiations with France can be regarded as reflecting a choice between alternative definitions of the issue at stake, or alternative tactics. Morocco was drawn into these negotiations prior to having had an opportunity to consider their impact on its relations with the Algerians.

Moroccan-French negotiations concerning Morocco's boundaries were a prolonged process, beginning with the Franco-Moroccan treaty of 1844 and continuing through the period prior to the French assumption of a protectorate over Morocco in 1912. According to the Moroccan view these negotiations continued even during the protectorate period, with Morocco opposing repeated French attempts to encroach upon Morocco's territorial integrity.

When negotiations about independence began, the struggle over the boundaries formed one aspect of the issues involved. According to the Franco-Moroccan agreement of May 28,

1956, Morocco recognized "that it assumed the obligations resulting from the international treaties concluded by France in the name of Morocco, as well as those resulting from international acts concerning Morocco about which it has made no observations."[7] According to the Moroccan view, the treaties concluded by France which related to Morocco's boundaries had not been recognized by Morocco, as Morocco had made "observations" about them, and they were therefore excepted from the above statement.

Since the independence instruments remained open to different interpretations, Morocco unofficially raised the matter of boundaries with France in June 1956, a few weeks after independence.[8] When, in August 1956, France invited Morocco to join the OCRS, Morocco took advantage of the opportunity to call again on France to enter into negotiations over the boundary problem.[9]*

Early in 1957 the operations of the Moroccan Liberation Army (MLA) began to influence Franco-Moroccan bargaining. When France protested the activities of the MLA Morocco responded by requesting that negotiations to determine the Moroccan Saharan boundaries be opened. After several weeks of negotiations about negotiations, it was announced in April that France and Morocco had agreed to negotiate about the boundaries.[10]

Despite the agreement to open negotiations on the boundary and the appointment by both Morocco and France of delegates to deal with the subject, negotiations never took place. As frontier incidents between Moroccan and French forces continued, France requested in 1959 that the joint commission on the boundary meet in order to settle the boundary question and prevent incidents. It became clear at this stage that Morocco was unwilling to enter into negotiations. The Moroccan explanation was that France had falsified the meaning of the agreement to negotiate by wishing to confine the negotiations to the delimitation of a de facto boundary, whereas Morocco interpreted the agreement as

---

*OCRS stands for Organisation Commune des Régions Sahariennes. It was established by France in 1957, and dissolved with Algeria's independence.

intended to cover negotiations concerning the full extent of Moroccan territorial claims.[11]

By this time the Algerian uprising had spread and intensified and had already received full political support from the Moroccan government. Thus, by 1959 Morocco no longer felt comfortable negotiating with France about its claims to French Algerian territory. Undoubtedly, the view began to be held that any meaningful negotiations would have to take the Algerian nationalists into account.

The Tunisian-Algerian border dispute represented another triangular situation. Since its independence in 1956, Tunisia had unsuccessfully pressed France to enter into negotiations concerning the delimitation of the Saharan border between Tunisia and Algeria. Despite Tunisia's close links with, and strong support for, the Algerian FLN, Tunisia until the very eve of Algerian independence continued its attempts to obtain a settlement of its boundary claims by negotiations with France. During his visit to Rambouillet on February 27, 1961, President Habib Bourguiba is reported to have raised the matter with General de Gaulle. By July, however, Tunisia's position had become more equivocal. In the course of a speech to the National Assembly on July 17, during the Bizerta crisis, President Bourguiba said that "France must restore to us what she has usurped," and he also declared that the delimitation of Tunisia's border with Algeria would be undertaken only with an independent Algerian government.[12]

While France had previously rejected the Tunisian claim because it did not want to surrender territory which it considered French, in 1961 France refused to negotiate with Tunisia on this question lest future French relations with an independent Algeria be prejudiced. President de Gaulle's response to the Tunisian claim was reiterated at his press conference on September 5, 1961: "We told M. Bourguiba at that time [at Rambouillet] that when we were bringing an Algerian State into being, which was bound to be interested in the Sahara . . . we were not going to cut up the rocks and sand and hand out sovereignty over them in slices."[13]

Somalia was more insistent than any other African state that its territorial claim be settled by the colonial power concerned. Somalia argued that since the British government held sovereignty over Kenya, it was Britain's responsibility to arrange for the exercise of self-determination in the Northern Frontier District. To this formal and legal argument, the ideological argument was often added that since Britain was responsible for the injustice of dismembering the Somalis and incorporating some of them into Kenya, it was Britain's responsibility to set right the situation it had created.

Britain, on its part, did not formally recognize the Somali government's competence to speak on behalf of the Somali population of Kenya, nor to give Britain advice on how to rule Kenya. Nevertheless, informally, the British and Somali governments maintained continued contact on the matter. Britain apparently believed that the damage to Anglo-Somali relations likely to be caused by the problem of the Northern Frontier District might be reduced by informal discussions.

In the course of these contacts, Britain advised Somalia to discuss the matter with Kenyan nationalist leaders. Indeed, Somalia itself seemed to recognize their interest in the future of the district. Thus discussions on the subject were held with Kenyan leaders parallel to the discussions with the British government. Nevertheless, Somalia stated in its talks with the nationalists that the decision on the future of the NFD was "a matter for the British Government alone."[14]

Somalia also took part informally in the consultations on the NFD during the Kenya Constitutional Conference, held in London in early 1962. Among several Kenyan delegations to the Constitutional Conference was that of the Somali leaders from the NFD. Also in London to advise the NFD Somalis was a government delegation from the Somali Republic, led by a cabinet minister (and subsequently prime minister), Mohamed Haji Ibrahim Egal. Formal discussions also took place, when the British and Somali prime ministers met in London in December 1962.[15]

As a result of the 1962 Kenya Constitutional Conference, a commission was set up "to ascertain, and report on, public opinion in the Northern Frontier District . . . regarding arrangements to be made for the future of the area in the light of the likely course of constitutional development in Kenya." The commission's report, published at the end of December, indicated that the Somalis in Kenya "almost unanimously" favored secession from Kenya, "with the object of ultimately joining the Somali Republic."[16]

The Somalis saw in the report a confirmation of their claim and assumed that the British government would act accordingly. On January 6, 1963, the Somali government formally advised Britain that "it is prepared to accept as its own duty the assumption of sovereignty over the territory and people in question." Somalia further proposed that a conference be held before the end of the month to make arrangements for the transfer of sovereignty.[17]   Britain's response, delayed until February 11, neither treated the substantive issues, nor replied to the Somali proposal. Yet Britain assured the Somali government that it would be consulted "before any final decision is taken on the future of the NFD."[18]

By all indications, Britain had already made up its mind, perhaps a long time before, not to alter Kenya's borders before independence. Yet diplomatic exchanges between Mogadishu and London continued for several weeks, until on March 8 Colonial and Commonwealth Secretary Duncan Sandys announced in Nairobi the arrangements which had been made for Kenya's independence. Among these was the decision that the Northern Frontier District would form one of the regions into which Kenya would be divided, and that its Somali population would enjoy a wide measure of autonomy within this framework. As the announcement signified Britain's decision to hand Kenya intact to its new African government, without meeting the Somali demand for secession, Somalia reacted by breaking diplomatic relations with Britain.[19]

During the spring and summer of 1963 Somalia's contacts with the Kenyan leaders became more regular. The African government, which assumed full responsibility for internal affairs on June 1, 1963, became a channel for communications between Somalia and Britain. Nevertheless, Somalia continued to insist that it regarded Britain as solely responsible for the settlement of the issue.[20]

In August 1963 it was announced that Britain and Somalia had agreed to hold talks in Rome on the question of the Northern Frontier District. The announcement was followed by some confusion concerning the composition of the British delegation. Britain insisted that Kenyan ministers be present as members of the British delegation. To this Somalia objected, thus provoking some resentment from the Kenyan side. In the end four ministers from Kenya participated in the talks, in addition to Peter Thomas, minister of state in the Foreign Office, who led the delegation.

Both sides hoped that the conference would produce a face-saving formula that would enable the other side to yield, but the negotiations failed. The proposals that Britain presented to the conference stated that Britain "will take no unilateral decision involving a change in the frontiers of Kenya before independence." It also declared that "the Kenya Government recognize the interest of Somalia in the future of any people of Somali origin reisiding in Kenya." Furthermore Britain proposed that Kenya and Somalia resume discussions on the problem and that in case the discussions did not result in an agreement, Kenya accept "that the Somali Government will be free after Kenya's independence to bring the matter to the notice of African states within the spirit of the Addis Ababa resolutions."[21]

The Somali proposals also contained no concessions, but only a formula intended to enable Britain and Kenya to yield without losing too much face. Somalia proposed that "as an interim measure, pending a final settlement . . . the Northern Frontier District . . . being a disputed area, should be placed under a special administration. Such administration should be either: (1) a joint Somali/Kenya administration, or (2) placed under United Nations administration." Reciprocating Britain's recognition of Somalia's interest in the Somali population, Somalia declared that it "likewise recognises the interest of Kenya in the same area."[22] But neither side was prepared to yield, and the negotiations were broken off.

Throughout this period all three governments had maintained somewhat inconsistent positions. Somalia insisted that the matter was entirely up to Britain, but nevertheless negotiated on the question with the Kenyan nationalists. Britain did not recognize Somalia's competence to raise the question, but nevertheless maintained discussions through diplomatic channels and later agreed to a formal conference. The African nationalists of Kenya insisted all along that any questions relating to Kenya must be discussed with them, but they too spoke in an equivocal voice. Minister of Finance James Gichuru, who acted for Prime Minister Kenyatta at the conference, was reported to have said on his departure for Rome that Kenya would not yield on the matter, but that he nevertheless hoped that Britain would find a formula.[23]

Britain did not find a formula. The moment when Britain and France were trying to patch previous quarrels with their colonial subjects and win their good will through the transfer of power to the new states, was most inauspicious for the presentation of territorial claims.

INTER-AFRICAN NEGOTIATIONS THAT FAILED

Negotiations can be considered failures if they did not result in conciliation between the parties. The *solution* of the boundary or territorial dispute is *not* the test here. Since the parties can agree to resume normal relations while continuing to disagree about the boundary.

In addition to the failures between revisionist governments and departing colonial powers discussed above, negotiations between two secessionist movements and the government of the territory they wished to separate from also failed. The secessionist movements were those of southern Sudan and Biafra. In a third case, that of Katanga, ostensible agreements were reached, but they were not implemented, and this, too, can be regarded as having ended in failure.

In the case of southern Sudan, negotiations with northern leaders had taken place between the mid-1940s and 1956, as Sudan went through successive stages of constitutional change leading to independence. The negotiations were held in the context of the general discussions at each stage of constitutional change.

In these discussions the south repeatedly demanded a federation, expecting to gain by it a measure of autonomy, whereas the north rejected federation and proceeded to construct a unitary, centralized state. Southern leaders continued to voice similar demands after independence, but discussions were suspended following the establishment of the military regime in 1958, when the constitutional-political framework was abolished.[24]

A major new attempt at a negotiated settlement was initiated following the overthrow of the military regime in October 1964. The attempt failed. Nevertheless, it is interesting to ask why the parties came together after several years during which no negotiations had taken place.

The background to the resumption of the negotiations was guerrilla-war attrition, which had imposed a great strain on both sides. After years of fighting it was evident that a stalemate had developed. Both sides could expect only more fighting and more casualties, without any prospects of a breakthrough. The strain on the Sudan government was already evident in the final months of the military regime. The appointment of a commission of inquiry "to study the factors which hinder harmony between the Northern and Southern parts of Sudan" suggests that a search for new alternatives had been opened.[25] The war was even more costly to the south and there were apparently important southern leaders who were considering ways out of the bloody stalemate.

An opportunity for a fresh start was provided by the revolution that took place in Sudan in October 1964. It appears that the initiative for negotiations was taken by some of the leaders of the Sudan African National Union. In a message sent under the SANU letterhead to the new regime in November 1964, a call was made for a round table conference to discuss "a working constitutional relationship between North and South." The letter actually amounted to capitulation by SANU as it declared the readiness of the exiled leaders to return to Sudan provided they were not prosecuted and on condition "that SANU be recognized as a political party to fight the coming general elections on the policy of a Federal Sudan." Thus the demands for self-determination and secession were dropped.[26] All that the letter claimed was the right to fight the general election on the federation issue.

The terms proposed in the letter did not reflect the consensus of SANU leaders. On the contrary, they induced the

polarization of rival groups and factions within the movement and resulted in the emergence of two camps. The letter
reflected the policies favored by William Deng, one of the
founders of SANU and its secretary-general. Its terms were
opposed by Joseph Oduho, the president, and by Aggrey
Jaden, who at the time held the post of deputy-secretary.

There seem to have been two principal reasons behind the
readiness of the Deng faction to offer these far-reaching concessions. One was the terrible cost of the guerrilla war, the
loss of life, and the suffering and the destruction it caused in
the south. The second was the pressure of the Uganda government for the cessation of Anya-Nya activities on Ugandan
soil, and for a settlement of the problem, which caused constant embarrassment to Uganda.

The revolution in Sudan, resulting in the fall of the military
regime, seemed to some of the southern leaders to offer an
opportunity to end the war without too much loss of face
and perhaps also as a moment at which northern leaders
might agree to some concessions.

Partly for tactical reasons, and perhaps partly out of persuasion, the authors of the letter identified themselves with
the revolution, and proclaimed that revolution was what they
had fought for all these years. The message congratulated the
prime minister, the new government, the political parties, the
University of Khartoum, the judiciary—and significantly
listed among those deserving congratulations also—"*ourselves*
and all the Sudanese people who have worked in one way or
another to retrieve political freedom and democratic life."
Elsewhere the message said: "*We* have forced the Army to
climb down and we are back to where we stopped in 1958."
The wish to return was also indicated in the identification
with Sudan: "Now that the Sudan has become once more a
democratic Republic under your guidance we would like to
express our desire to return to *our Motherland.*"[27]

The new regime's response was favorable. It agreed to a
conference of political parties and granted an amnesty. The
northern leaders' agreement to grant an amnesty and to sit
down at the conference table with exiles and rebels were not
difficult concessions. The war in the south had imposed a
great burden on the country as well, and its continuation was

likely to enable the army to continue to exercise greater influence than was agreeable to the politicians. The prospect of ending the war was therefore worth the price. Furthermore, the conference and the amnesty accorded well with the desire of the new regime to create the image of breaking with the past and of righting the wrongs perpetrated by the military government.

Probably the most difficult concession for northern leaders was their acceptance of the demand contained in the SANU letter that representatives of the OAU and of neighboring African countries attend the conference "in the capacity of observers and advisers." Their attendance could have weakened the Sudan government's argument that the conflict was an internal Sudanese matter. But, in view of the prevailing African sentiment in favor of the preservation of the territorial status quo, and of Uganda's attitude as indicated by its pressure on SANU to attend the conference, any inhibitions the northern leaders may have had about the presence of foreign observers at the conference were overcome.

The majority of SANU's leadership, headed by Oduho and Jaden, dissociated itself from the proposals contained in the letter and from Deng's position. They continued to stand by the goals of self-determination and secession. Yet, under the circumstances, it became increasingly difficult to oppose negotiations.

The conference was opened in Khartoum on March 16, 1965. Formally, it was a round table conference of northern and southern political parties rather than a confrontation between the government and the southern secessionists. Also present were observers from seven African states: Uganda, Kenya, Nigeria, United Arab Republic, Ghana, Tanzania, and Algeria. Since it soon became apparent that no progress toward a settlement was being made, after two weeks of deliberations the conference adjourned for three months. A committee of twelve was named to supervise the implementation of reforms proposed by the conference, and to continue searching for a solution.[28] Although no solution was found, the conference was at first regarded even by exiled southern leaders to have been successful, for it held out the promise of reforms in the south.[29] But, within a few weeks, as the reforms were not implemented, and as the conference was not reconvened, disillusionment set in. Insurgent activity in the south was again intensified, as were the government's repressive measures.

The conference had failed mainly because the goals of the two parties were incompatible. The northern delegates considered the preservation of the Sudan's political and territorial integrity as non-negotiable. The limit of northern concessions was indicated by a report of the Committee of Twelve set up by the conference. Published after a long delay, the report proposed a system of limited regional autonomy.[30] Even Deng's federal proposals were anathema to the north, since federation was viewed by it as a stepping stone to secession. The gap with the position of the other southern delegates (the radical wing of SANU and the Southern Front), who continued to insist on total separation, could not be bridged.

It is probable that the positions of both sides were influenced by certain political problems each faced within its own camp. The southerners' position was hardened by Anya-Nya's opposition to the negotiations and to any solution short of secession. The little influence that exiled political leaders still possessed over the Anya-Nya would have shrunk further had they agreed to anything less than secession and separation. The north's unyielding attitude was influenced by concern that concessions to the southerners might encourage separatist sentiments among other groups and tribes, and also that concessions would be likely to destroy the unstable coalition which had been established following the overthrow of the military regime.

The influence of the intermediaries, and notably of Uganda, was strong enough to force the SANU irreconcilables to attend the conference, yet the intermediaries were unable to persuade either side to modify its position.[31] They, too, were interested in the preservation of the territorial status quo and could not press upon the northern Sudanese an opposite point of view. Their ability to influence the south was also limited, especially since they were not prepared to interfere with the southerners' sources of support and supplies. For its own domestic reasons, Uganda displayed no inclination to take resolute action against the southern refugees within its borders. Moreover, support for a policy of suppression against exiled southern groups by the other states contiguous to the south, notably Ethiopia, Congo, and the Central African Republic (which were not present at the conference), was unlikely to be forthcoming because of strains in their relations with the government in Khartoum.

After the conference ended in deadlock, it was reported that Ghana was considering placing the issue on the agenda of the OAU meeting in Accra. Following Sudanese representations and lack of support from other African states, the idea was dropped. The OAU's only formal concern with the southern Sudan problem was through its Refugee Commission. The OAU, however, played an informal and indirect role, since the occasion of OAU conferences was used by the interested parties for propaganda and lobbying.[32]

Neither the attrition of the war, nor the pressure of friends and intermediaries, were able to change the positions of the two sides. These positions can be described as anchored to "core values": for the north—the preservation of Sudan's territorial integrity, and for the south—the right to separate existence. The clash between the conflicting values of unity and separation is probably one of the most difficult to reconcile.

Chapter **8** *Disengagement, I*

In several disputes disengagement and détente have taken place. By *disengagement* is meant that for an indefinite period the parties suspended their dispute. The border or territorial dispute was not resolved. Indeed, in some cases the revisionist side reiterated its claim. Yet, while not withdrawing the claim, the revisionist side nevertheless ceased its campaign against its adversary. The side defending the status quo, for its part, also ceased its countermeasures. Thus, disengagement required definite changes in the policies of both sides. Disengagement was usually accompanied by détente—the relaxation of tension and improvement of relations. Agreements were concluded on matters other than the border or territorial dispute and the parties entered into collaborative relations.

Disengagement both resembles and differs from some of the processes terminating conflict that have been discussed by Boulding and by Holsti.[1] One such process is "avoidance," described by Boulding as the separation of the disputants "to the point where the conflict ceases from sheer lack of contact." But in the cases before us, disengagement was accompanied by détente and the multiplication of collaborative contacts. Holsti described "avoidance" as the withdrawal of demands and cessation of acts that caused hostile responses. The difference between the disengagement cases before us and avoidance thus described is that in these African disputes the parties did not withdraw their claims but only ceased to pursue them actively. In fact, in some cases, they continued to declare their dedication to the goals which had originally caused the conflict.

In some respects, disengagement resembles, though it also differs from, the process of "reconciliation" described by Boulding. He definied "reconciliation" as a process "in which the value systems of the images of the parties so change that they now have common preferences." The modification of images is reached through "conversation, argument, discussion or debate." The disengagement cases differ in two respects. First, the change in policies reflects a revision in priorities, which may, but does not necessarily, reflect a change in the "value systems of the images." Secondly, in the African disputes discussed here, the change was brought about both by bargaining, which may involve "conversation, argument, discussion or debate," and by changes in the environment and in the personalities involved.

The agreements accompanying disengagement also differ from Boulding's "compromise," in which each party settles "for something less than his ideal position rather than continue the conflict," because the agreements did not concern the boundary or territorial conflict. No agreements were reached on these problems, and the border or territorial issue remained unresolved. The agreements concerned cooperation on problems unrelated to the border dispute.

Holsti has identified as "passive settlement" the process in which the parties quietly reduce their commitment to the contentious objective and implicitly accept the status quo as partially legitimate. Disengagement is different because its style and character are neither "passive" nor "quiet." It is sometimes accompanied by public statements by the parties that they had agreed to disagree on the border or territorial issue and wished to cooperate on a number of other matters of joint interest.

Several of the disputes in which disengagement took place concerned values that formed part of the states' self-image, or to use Boulding's term "core values."[2] In this chapter and the next we shall discuss the phenomenon of change from confrontation to disengagement. What produced the shift in course and the modification of policy? What systemic changes caused the policy change or enabled it to take place? What processes of negotiations were conducive to such an outcome?

EGYPT AND SUDAN

There is no published official account of Egyptian-Sudanese negotiations concerning their border dispute. The record indicates that on February 1, 1958, Egypt sent a note to Sudan requesting an urgent settlement to the boundary problem so that the inhabitants of the area claimed by Egypt could vote in the plebiscite scheduled for February 21, 1958. Sudan rejected the request, and Egypt sent police and troops into the disputed area. This led to the Sudanese complaint to the United Nations Security Council. At the council's meeting on February 21, 1958, Sudan argued that it had tried to settle the dispute through bilateral negotiations, but failed. The Security Council's consideration of the dispute ended when Egypt declared its readiness to postpone the settlement of the issue until after the Sudanese elections scheduled for February 27.[3]

This crisis in Egyptian-Sudanese relations was precipitated by the Egyptian plebiscite scheduled for February 21 and the Sudanese elections scheduled for February 27. Egypt wanted the population of the disputed area to participate in the Egyptian plebiscite and wished to prevent their voting in the Sudanese election. But the circumstances in which previous plebiscites and elections had been held suggest that this is only a partial explanation for the dispute. The same population had not been invited to vote in the previous Egyptian plebiscite in 1956 and the general election in 1957. Furthermore, no objections had been raised by Egypt at the time of the previous Sudanese elections, in 1953. In fact, those elections were supervised by an international commission that contained two Egyptian members.[4]

The February 1958 crisis was related to other problems in Egyptian-Sudanese relations. A few weeks earlier, the protracted negotiations on Sudanese claims resulting from the construction of the Aswan Dam had ended in deadlock. For Egypt, the matter was urgent since it threatened to hold up construction. The raising of the boundary question at that particular time can be interpreted as an attempt to exert pressure on the Sudan to accept Egyptian proposals for a settlement. In particular, the Egyptian claim for Wadi Halfa undermined Sudan's argument that it was entitled to compensation for the flooding of the area which was due to take place when the Aswan Dam was built.

Following the Security Council meeting, Egypt apparently did not continue to press for the settlement of the boundary issue. Negotiations between Egypt and Sudan continued, however, on the question of compensation and resettlement costs for the population of the Wadi Halfa area. Sudanese requests to increase the quota of waters allocated to it by the Nile Waters Agreement of 1929 were also discussed. In November 1959, it was announced that the two countries had reached agreement on these questions. There is no public evidence that the boundary question was raised in the negotiations. It seems that Egypt had decided to suspend the issue indefinitely.

Confirmation for this can be found in the interview given by President Nasser of Egypt in 1966 to the editor of the *Guardian*. When asked whether there had been any serious problems between Egypt and Sudan, President Nasser acknowledged that there had been a serious problem concerning the waters of the Nile, but this was now settled. Then the *Guardian* editor proceeded to ask about the boundary dispute:

> Question: There was also one question of frontier rectifications, wasn't there? I think it would be forgotten about now.
>
> Answer: Yes. You know it is a well known question of the political and the administrative borders. We have tried not to create a problem about them.[5]

The dispute was very much a secondary issue in Egyptian-Sudanese relations, and, therefore, its suspension was not too difficult. The border dispute can be regarded as a symptom of the strains caused by Egypt's disappointment at Sudan's having opted for independence rather than for union with Egypt. It also served as a leverage for the settlement of the compensation problem and the Nile waters question. It was not a major issue on its own merit.

CONGO (BRAZZAVILLE)-GABON

The conciliation of Congo and Gabon in 1962 is interesting because the procedural aspects of the peacemaking effort led to so much maneuvering.

The immediate cause of the crisis were the "football riots" that erupted in September 1962, during which Congolese were molested in Gabon and Gabonese in Congo. (Other foreign Africans were also hurt.) A general climate of antagonism also characterized relations between the two governments. Congo's territorial claims against Gabon were one cause for this antagonism; another was Gabon's reluctance to cooperate with the UDE lest Gabon be put in a position of having to disburse support for the other members of the organization.*

The riots rocked the family of states that had formerly been French Africa. Several leaders promptly reacted by suggesting that one of the "family elders" mediate between the disputants. One of the first proposals came from President Youlou of Congo, who suggested that General de Gaulle be invited to mediate. This idea was almost immediately superseded by others, all of which envisaged the reconciliation as taking place within an African framework. The question of which framework would be charged with the task aroused some controversy. Congo did not want formal UAM involvement, and preferred that the reconciliation take place within the UDE. One reason for this was that the incumbent president of the UAM happened to be President Leon Mba of Gabon. The UDE included only the more immediate family of French Equatorial Africa, and, what may have been more important, Gabon was not a popular member of this group. As Gabon and perhaps other states as well, preferred the

*UDE—Union Douaniére equatorial—the customs union between the states of former French Equatorial Africa and French Cameroon.

UAM, a compromise was worked out. A conference was convened on November 3, 1962, in Douala, Cameroon, by President Tombalbaye of Chad, who was at the time serving as president of the UDE. In addition to the heads of state of the five members of the UDE (Cameroon, the Central African Republic, Chad, Congo and Gabon), the president of Niger, a representative from the Ivory Coast, and the secretary-general of the UAM were also present.

Significantly, the grievances presented by each side at the Douala conference concerned different issues. Gabon complained against Congo's designs to annex Gabonese territory and Congolese attempts to organize subversion against the Gabon government. Congo, on the other hand, accused Gabon of responsibility for the riots and of violating the UAM Charter by expelling Congolese nationals. President Youlou sought to evade the question of Congo's territorial claims. His only response to Gabon's accusations on this issue was that they should have been raised through appropriate UAM procedures.

The task of conciliating the parties was in the main carried out at informal meetings. The communiqué issued at the end of the conference stated that the two governments affirmed their resolve "to effect a final reconciliation and to normalize the good relations which they have always enjoyed in the past."[6] To this end agreements were reached on payment of compensation and the return of the expelled Congolese to Gabon and of the expelled Gabonese to Congo. The final paragraph of the communiqué said that the conference "noted with pleasure" that Gabon and Congo "reaffirmed their complete adherence to all the principles and agreements of the UDE and of the UAM . . . respecting duly the sovereignty and territorial integrity of each state."[7]

According to Albert Tevoedjre, who was secretary-general of the UAM at that time, this last clause "was inserted in particular to satisfy the Gabonese and to give warning to the Congo Republic regarding the Franceville area" (the area claimed by Congo.)[8] Its phrasing in a formula which has become standard in international communiqués could hardly be objected to by Congo.

The conciliation of the two states must be credited to the Douala conference. It should be noted that the Douala conference did not take place within the framework of an existing organization, the UAM or the UDE. Conciliation took place at an ad hoc gathering; it could have been convened because the "conference habit" had become the accepted style of behavior in the "culture" of interstate relations in Africa.

Public opinion is also of interest in this dispute. Mob action precipitated the crisis, yet the two governments apparently had no difficulty at all in "selling" the reconciliation agreement to the same publics that only six weeks earlier had seemed unable to control their hatred toward the nationals of the other state.

DAHOMEY AND NIGER

The Dahomey-Niger dispute over Lété island was a problem of long standing, suddenly projected into prominence in November 1963, but not on its own merits.

The problem of Lété island first emerged during the colonial period, when it was the subject of argument between French administrators. In 1960, on the eve of independence, an incident on the island between those loyal to Dahomey and those loyal to Niger served to awaken the two African governments to the question of jurisdiction over the island. Following the accession of the two territories to independence, negotiations concerning the island were initiated. Conducted in a friendly atmosphere, these negotiations nevertheless reached a deadlock, and in July 1963 representatives from Dahomey and Niger agreed that the matter be referred to a meeting between the heads of state for settlement. But the revolution in Dahomey intervened. Shortly thereafter, the problem assumed major proportions. Simultaneously, other issues came to the fore, and Dahomey-Niger relations entered into a phase of serious crisis.[9]

The crisis was not caused by Lété island; indeed, the deterioration of the Lété island dispute was a symptom of the crisis, rather than its cause. The origin of the crisis can be traced to the revolution in Dahomey in October 1963, which led to the removal of President Hubert Maga. As long as he was at the helm, the close personal relations between him and President Hamani Diori of Niger helped smooth problems between the two countries. The new Dahomeyan regime, on the other hand, evoked deep distrust in Niger, and was suspected of aiding Djibo Bakary's Sawaba party, the outlawed Niger opposition movement. This mistrust and political antagonism precipitated the crisis. In addition to the question of Lété island, the long-standing problem of the terms for the transit through Dahomey of Niger's imports and exports also led to bitter controversy. Another acute conflict was caused by the expulsion from Niger of a large number of Dahomeyans working there.

Since attempts to settle the crisis through bilateral negotiations between Dahomey and Niger were unsuccessful, several African leaders began calling for mediation and conciliation by the African family. The Entente Council, to which both Dahomey and Niger belonged, (along with the Ivory Coast and Upper Volta), was handicapped in its attempt at conciliation because of the antagonism that developed between the new Dahomeyan regime, and President Houphouët-Boigny of the Ivory Coast, the leader of the Entente group. The Entente Council's action was therefore limited to a meeting of the heads of state of the Ivory Coast, Upper Volta, and Niger in Abidjan in January 1964 (Dahomey was absent), at which the presidents of the Ivory Coast and Upper Volta appealed to their two colleagues to settle their dispute amicably.[10]

Immediately after the Entente meeting, an attempt was made to convene a UAM conference in Abidjan on January 15, 1964. However, the conference did not take place, ostensibly because the elections in Dahomey prevented the attendance of the Dahomeyan leaders. A more weighty reason was the tension between the new Dahomeyan regime and the Entente leaders, and the Dahomeyans' consequent reluctance to attend a conference in Abidjan.[11]

A conference of the UAM heads of state finally did take place in Dakar, from March 7 to 10, 1964; among other subjects it dealt with the Dahomey-Niger dispute. At the conference President Hamani Diori of Niger assured President Apithy of Dahomey that Niger would indemnify the Dahomeyan civil servants dismissed from their posts in Niger and would not expel the Dahomeyans working in the private sector in Niger. Concerning Lété island, the UAM heads of state called upon Dahomey and Niger to withdraw their troops from the border and reopen negotiations.[12]

Accordingly, bilateral negotiations were reopened. At these, Dahomey requested that Niger compensate those Dahomeyans who were dismissed from private employment in Niger. Furthermore, Dahomey proposed to partition Lété island between the two states. However, since Niger refused to undertake the payment of compensation and rejected the proposal to divide Lété island, the talks reached a deadlock.[13]

By November relations were again at a crisis point, with the two states accusing each other of aiding subversive movements aiming to overthrow their respective governments. Significantly, the new crisis coincided with mounting internal tension in Dahomey resulting from intensification of the competition between President Apithy and Prime Minister Ahomadegbé.

The internal struggle in Dahomey led to an increase in Prime Minister Ahomadegbé's influence. This internal development had important consequences for the dispute with Niger. Ahomadegbé's rise opened the way for a reconciliation with President Houphouët-Boigny of the Ivory Coast.[14] The reconciliation led to Dahomey's return to the Entente Council whose meetings it had boycotted for over a year.

When the Entente Council met in Janaury 1965, with Prime Minister Justin Ahomadegbé representing Dahomey, it assumed the task of reconciling Dahomey and Niger. (The UAM had formally ceased to exist by then, in accordance with OAU decisions, and was in no position to continue the mediation.) After a formal meeting in Abidjan, the four leaders retired to Houphouët-Boigny's farm at Yamoussoukro for private talks. They reemerged after forty-eight hours and announced that the dispute between the two states had been settled. On the question of Lété island, it was agreed that nationals of both countries would continue to reside on the island until a final solution to the problem was reached.[15] In subsequent bilateral meetings further details on the questions of Niger's transit trade and compensation for Dahomeyan citizens expelled from Niger were settled. On June 15, 1965, the prime minister of Dahomey and the president of Niger met at the border and ceremoniously announced that the dispute between the two states had been solved.

Actually, the problem of sovereignty over Lété island was not solved. The formula agreed upon was vague and merely made formal the de facto situation that existed. Still, the matter was considered resolved, because the primary cause of the conflict had been eliminated. Political confidence between the leaders of Dahomey and Niger had been reestablished. This was reflected by the announcement, soon after the meeting, that "the whole of Dahomey is mobilized to find the Sawaba commandos,"[16] an opposition group in Niger. With the restoration of political confidence, the problem of Lété island ceased to be important, and was once again relegated to obscurity.

A number of factors contributed to a change in the parties' views of the dispute. Among these was Dahomey's desire to justify the construction of the new port at Cotonou, which necessitated an agreement with Niger. Another factor was Niger's demonstrated capacity to reciprocate Dahomey's support for the Sawaba by supporting Dahomeyan opposition movements and thus disturbing Dahomey's internal peace. Also important were the internal changes in Dahomey. The rise in Ahomadegbé's influence led to the restoration of close relations with the Ivory Coast and the Entente Council and opened the way to reconciliation. The UAM and Entente Council performed the task of conciliating the parties. Finally, the valued image of the closely knit "family" of former French Africa, which was shared by both antagonists, facilitated the settlement.

In none of the three cases reviewed (Egypt-Sudan, Congo-Gabon, Dahomey-Niger), was the territorial dispute resolved. But in all of them it lost its importance and therefore ceased to disturb the relations between the neighboring states. In part, this can be explained because the crises were not caused by the boundary dispute but by other problems. The boundary disputes had existed before the crises but had not taken an acute form. They had not attracted attention as long as there were neither incentives nor pressures upon the parties to seek a settlement.

On the other hand, the problems that produced the crises had pressed for urgent settlement. The question of the compensation due to the Sudan was regarded urgent by Egypt because it hindered progress on the Aswan Dam project. Sudan, for its part, was interested in maintaining normal relations with Egypt for reasons of domestic politics and to prevent the question of the relationship with Egypt from disturbing Sudan's precarious domestic stability. The Congo-Gabon dispute was tackled urgently because the leaders of other states feared that it might disturb the functioning and development of the UAM. The urgent problem of Congo nationals expelled from Gabon, and Gabon nationals expelled from Congo and left without jobs, served as another inducement for a settlement.

The Dahomey-Niger dispute also contained elements that pressed for settlement. Niger was greatly worried about the possible support which the Sawaba rebels could receive from an unfriendly Dahomey. Furthermore, Niger was interested in having Dahomey stop its interference with the transit of Niger goods passing through Dahomey. As for Dahomey, it found itself suddenly burdened with several thousands of its citizens expelled from Niger. They not only presented economic and social problems, but were potentially a political threat to the stability of the regime. To soothe their feelings and to alleviate somewhat the economic burden, Dahomey was interested in receiving compensation from Niger as soon as possible. Furthermore the new regime in Dahomey was worried because of the dissatisfaction in the north of the country over the dismissal of former President Maga. Riots had already occurred there and were particularly serious at Parakou. The Dahomey government was afraid that, in the disturbed state of relations between Dahomey and Niger, Niger might lend support to dissatisfied elements in the north. Finally, the diversion of some of Niger's transit trade to Nigeria hurt Dahomey financially: it was in Dahomey's interest to normalize the transit of Niger goods through Dahomey territory. These interests and pressures, on both sides, combined to prod both governments to seek an urgent solution to their problems.

Yet there was no pressure or incentive to seek solutions to the territorial disputes as well. Apparently the territorial disputes did not touch upon issues regarded as vital or pressing. Egypt, Congo, and Dahomey were prepared to institute normal relations with their adversaries while leaving the respective territorial problems unresolved. These problems reverted to their previous latent form, without further disturbing the relations between the respective states.

GHANA AND TOGO

The Ghana-Togo dispute raged on at a high level of hostility for several years. Following the death of President Olympio in Janaury 1963, a measure of disengagement took place. But relations remained disturbed until the overthrow of President Nkrumah in February 1966. Shortly thereafter, talks between the new Ghanaian regime and the Togo government led to a reconciliation. Personal changes—the death of Olympio and the removal of Nkrumah—provide partial explanations of the disengagement between 1963 and 1966. An analysis of the attitudes of the parties and the negotiations between them may help to explain the process.

The origin of the Ghana-Togo dispute can be traced to the incompatible goals that Gold Coast and Togo nationalists set for themselves after World War II. (The origin of the Togo problem as distinct from the Ghana-Togo dispute can be traced much further back to the partition of German Togoland by Britain and France.) The primary aim of Sylvanus Olympio and his political allies in the 1940s and early 1950s had been Ewe unification. But as it appeared that this goal was unlikely to win sympathy at the United Nations, and as a split had developed between the Anlo Ewe in the Gold Coast proper and the Ewe of British Togoland, the goals of the movement were redefined. The focus was shifted to the reunification of the two Togolands. Ewe unification was relegated to secondary place. Togo reunification meant that British Togoland would sever its links with Ghana, and unite with French Togoland.

On the other hand, both anticolonialism and Pan-Africanism led Nkrumah to aim at the unification of British Togoland with Ghana. This goal accorded well not only with ideology but also with Ghana's state interests. Since Ghana's independence was near at hand, whereas the independence of
French Togoland seemed remote, anticolonialism called for
the joining of British Togoland with Ghana, so as to enable it
to attain independence with Ghana, in 1957. Furthermore,
the call for Ewe unification presented Ghana with a challenge. The goal of reunifying peoples divided by colonialism
appealed to Nkrumah's Pan-Africanism. The question was
only in which direction unification ought to begin. In view of
Ghana's rapid progress toward independence the Ghanaians'
argument that unification ought to begin by going with
Ghana could be presented as the proper Pan-Africanist
course. Furthermore, the alternative—of Ewe unification
directed toward the pole of French Togoland—could threaten
Ghana's territorial integrity if Ewes in Ghana proper (the
former Gold Coast) became attracted to it. To avert such a
threat, Ghana came to argue that the best way for French
Togoland to become reunited with British Togoland, and the
best course for Ewe unity, would be to join French Togoland
to Ghana.

These differences over the direction of the unification
process developed into sharp controversy after the Nkrumah
government proceeded to integrate British Togoland into
Ghana, in accordance with the outcome of the 1956 referendum. Yet, since Nicolas Grunitzky and his political allies who
were in power in French Togoland at that time were indifferent, if not opposed, to reunification (partly in deference to
French views), the integration of British Togoland with
Ghana did not disturb relations between the official leader-
ships of the two territories.

This changed when Sylvanus Olympio and his party, the
Comité de l'Unité Totolaise (CUT), won the Togo election in
February 1958. Olympio came to power as leader of the
independence movement (as distinguished from the incumbent coalition which favored continued membership in the
French Union). His background as leader of the reunification
movement inevitably raised the question of the policies

which he would adopt on the reunification issue. Because of his past anti-French attitudes and connections with English-speaking Africa, the French suspected that Olympio would seek to detach Togo from France and associate it with Ghana.[17]

Immediately after his victory Olympio proceeded to hold a series of interviews with journalists. These served the double purpose of reassuring the French and opening a dialogue with Ghana. It was a public dialogue rather than an attempt to negotiate with Ghanaian leaders. On April 30, 1958 Olympio told a press conference that there now existed better conditions for realistic cooperation with France and that he wanted to see progress toward independence. As for relations with Ghana, he hoped that these would find a solution within the context of a West African Federation. Olympio also expressed the hope for an agreement on economic relations with Ghana.[18]

Nkrumah's response was cautious. In a public statement at the end of May, Nkrumah announced that the Ghana government was planning to hold talks with the new government of French Togoland, and was to work toward the removal of customs barriers and frontier transit problems. Nkrumah's statement further stressed "the intensely human problem created by the artificial boundary dividing an area populated by the same indigenous tribal groups."[19]

The dialogue assumed a new dimension when, early in August, Olympio raised the question of British Togoland, and expressed opposition to its integration in Ghana. Olympio was reported in the press to have said that it was extremely important that relations between Ghana and Togo be amicable because of the tribal links of the populations of the two countries. But Togo was "categorically" opposed to any integration with Ghana, including the integration of British Togoland. He favored federation, and believed that the first concrete aim should be a customs union.[20] But once Olympio raised the question of British Togoland, the break with Ghana became inevitable. In October Ghana responded by accusing Togo of supporting subversion in former British Togoland.[21]

The Togolese challenge, and the continued opposition to

integration among important sections of former British Togoland, induced Ghana to respond by reiterating its proposal
for an alternative way to Togo and Ewe unity. In October
1959 Nkrumah made a much publicized statement at Ho in
former British Togoland. He declared that after French Togoland became independent, the Ghana government would
undertake discussions with political leaders of that country in
order to work out a plan for the integration of Ghana and
French Togoland. He said that the artificial boundary was
anachronistic, and that it could be removed only by the total
integration of Togoland with Ghana into a "single and indi-
visible nation." Finally Nkrumah said that he knew that he
spoke also for "our kinsmen" across the border.[22] His statement implied that French colonial rule prevented integration,
and that the population of French Togoland wished to become part of Ghana. Olympio answered at a CUT rally two
days later. He said that Togo would never accept integration
and accused Nkrumah of expansionism. He repeated his view
the next day at a press conference.[23]

Togo's independence was scheduled for April 27, 1960, and
as that date approached the exchanges became angrier. Early
in February Olympio said that Nkrumah's proposals for integration were insulting. He favored a link with Ghana, at least
a customs union, but would never accept a unitary state and
give up independence. Indicating disquiet at Ghana's ambitions he announced that Togo might ask the United Nations
to guarantee its borders.[24]

In the debate, frequent appeals were made to Ewe nationalism. The Ghana government spokesman insisted that Nkrumah's office was being flooded with messages to press for
integration "in the interest of the Ewe people." This was
countered by Olympio who said that had Nkrumah shown
better intentions, by first handing British Togoland over to
the Ewe people, French Togo would have seriously considered some form of loose federation between Togo and
Ghana. He further accused Nkrumah of opposing Ewe unification and said that Togo wanted to remove the old artificial
border, but that the Ewe belonged to the Togolese side of the
border. A few days later Olympio compared Ghanaian policy
to Nazi Germany's Sudetenland policy. He said that Nkru-

mah should have thought of the hardship caused the Ewes when he insisted on the integration of British Togoland with Ghana. Olympio also warned that Ghana would have "an Irish problem" on its hands, since "our brothers" in British Togoland remained opposed to integration.[25]

The public recriminations were accompanied this time with diplomatic protests from Ghana to France, which was still responsible for Togoland. Ghana protested that a document purporting to be a draft constitution of Togoland, and defining a considerable area of Ghana as Togolese territory, was being circulated in Togoland. It also accused Togo of serving as a base, and providing facilities, for people organizing subversion and preparing to create disturbances in Ghana.[26] Following Togo's independence Ghana took the initiative in attempting to mend relations. In June, Nkrumah, accompanied by Foreign Minister Ako Adjei, paid a five-hour visit to Lomé. The meeting between Nkrumah and Olympio failed to produce an agreement. Nkrumah spoke of the need for a political union between Ghana and Togo, whereas Olympio argued that only economic union was practicable. The visit was followed by correspondence between the two leaders. According to Olympio, Nkrumah proposed in these exchanges the opening of negotiations on economic union, as a preliminary step toward a political union. Olympio's reply was that he was ready for immediate talks on economic cooperation, but that his opposition to political union was irrevocable. As these exchanges failed to produce agreement, Ghana reverted to a hostile posture and imposed restrictions on economic relations with Togo.[27]

It is interesting to speculate about the causes of Ghana's initiative. It seems that it stemmed from Nkrumah's belief that much of the trouble between Ghana and Togo had been caused by France, which had influenced Olympio to adopt "anti-Ghanaian" policies. Now that Togo had obtained independence, Nkrumah apparently expected that Ghana would be able to counteract these French influences and encourage Olympio to change his policies.

After this failure, relations between the two countries deteriorated sharply. Apparently assuming that economic pressure might soften Togo's position, Ghana closed the border with Togo. But in addition to economic warfare, in which Togo was at the receiving end, both states apparently engaged in subversion. Togo assisted leaders from British Togoland to organize opposition to the integration of the territory, as well as other Ghanaian groups opposing the Nkrumah regime. Ghana aided opposition leaders from Togo. Among the Ghanaian complaints against Togo was the allegation that President Olympio met Dr. K.A. Busia, head of the Ghanaian opposition, and promised him assistance, and that in return Dr. Busia promised to cede former British Togoland to the Togo Republic. An attempt on Olympio's life, in January 1962, from which he escaped unhurt, brought Togolese charges of Ghanaian complicity. An attempt on Nkrumah's life in December 1962 led to similar accusations by Ghana against Togo.[28]

Attempts by third parties to mediate the dispute all came to nothing. Of particular interest was Dahomey's abortive attempt at mediation. The Dahomeyan initiative seems to have been stimulated, in part, by the commitment to Pan-Africanist ideology of some of the personalities involved, notably Albert Tevoedjre. But it can also be attributed to Dahomey's own interest in the fate of Togo. The Dahomeyan interest is understandable, because the triumph of Ewe irredentism would have posed a threat to Dahomey's territorial integrity. Yet Dahomey would have faced an even greater threat if Ghana were to annex Togo. In such a case Ghana, cast in the role of savior of divided tribes, would have become Dahomey's immediate neighbor.[29]

Following President Olympio's assassination on January 13, 1963, a new government was formed in Togo, headed by Nicolas Grunitzky. Since Grunitzky had not associated himself with claims for Togolese or Ewe unification, it seemed that a new era in Ghanaian-Togolese relations was about to begin. Ghana was the first state to announce the recognition of the new Togolese government. At the same time President Grunitzky declared that he would seek contact with Nkrumah to reestablish commercial relations. This was followed by a relaxation of the restrictions imposed at the Ghanaian-Togolese boundary. A few days later President Grunitzky paid a "courtesy call" on President Nkrumah. In February the border was opened, but in June it was closed again. Another visit by Grunitzky to Nkrumah failed to resolve the problem.[30]

Negotiations in 1964 resulted in an agreement to reopen the border. But the implementation of the agreement was repeatedly delayed as Togo rejected Ghanaian requests for closer economic association. In 1965, as Togo joined the Organisation Commune Africaine et Malgache (OCAM), and thus associated itself with the activities of the anti-Ghanaian coalition of the French-speaking states, Ghana made several gestures to appease Togo. The reopening of the border in July was one such gesture. But toward the end of the year relations worsened, and the border was closed again.[31]

Compared with the 1958-1962 period, relations showed a marked improvement. The mutual involvement in subversion and the accompanying suspicions had been greatly abated following President Olympio's death. The irredentist zeal in both Ghana and Togo seems also to have subsided. The author's impression on a visit to Togo in January 1966 was that unification had been demoted in the order of priorities, and that it no longer played a primary role in Togolese politics. Yet, while the commitment to unification seems to have weakened, members of the Togolese elite retained reservations about the status quo. This attitude was reflected by a statement of a senior government official who was asked by the author whether Togo now accepted existing boundaries. He replied: "No Togolese can say that he accepts the border as it is." Nevertheless, Togo's claims were not proclaimed as frequently, on public or official occasions, as during Olympio's tenure of office. An Ewe rally in Lomé in September 1965 which called on the government to work for unification was the only "loud" reminder of the persisting claim.[32]

As the irredentist issue declined in prominence, improvement of Ghanaian-Togolese relations was hindered by what might be called the "systemic drag." The polarization of regional alignments, accompanied by the growing conflict between the OCAM states and Ghana, affected Ghanaian-Togolese relations and prevented reconciliation.

A definite change occurred following the overthrow of President Nkrumah on February 24, 1966. The new Ghanaian regime blamed Nkrumah for the bad relations and boundary disputes between Ghana and its neighbors. Seeking to present the image of breaking with Nkrumah's policies, the new men made great efforts to establish normal relations with Ghana's neighbors, and they dispatched goodwill missions to neighboring countries, including Togo. These efforts made an impression, and alleviated Togolese suspicions. After meeting the Ghana delegation President Grunitzky declared: "Ghana and Togo are friends again."[33] It took, nevertheless, more than two months for the border to be formally opened, and a few more months for the conclusion of a detailed agreement on the frontier regime. All in all, relations had become normal and smooth.

Territorial claims were not formally abandoned; but neither did they evoke controversy. At the very time that preparations were being made for the formal reopening of the border, President Grunitzky publicly called for the reunion of former British Togoland with the Togo Republic. He declared that there were now excellent relations between Ghana and Togo, and suggested that this was a right time to solve their territorial dispute.[34] But the new Ghanaian regime was not drawn into the controversy. Grunitzky's statement notwithstanding, the border was reopened as scheduled, and relations continued to improve.

The explanation for the success of reconciliation despite the persistence of the Togolese claim can be sought in the new circumstances, which differed markedly from those prevailing between 1956 and 1962. In 1958, the Ghana government was still worried about resistance in British Togoland to integration. By 1966, British Togoland had been absorbed, and the worry no longer persisted. Togo was most unlikely to serve as a base for Nkrumah's supporters who plotted his return to power. The immediate environment had also become more favorable, as Ghana's relations with the OCAM states had become normal. Thus, the "systemic drag," which was an obstacle to a Ghanaian-Togolese rapprochement, also ceased to operate. In these circumstances, the reiteration of the Togolese claim could be dismissed by Ghana as being a ritual, performed perhaps in deference to domestic political needs, but harmless as far as Ghana was concerned. Conversely, Togo's readiness for a reconciliation with Ghana was influenced by the removal of Nkrumah and the pronounced change in Ghana's foreign policy. Furthermore, the disappearance of the threat from Ghana served to reenforce an existing tendency to demote the reunification issue in the rank of Togolese priorities. Another factor contributing to this process was the recognition by Togo's leaders that Togo lacked the capacity to realize reunification. Togo's internal problems, and the concern of some political groups that unification would weaken their political influence by altering the tribal balance in favor of the Ewes, reenforced the tendency to remove the unification problem from the list of immediate and practical concerns.

Thus, the internal changes in Togo, followed by the changes in Ghana and in the atmosphere of interstate relations in West Africa, all contributed to a gradual deescalation of the conflict, and the eventual détente.

Perhaps the most striking case of disengagement took place in the Somali disputes during 1967 and 1968, when, within a few weeks, relations between Somalia and its neighbors were radically transformed and bitter hostility was replaced by expressions of good will and by friendly cooperation. The change was striking because Somalia, Kenya, and Ethiopia had regarded their disputes as involving "core values" concerning the definition of the "national self." Moreover, Kenya and Ethiopia had felt that the Somali claim challenged their survival as states. The vehemence of conflicting attitudes and the bloodshed and misery which resulted from the disputes contributed to bestow upon them the image of most intractable, if not insoluble, conflicts.

ESCALATION, 1957-1967

Notwithstanding numerous contacts between Somali representatives and neighboring governments, Somalia's relations with its neighbors steadily worsened until 1967.

Early Contacts. One of the earliest opportunities for Somali-Ethiopian discussions took place before Somalia's independence. It was in 1957, when Aden Abdulla Osman (then president of the Somali National Assembly, and later president of the Republic, 1960-1967) and Abdullahi Issa (then prime minister) visited Addis Ababa. Although the talks failed to bridge the gap between the parties, they ended on a note of good will. The communiqué issued at the conclusion of the visit declared the two sides desire for harmonious relations and contained a mutual pledge to take measures to prevent the dissemination of propaganda hostile to the other side.[1] The pledge was the first of several which were not respected.

Following Somalia's independence in 1960, diplomatic relations were established between the two countries. No significant negotiations ensued, however. Somali and Ethiopian representatives also met at United Nations gatherings and at occasional conferences in Africa. A Somali delegation attended the 1960 conference of independent African states in Addis Ababa. The Somali-Ethiopian dispute came up for discussion at the Monrovia conference in May 1961, and at the African summit conference in Addis Ababa in May 1963. Despite the fact that the meetings provided an opportunity for the two sides not only to talk at each other, but also with each other, relations did not improve. On the contrary, relations deteriorated as a result of clashes between Somali tribesmen and Ethiopian authorities and the spread of the shifta movement, supported from the Somali Republic.

In 1962, when the first formal talks between Kenya and Somalia were held, their character and atmosphere were quite different from the early phases of Somali-Ethiopian talks. It is unlikely that Somali leaders expected Ethiopia to concede Somali claims. Yet, at the time of their 1962 talks with Kenyan leaders, the Somalis apparently believed that Britain could be persuaded to hand the Northern Frontier District (NFD) over to them prior to Kenya's independence. The discussions with the Kenyan leaders were designed to weaken their opposition, and to make it easier for Britain to hand over the territory.

The talks were held in July and August 1962 during separate visists to Mogadishu by two delegations, representing Kenya's major political parties, KANU and KADU, respectively. Jomo Kenyatta led the KANU group, and Ronald Ngala the KADU delegation. The Somali government extended a warm and festive welcome, but the talks could not bridge the gap between their respective viewpoints. They also failed to soften Kenyan opposition to the separation of the NFD. In fact, Kenyatta emphatically stated that the NFD problem was a domestic Kenyan affair in which Somalia was not to interfere.

The Somali prime minister, Abdirashid Ali Shermarke, responded by saying that if the phrase "interference in domestic affairs" was used, then "any external opposition to Somali reunification is considered as interference in the domestic affairs of the Somali people." He also expressed the hope that if the NFD commission found that the population of the area wished to unite with the Somali Republic, arrangements to that effect would speedily be made with the British government. In the Somali view, this was "a matter for the British government alone."[2]

One of the ideas current in 1962 was that a solution might lie in an expanded East African Federation: in addition to Kenya, Uganda, and Tanganyika (the original sponsors), such a federation was to include Ethiopia and Somalia as well. A tentative step toward broadening the East African association, taken at the end of 1961, had been the expansion of the Pan-African Freedom Movement for East, Central and Southern Africa (PAFMECSA) to include Ethiopia and Somalia.[3] As a result of this step, Ethiopia and Somalia were among the fourteen countries represented at PAFMECSA's annual conference in February 1962 in Addis Ababa. The idea that federation might supply a solution was implied in the conference resolution calling for the establishment of an East African federation also comprising Ethiopia and Somalia.[4] However, the dispute between Somalia and Ethiopia and the developing crisis in Somali-Kenyan relations cast a deep shadow on the scene.

The hope that a federation might render the territorial dispute between Somalia and its neighbors no longer relevant foundered upon the Somali claim that boundary revision must precede federation. This was made clear when, in the course of Ngala's visit to Mogadishu, in August 1962, Prime Minister Shermarke responded to Ngala's suggestion that Somalia join an East African federation:

> The Somali Republic, though otherwise more than willing to do so, can only enter into a political federation on the

prior condition that the constituent part, comprising all Somalis who wish to be reunited, is established before the Republic enters into the proposed federal relationship. The reason for this is obvious. No state, regional or administrative boundaries within a federation have yet been revised without at least a two-thirds majority in the Federal Legislature. This is a political risk which the Somali people, being in a minority, would not be prepared to take. It is absolutely necessary, therefore, that all constituent boundary arrangements should be settled before an act of federation is passed.[5]

Despite these disagreements, contact between Somali and Kenyan leaders continued. There were many opportunities for talks at the cabinet ministers' level in the months which followed. The story of the Rome conference has been related.[6] In addition, before Kenya's independence the Somali Foreign Minister, Abdullahi Issa, stopped over in Nairobi several times in his travels. His more important conferences in Nairobi were in June and November 1963. In the course of the November talks, the Somali Foreign Minister denied that his government was in any way implicated in the shifta movement in the NFD. He promised that Somalia would stop inflammatory propaganda broadcasts over Radio Mogadishu, and suggested the establishment of diplomatic relations between the two states.[7]

On both occasions Issa's talks in Nairobi were conducted with Prime Minister Kenyatta. But the principal responsibility for Kenya's relations with Somalia was in 1963 placed in Joseph Murumbi, who served as minister of state in the prime minister's office, directly responsible to Kenyatta. Murumbi had lived in Mogadishu in the 1940s, and had many friends among Somali leaders. The Kenyans hoped that Murumbi's connections in Mogadishu would, in addition to his other qualities, help to prevent the worsening of relations.

Murumbi's personal connections and Abdullahi Issa's moderation facilitated contacts. Yet Issa's influence in the Somali cabinet was limited, and insufficient to prevent the initiation of the shifta campaign against Kenya. As shifta activities intensified, Kenya-Somali relations deteriorated rapidly. In these circumstances, Kenya refused to establish diplomatic relations, and in April 1964 even expelled M. A. Murgian, the Nairobi lawyer who had acted as Somali representative in Kenya.[8]

The 1964 crisis and OAU involvement.   At the end of January 1964, a series of shifta incidents escalated into fighting between the Somali and Ethiopian regular armies, and the Somali government sought international intervention. As in the case of the Algerian-Moroccan fighting, the first question to arise concerned jurisdiction over the dispute. Somalia informed the OAU secretariat about the fighting. But Somalia feared that because of the commitment of most African states to the status quo, the OAU might be unsympathetic. Therefore Somalia clearly preferred that the UN Security Council handle the matter, rather than the OAU. On February 9 the Somalis requested an urgent meeting of the Security Council.[9]

The Somali request for a Security Council meeting was not favorably received at the United Nations. Some of the African delegations felt that the dispute should first be referred to the OAU, which, as a regional organization, should have primary jurisdiction over disputes among African states. Secretary-General U Thant either shared or accepted their view, since his message to the Somali and Ethiopian governments calling for a peaceful settlement contained a specific reference to the OAU.[10]

On February 9, the day that Somalia requested the Security Council to meet, Ethiopia asked that the OAU consider the dispute. Ethiopia requested that an extraordinary session of the OAU Council of Ministers be called to consider its complaint accusing Somalia of aggression. On the following day, Somalia too requested that the OAU meet.[11] OAU efforts to resolve or alleviate the dispute failed. A detailed analysis of these efforts will throw some light on the reasons for its ineffectiveness as a peacemaker.

An extraordinary session of the Council of Ministers had already been called to meet in Dar es Salaam on February 12, 1964 at the request of Tanganyika, to consider the situation arising from the army mutinies in East Africa. The later inscription of the Somali-Ethiopian dispute on the agenda aroused objections from a few of the delegations on the grounds that they had received no instructions from their governments on this matter, and, moreover, that the dispute could be examined at the ordinary session of the Council of Ministers due to meet two weeks later. But the majority of the delegations felt that the fighting merited urgent consideration. Kenya's subsequent request that its dispute with Somalia also be placed on the agenda was accepted somewhat reluctantly by the council by a vote of 9 to 1, with 9 abstentions.

Although now participating in the intiative for OAU intervention, Somalia did not entirely abandon its original intention to have its dispute with Ethiopia placed before the Security Council. On February 12, as the OAU extraordinary session of the Council of Ministers met in Dar es Salaam, the Somali government appealed to the secretary-general of the United Nations, asking that a commission be sent to the area to ascertain the responsibility for the fighting and to supervise the expected cease-fire. On his way to Dar es Salaam, the Somali foreign minister announced that Somalia would take the matter to the United Nations if it did not receive satisfaction at the OAU conference.[12]

The question of jurisdiction was raised at the Council of Ministers meeting, when, in the course of the debate, both parties were called upon to refrain from appealing to other international organizations. Somalia's reservations on the subject were significantly supported by Morocco, which had been reluctant to submit its territorial dispute with Algeria to OAU jurisdiction.

In the end, a formula was found by which Somalia agreed that its complaint to the Security Council be kept in abeyance. On February 14, the Somali delegation notified the secretary-general that "it is the desire of the Somali Government not to raise the matter with the Security Council while the problem is in the hands of the OAU."[13]

The objectives of the parties at this stage of the diplomatic battle were quite dissimilar. Somalia did not wish to raise the wider issue of its territorial claims, fearing that such a discussion might turn to its disadvantage. Rather, Somalia hoped that the debate could be limited to the more immediate ques-

tion of the disengagement of the regular armies. Concerned
also about the possibility that Ethiopia might react to shifta
attacks by launching reprisals across the border into Somali
territory, Somalia concentrated on requesting the creation of
a demilitarized zone along the border and the posting of
neutral observers in this area. Somalia probably hoped for an
additional benefit from such measures: an implicit international recognition that the Somali-inhabited areas of Ethiopia
and Kenya, over which these two states claimed exclusive
sovereignty, were actually disputed territories, with respect
to which the international community might have to play a
role. These objectives were more likely to be achieved
through placing the issue before the United Nations Security
Council than by referring it to the OAU. Ethiopia and Kenya,
on the other hand, wanted the basic issue of Somali territorial ambitions discussed because they expected that Somalia
would find itself isolated. They preferred the OAU as a
forum for such a debate, since isolation at a conference at
which all African states were represented would have been
more damaging to Somalia than a rebuff by the Security
Council.

When the debate opened in Dar es Salaam, Ethiopia and
Kenya both emphasized the political roots of the dispute and
the questions of principle involved. Both called on the council to help end the fighting, and to consider measures which
would pave the way to a permanent solution, on the basis of
respect for the territorial integrity of states and the acceptance of existing borders. The Kenyan delegate also suggested
that another charter be drawn up, by which all African states
would bind themselves to desist from making territorial
claims against each other. The Somali delegate refused to be
drawn into the discussion of the wider issues. He requested
that the council call for a cease-fire, and send observers to
supervise it.

The drafting of a resolution on the Somali-Ethiopian dispute was entrusted to a committee of twelve: Ethiopia, Somalia, Morocco, Dahomey, Tunisia, United Arab Republic,
Cameroon, Liberia, Ghana, Upper Volta, Sierra Leone, and
Mauritania.

The resolution adopted by the council referred in its preamble to the question of jurisdiction, proclaiming that "the Unity of Africa requires the solution to all disputes between Member States be sought first within the Organization of African Unity." The operative paragraphs of the resolution called for a cease-fire, the cessation of hostile propaganda, and negotiations for a peaceful settlement of the dispute. The resolution further called upon "all African States with diplomatic or consular missions in Ethiopia and Somalia to do their best to assist in the implementation of the cease-fire." The council also placed the issue on the agenda of its forthcoming meeting in Lagos.[14]

In the resolution on the Somali-Kenyan dispute, the council called on the two governments to take steps to settle the dispute "in the spirit of paragraph 4 of Article III of the Charter," without specifically suggesting negotiations as it had done with respect to the Somali-Ethiopian dispute. It also asked the parties to refrain from hostile propaganda, and decided to keep the dispute on the agenda "of all subsequent Sessions" of the Council "until a final settlement has been achieved."[15] A cease-fire agreement between Somalia and Ethiopia was subsequently negotiated. It is significant that this was accomplished not through the OAU, but with the help of General Abboud, the Sudanese president, who acted as intermediary between the parties.[16]

At the Council of Ministers meeting in Lagos,[17] which opened on February 24, Somalia asked that a demilitarized zone be created along the borders and repeated its request that observers be sent to supervise the cease-fire. The posting of observers was strongly supported by Ghana, which at that time was interested in promoting its proposals for an African military force. Nigeria, Libya, Tunisia and Congo-Brazzaville also spoke in favor of the Somali proposals.

Ethiopia again asked that the council take action with respect to the basic problem of the dispute. The Ethiopian representative requested that the council enjoin Somalia to renounce its territorial claims on Ethiopia and call on it to recognize and respect international borders. He also asked that the council call upon Somalia to desist from sending shiftas and to stop its propaganda campaign and other forms of aggression against Ethiopia.

In the exchange between Somalia and Kenya, the Somali representative reiterated the Somali position on the NFD, and claimed the right of self-determination for its population. But his attitude seemed more conciliatory than in the debate with Ethiopia. The Kenya delegate argued that the principle of self-determination was inapplicable to people living in an independent state, and that the redrawing of borders on ethnic grounds would affect many African states. He too requested that Somalia renounce its territorial claims.

Both disputes were referred to committees, whose membership was identical with that of the committee of twelve which had discussed the matter in Dar es Salaam plus the Sudan. The committees did not enter into the substance of the disputes, but concentrated on the discussion of measures to ease the immediate tension. Some pressure was exerted upon Ethiopia in an attempt to obtain its consent to the posting of observers along the border. But Ethiopia objected, arguing that these measures would be irrelevant to the main problems of bringing an end to the shifta activities and Somalia's renunciation of its territorial claims.

The resolution on the Ethiopia-Somalia dispute which was finally agreed upon did not mention observers. This resolution, as well as the resolution on the Kenya-Somalia dispute, confirmed those passed earlier in Dar es Salaam. This time, the request to the parties to open "direct negotiations" also included a reference to paragraph 3 of Article III of the Charter (respect for the sovereignty and territorial integrity of states), which the resolutions passed in Dar es Salaam had not contained.[18]

If the Council of Ministers failed to give comfort to either side at Dar es Salaam, the outcome of the Lagos meeting seemed to indicate, without stating so explicitly, that an important number of states sympathized with the Ethiopian and Kenyan positions. Nevertheless, the Somalis claimed to be satisfied. *The National Review*, published by the Somali Ministry of Information, stated:

> For the first time in recent history, the existence of a problem along Somalia's borders had been openly recognized at an international level . . .

So Africa and the world now know that the rightful claim of the Somalis still under foreign rule must be accepted before there can be a just and permanent peace in East Africa, and the OAU Charter becomes a reality.[19]

In March 1964, a meeting between the Somali and Ethiopian foreign ministers took place in Khartoum. The meeting was unexpectedly successful, and agreements were reached for the maintenance of the cease-fire, the creation of a demilitarized zone along the borders, the establishment of a joint commission to supervise the withdrawal of forces, and the cessation of hostile propaganda. The parties also agreed to resume negotiations before the next meeting of the OAU Assembly of Heads of State and Government.

The joint Somali-Ethiopian communiqué issued at the end of the talks stated that the meeting had taken place in pursuance of the Dar es Salaam and Lagos resolutions of the OAU Council of Ministers.[20] No doubt the OAU resolutions made it easier for the two sides to meet, and helped create a suitable atmosphere. Yet the meeting was arranged by the Sudan, which had the previous month also acted as intermediary in the cease-fire negotiations. Moreover, the Sudanese Foreign Minister, who was present through most of the negotiations, was instrumental in helping the parties to avoid a breakdown in the talks and in steering them to a successful conclusion.

The next meeting between the Somali, Ethiopian, and Kenyan foreign ministers took place in Cairo in July 1964. In accordance with the Lagos resolutions, reports on the negotiations were to be presented to the OAU summit conference a few days later. In their opening phase, the Somali-Ethiopian talks produced a disagreement about the agenda. Whereas Ethiopia maintained that only the long-disputed interpretation of the 1908 Ethiopian-Italian treaty delimiting the Somali-Ethiopian border should be discussed, Somalia insisted that its wider territorial claims should be the subject of the negotiations. At this stage, a government crisis in Somalia intervened, since the newly formed government failed to obtain a majority in the National Assembly. As a result, Somalia requested the postponement of the talks, and the deletion of the item concerning the Somali-Ethiopian and Soma-li-Kenyan disputes from the summit agenda.[21]

Two other events closely related to these disputes occurred in Cairo at this time. One was the adoption by the Assembly of Heads of State and Government of a resolution on border disputes (this was discussed in Chapter 4). The other, at the Council of Ministers on July 14, was a discussion of an agenda item proposed by Somalia concerning bilateral or regional military alliances among African states. Aiming at the recently concluded Ethiopian-Kenyan defense agreement, the Somali delegate argued that such alliances might upset the balance of power in Africa and consititue a "threat to the concept of African Unity." He called upon the OAU "to denounce such pacts."[22] This argument was rejected by Ethiopia and Kenya. Ghana suggested that discussion of the problem be deferred, to be taken up when the question of the African High Command was discussed. Other states considered any discussion of this issue inopportune, and feared it might harm the Lagos and Khartoum spirit of negotiations between the disputants. At the suggestion of the United Republic of Tanganyika and Zanzibar the item was dropped from the agenda.[23]

In March 1965 Somalia made another attempt to press its claim against Ethiopia through the OAU. Charging that Ethiopia had concentrated troops and undertaken "oppressive measures" against the Somali inhabitants in the Ogaden, Somalia requested that the OAU send a "fact-finding commission" to examine the causes of the unrest. Somalia also asked the OAU Commission on Refugees to visit Somalia to talk to Somali refugees from Ethiopia. Because Ethiopia objected, the OAU did not act on these requests, but Somalia's appeal to the OAU may have hastened Ethiopia's agreement to discuss the border situation with Somalia, and to reactivate the joint commission to supervise the implementation of the Khartoum agreement.[24]

In the meantime, attempts to resume the substantive negotiations for a final settlement of the Somali-Ethiopian dispute had run into repeated difficulties. The ostensible reason for the failure to resume the talks was the parties' inability to agree on a venue. But the real obstacle was their disagreement

on the agenda of their proposed negotiations. Opportunities
for informal talks presented themselves, nevertheless, at various international conferences. At the Accra summit conference in October 1965, such contacts resulted in agreement
between the two states on the definition of hostile propaganda, thus supplementing the Khartoum agreement of
March 1964.[25]

Fiasco at Arusha, 1965. In the fall of 1965, while Somalia
and Ethiopia were unable to agree on the resumption of their
talks, a meeting between the Somali and Kenyan presidents
took place. The meeting failed to produce an agreement, and
Somali-Kenyan relations worsened.

The initiative for the conference came from Somalia. It
stemmed, at least in part, from a conversation between
Joseph Murumbi, the Kenyan foreign minister, and Somali
leaders at the OAU conference in Accra in October 1965, at
which the desirability of resuming the negotiations interrupted in July 1964 was mentioned. It is unclear whether the
Kenyan foreign minister overstepped his authority by acting
out of step with President Kenyatta's thinking, or whether
his words were misinterpreted by the Somali delegates. In
any event, following the conversation, Somali representatives
approached President Nyerere of Tanzania, who was present
at the Accra conference, and asked him to help them improve
relations with Kenya. President Nyerere acted upon the
Somali request and suggested to President Kenyatta that he
meet with the Somali president, to which Kenyatta apparently agreed. Some attempt was made to prepare for the heads
of state conference through visits to Mogadishu and Nairobi by
a Tanzanian delegation headed by Bhoke Munanka, minister of
state in the president's office.

An opportunity for a meeting between the Somali and
Kenyan presidents offered itself during the visit of President
Aden Abdulla Osman of Somalia to Tanzania on the occasion
of Tanzania's independence anniversary in December. The
stage was set for the meeting of the Somali and Kenyan heads
of state, in the presence of President Nyerere, at the latter's
lodge in Arusha, on December 9. However, a few days before
the meeting, Kenyatta notified Nyerere that he would be

unable to come to Arusha because he would be busy with preparations for Kenya's independence anniversary celebrations, scheduled for December 12. Kenyatta proposed that the Somalis come to Nairobi and be his guests for the celebrations. When they refused, it was arranged that the Kenyan foreign minister, Joseph Murumbi, and Mbiyu Koinange, the minister of education (who had participated in previous talks with the Somalis) would meet the Somalis in Tanzania. After brief talks, the two ministers returned to Nairobi and succeeded in persuading Kenyatta to go to Arusha anyway. Kenyatta traveled to Arusha on December 13, and met the Somali leaders with Nyerere present as impartial chairman.[26]

It seems that Somalia's aim in initiating the talks was to find a face-saving formula that would enable the Somali government to disengage from the active pursuit of its irredentist goals, and to open the way to normal Somali-Kenyan relations.[27] The normalization of relations was expected to be of particular benefit to Somalia, since it would have enabled Somalia to become associated with some of the functions of the East African Common Services Organization (EACSO). In addition, Somalia was interested in obtaining air traffic rights between Mogadishu and East African capitals for Somali Airlines. Somalia also hoped that the state of emergency in the Northern Frontier District would be lifted.

The face-saving formula proposed by Somalia at Arusha contained several elements: (1) that the Somali government would declare that Somalia does not profess any territorial claims; (2) that Kenya would declare its recognition of Somalia's "interest in the welfare and destiny of the Somali people in Kenya"; and (3) that the two sides indicate their willingness to hold talks some time in the future in order to reach a solution to the problem. Somalia might have expected Kenyan acceptance of these proposals, since Kenya had accepted some similar formulations at the Rome talks in August 1963.[28]

But Kenya was suspicious of the Somali proposal. The formula whereby Kenya was to recognize Somalia's interest in the Somali people of Kenya could have other uses besides that of saving the Somali government's face, and of enabling it to disengage from the active pursuit of the dispute. It could also be interpreted as a Kenyan concession of principle, and it could serve as the thin wedge for further Somali efforts to obtain additional concessions from Kenya. Moreover, Kenya suspected that Somalia wished to disrupt the Kenyan-Ethiopian alliance. By agreeing to the Somali porposal, Kenya would have risked alienating Ethiopia and losing Ethiopian support in the event of a resumption of Somali pressure. Kenyan suspicions about the Somali initiative were indeed reenforced by Ethiopian misgivings which were communicated to the Kenyan government at the time.

Kenya therefore sought an assurance that Somalia really desired a détente and stipulated "prerequisites" to the normalization of relations. Among these was the condition that Somalia condemn the shifta and cease aiding them. Since the Somali government considered these Kenyan conditions tantamount to a public retraction of its policies it rejected the Kenyan proposals. With the discussions at a deadlock Kenyatta indicated that he saw no purpose in continuing the talks and the meeting was terminated.[29]

Instead of improving relations, the Arusha conference led to a worsening of the atmosphere between the two states. This was reflected in the personal attacks against Kenyatta over Mogadishu radio in March 1966, and the praise accorded by the Somalis to his political adversary, former Vice-President Oginga Odinga.[30]

Despite these deteriorating relations, the Somali prime minister attended the Nairobi meeting of East and Central African states in March 1966. At the conference, the disputants became engaged in a heated debate, in which the other participants did not wish to become involved. Prime Minister Abdirazaq Haji Hussein reported over Mogadishu radio that "the conference then requested us to take up this issue between ourselves and seek a solution in a brotherly and good neighbourly manner."[31] The final communiqué of the conference stated that agreement was reached among the eleven participating states to avoid propaganda attacks against each other and to control border incidents. But such an agreement was applicable to several situations involving participants at the conference, and was not aimed explicitly at the Somali disputes.[32]

The conference made little difference, and Somali-Kenyan relations continued to worsen. In July 1966 Kenya imposed a ban on all trade and all movement between Kenya and Somalia, by land, sea, or air. In April 1967, following the intensification of shifta activity, Kenya launched a diplomatic campaign accusing Somalia of responsibility for the shiftas. Kenyan statements also contained an implied warning that Kenya might abandon its restraint and consider new forms of response. At the same time Kenya reiterated its readiness to establish normal relations, but listed several "prerequisites to the opening of . . . negotiations." These included the explicit renunciation of territorial claims and the withdrawal of support for the shifta. Since at Arusha, in 1965, Kenya's prerequisites were conditions for the *normalization* of relations, the listing of prerequisites for mere *negotiations* reflected a hardening of the Kenyan position.[33]

Djibouti.   The third dispute that arose from Somali irredentist aspirations, was over the French territory of Afars and Issas (formerly French Somaliland). It was not raised explicitly as a territorial claim, but as a question of decolonization. Therefore, the issue was pressed mainly through the United Nations and the Organization of African Unity.

French Somaliland was first placed on the agenda of the OAU Liberation Committee in June 1963. Established by the summit conference in 1963, the committee was charged with coordinating aid to liberation movements. Apart from disbursing financial assistance to nationalist leaders, no action was taken by the committee on this question until January 1965, when a subcommittee was appointed to prepare a report on the situation in the territory. The subcommittee visited the Somali Republic and Ethiopia but was refused permission to enter French Somaliland itself. The nationalist leaders from French Somaliland who were interviewed by the subcommittee in Somalia claimed that their aim was union with the Somali Republic. Those interviewed in Ethiopia stated that the population desired union with Ethiopia. The Liberation Committee, avoiding involvement in the Somali-Ethiopian competition over the territory, maintained that the future political status of the territory would have to be decided by the population itself.[34]

The United Nations Committee on Colonialism (Committee of twenty-four) also treated the matter cautiously. On the occasion of its visit to Africa in 1965, the committee decided not to include the question of French Somaliland on its immediate agenda. When the committee revisited Africa in 1966, it too, like the OAU, heard both pro-Somali and pro-Ethiopian spokesmen, all of whom claimed to represent the population of the territory. Ethiopia and Somalia pursued different tactics. Ethiopia told the committee that French Somaliland was neither French, nor Somali, but Ethiopian. On the other hand, Somalia urged the United Nations to press France to grant immediate independence to the territory, and to call on all states to abstain from "pressure . . . calculated to distort free expression of the right to self-determination."[35]

Somali-Ethiopian competition over the territory was greatly intensified in the wake of the riots during de Gaulle's visit there in August 1966, and the French promise of a referendum to decide the future of the territory. Although Somalia continued to claim the territory, it reiterated the view that the territory ought to be placed under a temporary administration by the United Nations or the OAU, to ensure the fairness of the plebiscite. Emperor Haile Selassie indicated that if France withdrew from the territory, Ethiopia might occupy it. He also declared that Ethiopia "will never accept a solution . . . which is in contradiction to the interests of the people concerned and in violation of the rights of the Ethiopian people."[36]

Both Ethiopia and Somalia attempted to raise the problem with France. In discussions between the emperor and President de Gaulle in Addis Ababa (in August), and in Paris (in October), as well as in talks at the ministerial level, France apparently made it clear that it intended to stay in Djibouti, and assured Ethiopia of France's sympathy with the Ethiopian interest in the territory. A Somali request for a meeting between Prime Minister Adbirazaq Haji Hussein and the French government was at first turned down because of "prior commitments." Subsequently a meeting was arranged, and the Somali prime minister met the French prime minister and foreign minister in Paris on October 28. Their talks were inconclusive, however, since Somalia wanted assurances about the conduct of the forthcoming referendum and the franchise rights of the Somali inhabitants, while France refused to discuss these matters on the ground that they fell within domestic jurisdiction.[37]

On Somali initiative, the question of French Somaliland was placed on the agenda of the OAU conference which met in Addis Ababa in November 1966. The delegates saw the crystallization of conflicting attitudes. Somalia and the more radical states pressed for an unequivocal endorsement of independence, regardless of the consequences. They also supported the demand that the referendum be supervised by the OAU or by the United Nations. The other point of view reflected the concern that France's withdrawal might result in a serious confrontation between Somalia and Ethiopia. The states holding this view maintained that the OAU should not encourage the population to vote for independence, and opposed the involvement of the OAU in the plebiscite.

In the Liberation Committee, which was the first to discuss the issue, the radical view prevailed. On October 31, the committee adopted a resolution calling on the population to vote for independence in the forthcoming referendum, and condemning alleged French intimidation. The Council of Ministers did not accept this text and a sharp debate ensued. A Somali proposal called on the population to choose independence, criticized French policy, and demanded that the referendum be supervised by the United Nations or OAU; it failed the vote, as did an Ivory Coast proposal merely taking notice of the French promise to hold a referendum. A compromise resolution was finally adopted on November 4, expressing the hope that the referendum would be free and impartial and pledged the member states to accord the population all necessary assistance in case of need.

The matter was next discussed by the heads of state. Reflecting the cautious attitude of the majority of states, the resolution approved took note of France's decision "to grant the people self-determination by means of referendum"; expressed "fervent desire" that the voting be "free," "democratic," and "impartial"; appealed to the population "to unite in confronting its destiny"; and, finally, assured the "people of so-called French Somaliland (Djibouti)" of OAU's "active solidarity, designed to bring about and consolidate the independence of that people."[38]

After failing to obtain OAU support for international supervision of the plebiscite, Somalia pressed for the adoption of a resolution to that effect by the United Nations General Assembly. Such a resolution was indeed adopted on December 21, 1966. African states divided on the issue: fifteen, Ethiopia among them, abstained from voting on the controversial paragraph calling for United Nations supervision; twenty, among them Kenya, voted for it.[39]

As expected, France ignored the call for international supervision. The referendum was held as scheduled on March 19, 1967. The vote was 22,523 for continued association with France and 14,734 against.[40] The Somalis could console themselves, however, that in the town of Djibouti itself, 6,862 voted against, and only 2,798 voted to continue the association.

The Somali and Ethiopian reactions were predictable. Somalia claimed fraud and called for an investigation of the manner in which the referendum had been conducted. Ethiopia, on the other hand, accepted the result, which, it considered, a reflection of the peoples' free exercise of self-determination. Opinion in Africa was divided, with most French-speaking states defending the conduct of the referendum, and most states with a radical orientation condemning it. To Somalia's satisfaction, its viewpoint—that the people of the territory could not have voted freely to remain under colonial subjection, and that the referendum had not been fairly conducted—enjoyed some sympathy among African states. This was in sharp contrast to the isolation in which Somalia found itself during the OAU's consideration of Somalia's disputes with Ethiopia and Kenya.[41]

Yet the result was that Somali efforts were again frustrated. To add to the insult, the territory's legislature and the French National Assembly approved a proposal to change the territory's name: it now became the French Territory of Afars and Issas. The name "Somaliland" was dropped.

DISENGAGEMENT

There is a sharp contrast between the growing bitterness and the continuously increasingly tension which characterized the situation until mid-1967, and the détente which began in the second half of 1967. The first major landmark in the development of détente was an agreement between Kenya and Somalia, reached with the help of President Kaunda of Zambia during the OAU summit conference in Kinshasa in September 1967. The agreement, labeled "Joint Declaration," expressed the desire of the two governments "to respect each other's sovereignty and territorial integrity." It also contained undertakings to resolve their differences, to ensure peace, and to refrain from hostile propaganda. Finally, the two governments agreed to meet again in the following month in Lusaka.[42]

The next event, merely five days after the Kinshasa summit had ended, was the arrival of a Somali ministerial delegation in Addis Ababa. Within three days a series of agreements had been reached. These included the reaffirmation of the Khartoum and Accra agreements, the reactivation of the Somali-Ethiopian joint military commission set up by the Khartoum agreement, and the convening of periodic meetings of regional administrators to discuss frontier problems. A vague but significant clause stated that it was agreed to take steps for the removal of "conditions which affect adversely relations between the two countries." It was also agreed to lift the restrictions on the movement of diplomatic personnel, to grant exit permits to persons who had taken asylum in their respective embassies, to examine the cases of the other side's imprisoned nationals, to return seized aircraft and other property, and to investigate complaints on seizure of property. Finally, Ethiopia and Somalia agreed that their talks would be continued in Mogadishu.[43]

The Somali-Kenyan meeting agreed upon in Kinshasa took place on October 28, in Arusha (instead of Lusaka). The Somali delegation was headed by Prime Minister Egal, and the Kenyan by President Kenyatta. President Kaunda chaired the meeting; also present were Presidents Nyerere and Obote. The two governments reaffirmed their adherence to the Kinshasa Declaration and pledged themselves to exert all efforts to create good neighborly relations. In order to facilitate a solution to their dispute, they agreed to preserve peace on both sides of the border, gradually suspend the state of emergency along the frontier, refrain from hostile propaganda and encourage propaganda which promotes friendly relations, reestablish diplomatic relations, and consider measures encouraging economic relations. Finally, they agreed to set up a "working committee," in which Zambia would participate, which would meet periodically to review the implementation of the agreements and "to examine ways and means of bringing about a satisfactory solution to major and minor differences between Kenya and Somalia."[44]

The following months saw intense diplomatic activity and very slow progress. A chronological summary of the main events indicates how much effort was invested, and how slowly the results came to fruition:[45]

October 26, 1967. Somalia and Ethiopia exchange seized aircraft, in accordance with September agreements reached in Addis Ababa.

November 23-30, 1967. Somali-Ethiopian negotiations at ambassadorial level take place in Addis Ababa on the implementation of the September agreements.

December 1, 1967. Talks take place "at summit" on the occasion of ceremonies inaugurating the East African Economic Community in Arusha. Present (among others): Emperor Haile Selassie, Presidents Kaunda, Kenyatta, Shermarke.

December 15-16, 1967. Talks take place at East and Central African Summit Conference, Kampala. Present (among others): Emperor Haile Selassie, Presidents Kaunda and Kenyatta, Prime Minister Egal. Kenya and Somalia reach an agreement on the terms of reference of the working committee decided upon at Arusha. Somalia formally applies for membership in the East African Economic Community.

January 27, 1968. Kenyan ministerial delegation visits Mogadishu. Subsequent announcement on the establishment of diplomatic relations and the lifting of trade embargoes.

February 5-8, 1968. Ethiopian Foreign Minister visits Mogadishu. Progress on the implementation of the agreements reached in Addis Ababa in September.

July 24-28, 1968. President Shermarke and Prime Minister Egal on an official visit to Kenya (Kaunda not present).

Agree to convene the working committee, decided upon in Arusha in October, "soon."

August 30, 1968.   Conclusion of Kenyan-Somali talks in Kismayu. At the administrative level, they deal with security along the border, land communications, and trade. (This was not the working committee of Kenyan, Somali, and Zambian representatives mentioned above).

September 1-5, 1968.   Prime Minister Egal visits Addis Ababa. Progress on previous year's agreements for exchange of seized property, with vehicles being exchanged on September 30. Additional points: the two governments undertake not to engage in subversive activities; Ethiopia grants provisional overflight rights to Somalia, pending conclusion of an air agreement; Ethiopia agrees to suspend the state of emergency along the border; negotiations to be held on a cultural convention, a telecommunications agreement, and a trade agreement. Communiqué emphasizes that the talks were of an exploratory nature, *aimed at the eventual* settlement of major issues (italics added).

September 5-16, 1968.   Parties meet again at the OAU summit at Algiers. Apparently no substantive negotiations on Somali disputes as participants preoccupied with other issues, notably the Biafran-Nigerian conflict.

September 20-21, 1968.   Prime Minister Egal visits Paris for talks with President de Gaulle. Communiqué: Egal explained his policy of détente toward all neighboring countries; both governments stated that they are inspired by the same principles—respect for independence, the right of all peoples to self-determination through democratic procedures and without foreign interference, noninterference by any state in the internal affairs of others—and agreed on good-neighbor policy; France stated that it would examine sympathetically Somali suggestions for French cooperation in Somalia's development (i.e., Somali requests for aid).

February 21, 1969.   Prime Minister Egal and President Kenyatta hold talks in Nairobi, with President Kaunda present. Communiqué: satisfaction expressed at progress in normalization of relations; Kenya agreed to grant an amnesty to political offenders who fled the country and to lift the state of emergency in the Northeastern Province; both sides will ease restrictions on the movement of livestock across the border; will cooperate in improving communications and in joint development projects; will discuss further relaxation of currency exchange restrictions.

March 15, 1969. Emergency regulations lifted in Kenya's Northeastern Province.

These agreements, and the rapid change from hostility to conciliation, became possible because of a modification in the attitudes and positions of the disputants. Before 1967 the attitude of the parties had been that no real improvement in relations between them was possible unless the principal issue in dispute—the Somali territorial claim—was resolved. As Somalia, Ethiopia, and Kenya all regarded this issue as touching upon "core values," they were unwilling to make any concessions on it. Their changed positions were reflected in their willingness to conclude a series of agreements *without* requiring a prior solution to the question of the territorial claims.

Yet, while accepting the approach that instituting normal relations was possible even though the territorial conflict remained unresolved, each of the parties continued to insist that its core values were to remain intact. Therefore, agreements reached had to be formulated in a manner consistent with the position of each party on the principal issue in dispute. This required formulas that lent themselves to different interpretations.

Somalia claimed that the agreements concluded contained two major gains for its position. One, that Kenya and Ethiopia "now explicitly recognize the existence of a dispute and both have expressed willingness to try to find ways of solving it." According to the Somali view, this was the meaning of paragraph (f) of Article 4 of the Arusha agreement, which provided for the appointment of a working committee that would "examine ways and means of bringing about a satisfactory solution to major and minor differences between Kenya and Somalia."[46]

The Somali-Ethiopian agreements lend themselves to a similar interpretation. The September 1967 communiqué said that the talks held between the two delegations aimed at "paving the way for a future meeting between the Heads of State of the two countries to discuss major issues."[47]   The 1968 agreement contained a similar phrase.

Explaining the agreements in a radio speech Prime Minister Egal hotly denied that any principles had been abandoned:

> What my government seeks to do is to foster an atmosphere of goodwill wherein it will be possible to negotiate at a round-table conference an equitable solution for the problems of these peoples without exposing them to the scourge of War.
>
> I am therefore surprised that there are elements who would like, for some other baser ulterior motives, to make people believe that there has been a compromise on principle and a sell-out at Kinshasa, Addis Ababa and Arusha. Is it a sell-out to persuade Kenya to leave the people of the NFD in peace whilst still accepting to negotiate at the conference table the future of these people? Is it a sell-out to persuade Kenya to expose conditions in the area to the examination of a three-State Working Committee?[48]

It is more difficult to substantiate the second Somali claim (significantly not made at the time that the first agreements were concluded but only much later), that Somalia now "had a say" by way of "consultation" in the affairs and administration of the Northern Frontier District and the Ogaden.[49] Perhaps the fact that both agreements contained a statement about the suspension of the state of emergency in these areas can be interpreted as implying that Somalia "had a say." It is interesting, however, that the Kinshasa and Arusha agreements did not contain a paragraph expressing recognition of Somalia's interest in the future of Somalis residing in Kenya, which had been suggested by Kenya during the Rome talks in August 1963.

Kenya's changed attitude is reflected in its abandoning the demand that Somalia explicitly recognize the Northern Frontier District as "an integral and *de jure* part of the Kenya

Republic," which had been one of the prerequisites for negotiations presented by Kenya in April 1967. The substitute
formula in the Kinshasa Declaration, accepted by Kenya,
merely stated that "both Governments have expressed their
desire to respect each other's sovereignty and territorial integrity in the spirit of paragraph 3 of Article III of the OAU
Charter." The Somali government explained that this phrase
did not represent a concession since Somalia had already
espoused this principle by its signature of the United Nations
and OAU charters.[50]

The Somali-French understanding of September 1968 can
also be interpreted as consistent with the principles of both
parties. Somalia could point with satisfaction to the reference
to "self-determination," and France to the phrase on "noninterference."

Similar formulas could have been constructed before September 1967. Before that time, however, they were not considered satisfactory, since each side refused to accept anything less than a settlement of the dispute on its terms. The
détente became possible not because of any breakthrough on
formulations, but rather because the parties had tacitly
agreed that their fundamental disagreement should not prevent the restoration of normal relations. Once the parties
adopted this attitude, it followed that each was free to interpret the agreement as consistent with its core values. The
rules of the game also prescribed that they would refrain
from challenging the interpretations of the other side.

Having examined *what* changes took place in the attitudes
of the parties, we now turn to the *why* and *how* of the Somali initiative for disengagement, and of the Ethiopian and
Kenyan responses.[51] These are closely interwoven, and shall
be examined by distinguishing among five categories of factors influencing the attitudes and the process: (1) the impact
of the conflict upon the parties, and the incentives for disengagement; (2) the freedom of action enjoyed by the parties,
and the effect of domestic politics upon freedom of action;
(3) the impact of personalities; (4) tactics, sequence of
events, and the role of mediators and; (5) the external environment: the ideological and normative atmosphere and the
influence of third powers.

1. *The impact of the conflict and the promises of détente.* By the eighth year of Somalia's independence, nearly twenty-five years after the Somali Youth League had proclaimed the goal of Somali unification, its attainment appeared as remote as ever. Somalia's policy with respect to the territories claimed had not yielded any fruits, and its cause had made no progress. Ethiopia, Kenya, and France had made no concessions. Somalia's irredentism had not elicited political support from other states; on the contrary it had tended to isolate Somalia. Normal life in the Ogaden and in the Northern Frontier District was most seriously disrupted as a result of the shifta operations and of the Ethiopian and Kenyan anti-insurgency measures. The morale of the Somali populations in these areas was low, and they gradually ceased to provide the shifta with the local support they required. In addition, the Somalis of the French Territory of the Afars and the Issas began paying a heavy price for their support of Somali nationalism.[52] Under these circumstances frustration set in.

The economic burden of the policy of confrontation also pressed heavily, despite the massive foreign assistance which Somalia received. To be sure, the resources that Somalia invested in helping the shifta were relatively small, but the policy necessitated a vast expansion of Somalia's armed forces. Furthermore, the closure of the Ethiopian and Kenyan borders was beginning to hurt economically, since it interfered with the seasonal migrations of nomadic tribes in search of water and grazing land. The closure of the border also drastically reduced trade between Somalia and its neighbors; although relatively small in monetary value, the trade affected the livelihood of additional groups in the population.

The pressure of economic difficulties did not bring about policy changes. But the prospect that these difficulties might be eased was probably an inducement. Détente seemed to offer many advantages to Somalia. It promised to relieve the plight of the Somali populations in Ethiopia and in Kenya. The economic difficulties in which Somalia found itself would also be alleviated; trade, and especially the sale of cattle to Kenya, would be resumed. Also, normalization of relations with Kenya was believed to hold the key to Somalia's association with East African regional organizations. Somalia's air communications would be greatly facilitated if routed via Nairobi and Addis Ababa. And, perhaps no less important than all these considerations, was the assessment that since the irredentist cause had made no progress, it would not be damaged by a détente.

Ethiopia and Kenya responded favorably to the Somali initiative, since they also stood to gain by disengagement. They too were being hurt by the conflict. To be sure, normal life in the two countries was not much disturbed. But the economic cost of the anti-shifta operations was considerable. It became more burdensome as the economies of Ethiopia and Kenya became affected by the closing of the Suez Canal. However, a détente made sense for Ethiopia and for Kenya only if accompanied by a cessation of shifta activity. In that case they would be relieved of the economic burden of their military effort. Furthermore, a détente entailed no risks, since the pressure on Somalia could be turned on again in case the shifta war were resumed, or if Somali policies became objectionable.

2. *Freedom of action.*   Domestic pressures are generally assumed to restrict the freedom of leaders to pursue policies of détente. This assumption is based on the premise that détente policies are more vulnerable to criticism than policies exhibiting firmness toward the adversary. If these premises and assumptions are valid, then the ability of the Somali, Ethiopian, and Kenyan governments to follow policies of détente also requires explanation.

In fact, it seems that in Ethiopia and in Kenya, the governments did not encounter much of a problem. The emperor's policies are rarely, if ever, publicly criticized in Ethiopia. Yet policies are often debated in private among Ethiopian elites. In this case, it seems that no significant group raised objections to the policy of détente. Had there been objections, the government would have launched a campaign to justify the policy, or initiated countermeasures. But nothing of this nature took place.

In Kenya criticism of the government is quite common. Yet

no public criticism of any significance had been voiced on this issue. The opposition Kenya People's Union (KPU) was, in fact, reported to have expressed support for the Arusha agreement.[53] Considering that the Kenya government had committed itself in April 1967 to "prerequisites for negotiations," and that in September it modified its position, and agreed to negotiate without the prerequisites being fulfilled, the absence of criticism is remarkable.

In Somalia the tenure of President Aden Abdullah Osman came to an end in June 1967. The new president, elected by the National Assembly on June 10, was Dr. Abdirashid Ali Shermarke. The change in the presidency led also to a change of government, the new one being headed by Mohamed Haji Ibrahim Egal. Although the governing team changed almost completely, the new men were not so "new." Several of them bore chief responsibility for having initiated the abortive diplomatic and military policies of irredentism. President Shermarke had been prime minister from 1960 to 1964, and Prime Minister Egal had served as minister of defense and minister of education in Shermarke's governments.

Nevertheless, as a new government, it was disposed to demonstrate its newness and freshness by breaking with policies and practices of its immediate predecessor. Its nationalist-radical reputation was impeccable, and President Shermarke still enjoyed the popularity he had attained by concluding the military-aid agreement with the Soviet Union. Furthermore, the Egal government was based on broader parliamentary support than hitherto enjoyed by any Somali government: it was confirmed by a majority of 119 out of 124 members of the National Assembly.

All this combined to give the new team unprecedented freedom of action, a freedom which was not much restricted by a revolt within the ruling Somali Yough League (SYL) against Prime Minister Egal and his policy of détente. The party revolt was led by former Prime Minister Abdirazaq Haji Hussein who, despite losing the premiership, had remained secretary-general of the SYL, and retained control of the party's central bodies. The growth of opposition within the party led to the closing of party headquarters by the authorities. The central committee responded by expelling Prime Minister Egal from the party.[54]

The government, however, retained considerable support in the National Assembly, and overcame the party crisis by winning the battle in the assembly. By a majority of 89 to 1, with 4 abstentions, the assembly approved the agreements, and authorized the government to continue the policy thus initiated. To be sure the assembly's support was qualified by a provision calling upon the government to submit future agreements to the assembly for approval. Following the victory in the National Assembly, the government achieved the upper hand in the party as well, and Abdirazaq Haji Hussein resigned his post as secretary-general. Following this, Abdirazaq's political influence continued to decline. In the general election in March 1969 he ran on an independent list, the Popular Movement for Democratic Action (PMDA), and obtained two seats in the National Assembly, compared with the SYL's seventy-three.[55]

The internal struggle within the SYL was the significant contest. Since the SYL was a broad coalition comprising the most important tribal groups, the prospect of any opposition to government policies was usually decided by intraparty politics. Opposition parties, because of their narrow tribal base, were not powerful. Nevertheless, it is interesting to note that the two most important opposition parties, the Socialist National Congress (SNC) and the Somali Democratic Union (SDU), supported the government's policy of détente in the National Assembly.[56]

The government's freedom of action was greatly extended by its ability to control the guerrillas in the Ogaden and in the NFD. Ironically, former Prime Minister Hussein deserves much of the credit for the success of the disengagement policy. His tightening of the Somali government's control of the guerrillas, in contrast to the Shermarke policy prior to July 1964, provided the Shermarke-Egal team with the requisite freedom of action. Symptomatic of the government's control of the guerrillas were announcements by the guerrilla movement supporting the new policy of the government and condemning "political agitators."[57] The decline in guerrilla activity, timed to precede the Somali government's diplomatic initiative in September 1967, and the tapering off in activity since then, indicate that the government's control of the guerrillas was indeed effective.

The Somali government continued to enjoy considerable freedom of action in the months that followed, and this despite the fact that the promised negotiations aiming at the solution of major issues had not taken place. Other results of the détente policy, such as the lifting of the state of emergency in the Somali-inhabited areas in Ethiopia and Kenya, and the amnesty to Somali political prisoners in Kenya, probably compensated for this failure. Indeed the lifting of the emergency in Kenya's Northeastern Province on March 15, 1969, ten days before the Somali general election, suggests that the Kenya government cooperated in helping the Somali prime minister in the elections. The results of the election, in which the SYL won 73 seats, and following which 47 additional members joined the SYL, giving the government party 120 out of 124 seats in the National Assembly, confirmed that the government's assessment of its freedom of action was correct.

3. *Personalities.*   The change of government in Somalia resulted not only in greater flexibility, but also in the advent of a new negotiating team on the Somali side. It was headed by Prime Minister Egal, who was very much an extrovert and had greater facility in communicating and establishing rapport with the Kenyan leaders than his predecessors. President Osman and Prime Minister Hussein who conducted the 1965 talks spoke English well, but, hailing from the region formerly ruled by Italy, were not as much at home with the Kenyan leaders as Prime Minister Egal, who came from former British Somaliland and had lived in England for several years. President Shermarke, who possessed a somewhat reserved personality and came from Italian Somaliland, did not attend the Kinshasa and Arusha negotiations.

Personal changes on the Kenya side also tended to facilitate negotiations. The Kinshasa talks were conducted by Vice President Daniel Arap Moi, whose judgment on the Somali problem Kenyatta regarded as more trustworthy than Murumbi's. Murumbi, who was responsible for the preparatory talks for the 1965 Kenyan-Somali summit, was sometimes regarded as overly susceptible to Somali influence.

As for the mediator, Kaunda enjoyed an advantage over

Nyerere, who had performed this role in 1965. The close and intensive links between Kenya and Tanzania had produced occasional strains between the two countries, as well as between their leaders. On the other hand, Kaunda's relations with Kenyatta were less complex, and this probably enabled him to be a more effective mediator.

4. *Scenario and tactics.*[58]   Analysis of the Somali initiative suggests that the scenario and the tactics were very carefully planned. Among other details, it seems that much attention was paid to convincing Kenya and Ethiopia of the sincerity of Somalia's initiative. A most important signal aimed at conveying the image of sincerity was the marked diminution of shifta activity and the suspension of anti-Ethiopian and anti-Kenyan propaganda over Mogadishu radio, *prior* to the Kinshasa conference.

The next step in the Somali initiative took place at Kinshasa. Prime Minister Egal took advantage of the opportunities for personal contacts provided by the conference to approach Haile Selassie and the leader of the Kenyan delegation, Vice-President Daniel Arap Moi. The parallel approach to Ethiopia and Kenya seems to have been an essential feature of the Somali design. By making parallel progress with both adversaries, Somalia succeeded in avoiding one of the difficulties it had encountered in 1965, when Ethiopia had acted as a brake hindering the Kenyan-Somali negotiations.

In the talks between Egal and the emperor, it was agreed that a Somali ministerial delegation would come to Addis Ababa for negotiations immediately following the OAU conference. Although the agreement did not contain any substantive points, Somalia again indicated the seriousness of its intentions by pushing aside the three-year old controversy about the venue of Ethiopian-Somali talks, and making the gesture of sending a high level delegation to Addis Ababa.

At the same time, Somalia attempted to cover substantive points in the negotiations with Kenya. In the talks between Egal and Moi it was agreed that officials from both delegations would try to draw up an agreement. However, the officials soon reached a deadlock, as Kenya insisted upon the "prerequisites" to negotiations proclaimed in April. Another difficulty stemmed from the need to consult with Presidents Kenyatta and Shermarke, who were not present in Kinshasa.

The deadlock was broken by President Kaunda of Zambia who was asked by Egal to intervene. (The question of an approach to President Nyerere to resume his mediation efforts did not arise, as Nyerere was not present at Kinshasa.) Following talks between Kaunda and Moi, Kenya softened its conditions, and agreement on the declaration was finally reached.

The role of the OAU in this process was limited. It provided an opportunity for the parties to meet. Subsequently, after agreement was reached, the OAU summit conference endowed the declaration with its own prestige by adopting a formal statement embodying the declaration, which thus became an official OAU document. The heads of state also requested the parties to submit a progress report to the OAU. But the effectiveness of this device was doubtful, since a progress report had already been requested as early as February 1964.

A crucial move in the Somali diplomatic offensive was the visit of the Somali ministerial delegation to Addis Ababa. The delegation arrived in Addis on September 19, merely five days after the agreement with Kenya was concluded in Kinshasa. The seriousness of Somali intentions was suggested by the fact that the delegation was headed by Yassin Nur Hassan, the minister of interior, and probably the most influential member of the Somali cabinet after the prime minister. The agreements concluded on this occasion represented not only progress toward a Somali-Ethiopian détente, but also helped prepare the atmosphere for the forthcoming Somali-Kenyan negotiations.

The Somali-Kenyan meeting was indeed the subject of elaborate preparations. It was far better and more elaborately prepared than the Somali-Kenyan conference in 1965. Zambia took an active part. A week after Kinshasa, a Zambian delegation visited Nairobi and Mogadishu to help prepare the talks. Thought was given also to the composition of the two teams. To smooth and speed up the decisions on the Kenyan side, it was deemed desirable that President Kenyatta attend in person. To diminish Kenyatta's reluctance, it was arranged that the conference take place in Arusha, a few hours by car from Nairobi, instead of at Lusaka. Following a personal appeal by Egal, Kenyatta finally agreed to attend, despite the fact that the Somali head of state was not going to be present. It seems that in the course of the preparations for the conference, an understanding in principle on the general outline of the Arusha agreement had been reached. This is suggested by the optimistic atmosphere which prevailed in Arusha when the conference met, and by its ability to accomplish its work within a few hours.[59]

Further steps for the improvement of relations were taken concurrently in Somali-Ethiopian and Somali-Kenyan contacts. They were undoubtedly facilitated by an understanding reached between the two allies, Ethiopia and Kenya, to proceed on such a course. President Kenyatta went to Addis Ababa on a visit on October 31, almost directly after the Arusha conference, which took place on October 28. This visit served as an occasion to inform the Ethiopians about Arusha, and also to coordinate future policy toward Somalia.

The détente in Somali-French relations over the Afar and Issa Territory was a necessary corollary of the Somali détente with Ethiopia. It was necessary for the maintenance of the whole détente policy since a continuation of activist Somali policies on this subject would have undermined the understanding with Ethiopia. This, in turn, would have endangered the détente with Kenya. In other words, the disputes were interrelated, and, to be successful, the policy of détente had to embrace all three of Somalia's neighbors.

Somalia was probably encouraged to mend its relations with France by the prospect of the benefits likely to follow from such a policy. One benefit concerned the situation in the Afar and Issa Territory, from which many Somalis had been expelled, and where Somalis were being increasingly replaced in jobs and other positions by members of the rival Afar (Danakil) tribe. An understanding with France could be expected to lead to a more lenient attitude toward the Somalis on the part of the Djibouti authorities. Needless to say, the prospect of receiving some French economic or technical aid was an additional inducement.[60]

5. *The external environment.* The influence of the external environment also seems to have been conducive to a détente. One element in this environment was Pan-African ideology. Both the acceptance of the status quo, and the attempt to revise it, were justified by reference to different aspects of Pan-African ideology. Pan-Africanism was useful in justifying the policy of disengagement and détente as well. It is unlikely that the commitment to ideology brought about the policy changes. But, once the policy of disengagement was adopted, the idea of African solidarity was used to justify it.[61]

The policies of the major powers were also of some effect. On the Western side, both the United States and Britain encouraged the détente. In fact, the United States was at various times actively involved in attempts to improve Somali-Kenyan and Somali-British relations. As the dispute had, through the Soviet-Somali military aid agreement, served to introduce Soviet influence into Somalia, the United States could be expected to hope that a détente might help diminish Soviet influence. Britain, for its part, could expect that, following the normalization of Somali-Kenyan relations, diplomatic relations between Britain and Somalia would also be restored. Indeed, agreement on the resumption of relations was reached in December 1967.

The Soviet Union also seems to have favored a détente. Soviet support for the détente was reflected in the congratulatory telegram sent to President Kenyatta on the occasion of the conclusion of the Arusha agreement. Of greater significance were the Soviet expressions of support for Egal and his policy when the Arusha agreement encountered criticism in Somalia. At this critical moment the Soviet Union issued a statement praising the new government's policy, and criticizing Abdirazaq's government for "squandering" 30 percent of the national income "on dead end policies in violation of OAU decisions."[62] If any opposition group in Somalia hoped that its campaign against the détente might draw Soviet support, such hopes were greatly dampened by the Soviet statement. Soviet motives in supporting the détente are not entirely clear. It seems that since the Soviet connection was in Somalia regarded as an implicit alliance, the Soviet Union preferred the tension to subside so as not to be placed again in an embarrassing situation, which had happened in the Arab-Israeli war in June 1967, when it failed to prevent the defeat of its protegés.

The Arab-Israeli war of June influenced Somalia's attitude as well, serving to shake its self-confidence. Somalia's economic situation worsened as a result of the closing of the Suez Canal, at which time the economic consequences of its conflict with the neighboring states became more difficult to bear. The outbreak of the Arab-Israeli war, which exemplified a process of escalation resulting from Arab guerrilla activities against Israel, also aroused reflection about where the Somalis' guerrilla war might lead. The ineffectiveness of Soviet support for Egypt, and Egypt's own collapse in this war, were not encouraging to Somalia, which relied on Soviet military assistance. Moreover, with the closure of the Suez Canal, supplying Soviet assistance to Somalia became more difficult.

All these factors combined to induce and to facilitate the process of disengagement. The complementary perceptions by the parties of the circumstances and options faced by them, and their willingness and ability to take the reciprocal steps toward their common goal of disengagement, resulted in a détente.

This détente withstood the fall of Egal and the establishment of a military regime in Somalia. Shortly after taking power in October 1969, the new regime assured Ethiopia and Kenya that it would continue its predecessor's policy.[63]

The détente remains, however, highly unstable. Somalia continues to proclaim its dedication to its irredentist goals, and regards the 1967-1968 agreements as providing the setting and machinery for negotiations on the "major issues"— the separation of the Somali-inhabited territories from Ethiopia and Kenya. Ethiopia and Kenya, on the other hand, remain as opposed as ever to Somali secession. Not surprisingly, the negotiations on "major issues" have not yet begun (January 1972). In these circumstances, the détente can be upset not only by the volatility of Somali politics, but also by the periodic clashes between nomadic tribes, which might draw the governments into argument and thus lead to the resumption of conflict.[64]

In a number of cases, negotiations led to specific boundary agreements that terminated territorial disputes. Such agreements were made possible by changes in the policy of at least one party in the dispute. In most cases, the change of policy reflected a reordering of priorities and a modification of the value attached to the disputed territory in relation to other goals and values sought by the same government. Two kinds of agreements should be distinguished: agreements involving a territorial compromise and agreements ratifying the territorial status quo. In both kinds, a trade-off has occurred, with each side compensating the other for concessions the other has made. The difference between the two kinds of agreements lies in the quality of compensations and gains. In the territorial compromise both sides yielded and achieved some part of their territorial claims. In the agreements ratifying the status quo, the side yielding on the territorial claim was compensated in some other way.

TERRITORIAL COMPROMISE

Compromise agreements were reached between Mauritania and Mali and between Kenya and Ethiopia. By "territorial compromise" is meant an agreement representing territorial concessions by both sides.[1] Both agreements provided for the partition of the disputed territory between the parties. But

the area was not apportioned equally: Mali gained more territory than Mauritania, and Ethiopia gained the Gadaduma
wells, which were the main source of contention between it
and Kenya. Therefore, an explanation of the two disputes in
terms of territorial compromise must be supplemented by
another approach: why were Mauritania and Kenya willing to
give up the major part of their claims?

An explanation can be found in the fact that territories are
seldom assigned equal value by both sides. Each side is likely
to assess differently the importance of size, of natural resources available in the territory, and its strategic significance. Moreover, for each of the parties, the emotional and
symbolic value of the territory is likely to be different.

Initially the two disputes developed because the parties
involved assigned high priority to the control of the territories at question. The value attributed by Mali and Mauritania
to the territory disputed by them stemmed partly from its
considerable size and the wells located in it, which were of
vital importance to the nomadic tribes inhabiting the frontier
zone between the two states. The Malian outlook upon the
problem also had an emotional dimension, as the transfer of
the Hodh region to Mauritania by France in 1944 was still
resented at the time of independence. On the other hand, in
Mauritanian eyes, the incorporation of the Hodh into Mauritania in 1944 reinstated the region to its rightful owners—the
Moorish chiefs in Mauritania who regarded the inhabitants of
the Hodh as subjects who owed them tribute. At the time of
independence, in 1960, the Mauritanian leadership considered the Hodh to be part of the national partrimony, inherited from the colonial rulers.[2]

As for Ethiopia and Kenya, the area in dispute between
them was almost minute in size. The real subject of the dispute was not the territory but the Gadaduma wells located in
it. These were considered important because control of the
wells made possible control of the nomadic tribes of the area.

To be sure, in neither case was the disputed territory considered a core value in the sense that yielding it might undermine national identity, and concessions were not inconceivable. Nevertheless, the disputes continued for several years.

The subsequent compromise agreements were made possible by changes in the Mauritanian and Kenyan positions, which were reflected in their readiness to offer concessions.

1. *The Kenyan-Ethiopian dispute.* In the settlement of the Kenyan-Ethiopian dispute, Kenya recognized Ethiopia's ownership of the Gadaduma wells, while Ethiopia recognized Kenya's possession of the Godama wells. However, this trading of concessions seems to have been more a face-saving device for Kenya, than a real concession on the part of Ethiopia. The principal subject of contention were the Gadaduma wells and not the Godama wells. The main significance of the agreement is that it settled this long contested issue by Kenya's acquiescence in Ethiopian control.[3]

The change in the Kenyan position which made the agreement possible is clearly associated with the transfer of power from British to Kenyan officials and the problems thrust upon Kenya with independence. The insistence that the Gadaduma wells must be controlled by Kenya had come in particular from the British administration of the Northern Province.[4] The importance of the wells had not changed by 1963. The change in the Kenyan position became possible because the Kenyan ministers and officials were not committed to Gadaduma to the same extent that the British administrators had been. In addition, the general atmosphere was propitious to settlement. For one thing, there was no history of conflict between Ethiopia and the Kenyan nationalists. On the contrary, like many other African nationalist leaders, Jomo Kenyatta admired Ethiopia as a symbol of African dignity.

Security considerations also played a role. Kenya was concerned over the threat from Somalia, and, the boundary negotiations took place at the same conference at which defense cooperation between Kenya and Ethiopia was discussed. Since Kenya was eager for Ethiopian support against Somalia, Kenya made the concession over Gadaduma in order to remove any disagreements inherited from the colonial era and to smooth the way for future cooperation. Less experienced than their Ethiopian counterparts, the Kenyan negotiators were apparently unaware that Ethiopia was at least as interested in strengthening Kenya's ability to withstand Somali pressure as Kenya was in Ethiopian support.*

2. *The Mauritanian-Malian dispute.* The processes that brought about the agreement between Mali and Mauritania were very different. In this case, the changes brought by independence were not conducive to compromise. In fact, they hardened the attitudes on both sides.

During the first half of 1960, when the two states were already autonomous but not yet independent, two conferences on frontier problems had ended on a harmonious note.[5] Yet, after independence, relations soured. In Mali, irredentist sentiments came to the fore. This was the result of several factors, among them the continuous unrest along the border and the ideological gap between a radically inclined Mali and a more conservative Mauritania. But probably the main reason was Mali's desire to "receive its share" should Mauritania disintegrate under Moroccan pressure. As for the Mauritanian attitude in face of Malian claims, it was firm. Threatened by Moroccan-inspired subversion, the Mauritanian government could not concede Malian claims, lest this alienate the Moorish chiefs, whose tribute-paying subjects Mali wished to "liberate," and start the process of disintegration.

Mauritania began to soften its position toward Mali in early 1962. The new policy was signified by Mauritania's proposal to send a mission to Mali to seek ways to improve relations between the two countries. Probably the most important consideration behind Mauritania's change of attitude was the desire to drive a wedge between Mali and Morocco, and thus to ease the pressures to which Mauritania was being subjected

---

*It is interesting to note that both the border agreement and the defense treaty were negotiated and initialed in July 1963, before Kenya attained independence, that is—before the Kenya government was legally competent to do so. The Kenyan delegation was led by Oginga Odinga. The 1963 agreement did not settle the issue, and intermittent negotiations continued until 1970. A ceremonious signing of the border agreement by Emperor Haile Selassie and President Kenyatta took place in June 1970. (See *ARB*, June 1970, p. 1775.)

by the claims of these two states. The change in Mauritanian policy may have been facilitated by the Mauritanian government's success in overcoming the Moroccan-supported internal opposition. As a result, the Mauritanian government's domestic hold was strengthened and its freedom of action greatly widened. The Mauritanian initiative coincided with the intensification of Mali-based guerrilla activities in the disputed Hodh and statements by Mauritanian spokesmen accusing Mali of complicity. After agreeing at first to receive the Mauritanian mission, Mali reversed its attitude in early May and requested that the mission be cancelled on the grounds of the alleged "discourteous tone" of the Mauritanian president in a recent speech.

That Mauritania was already seriously committed to a conciliatory policy is evident from President Ould Daddah's response to the Malian rebuff. Toward the end of May he told a press conference in Paris that Mali's attitude toward Mauritania was very different from the Moroccan attitude, and that border incidents were less the acts of the governments concerned than "inherent in the nature of things."[6] Despite the president's conciliatory tone, negotiations did not start until November. It is possible that Malian support for the terrorist activities helped to increase Mauritania's readiness to negotiate about the boundary. In any event, it does not seem that the use of force inhibited Mauritania's desire for an accommodation.

In November a Mauritanian mission headed by the minister of interior was received in Bamako. The territorial dispute was not settled, but the talks helped to improve the atmosphere. It was agreed that the two heads of state would meet to try to solve the border dispute.[7]

An agreement was finally reached in February 1963. President Ould Daddah traveled to Kayes in Mali to meet President Modibo Keita. After lengthy discussions Ould Daddah offered the concessions which neither subordinate officials nor the minister of interior had dared to make. The border agreement was signed.[8]

The Kayes agreement on the boundary signified the beginning of a new era in Mali-Mauritanian relations. Additional agreements on trade, financial matters, and communications followed in April 1963 and relations rapidly improved. But, most important from Mauritania's point of view, the Bamako-Rabat axis was broken and Morocco was left isolated in its anti-Mauritanian policy.

In summary, the agreements were possible because both Kenya and Mauritania were able to yield some of the territory in question without compromising what they regarded as core values. Both agreements were associated with a change in the ranking of values and priorities by the decision makers. The change in Kenya came with the advent of new men at independence. In Mauritania the same man, President Ould Daddah, had in 1960 refused compromise, and in 1963 decided to yield. Changes in internal and external circumstances had made the territorial concession possible or perhaps even desirable.*

AGREEMENTS RECOGNIZING THE STATUS QUO

Agreements in which the disputants recognized the territorial status quo signified the renunciation of territorial claims by one side. Obviously such renunciation required a major policy change. The magnitude of the policy adjustment varied, of course, according to the previous commitment of the state yielding its claim.

1. *The Tunisian-Algerian dispute.* In 1961, while Tunisia was still pressing France on Tunisian territorial claims along the Algerian border, Tunisia also began to discuss the matter with the provisional government of the Algerian Republic, which represented the Algerian nationalists struggling for independence from France. The Tunisian-Algerian negotiations continued intermittently through 1961 and 1962. They were interrupted in January 1963, when the two countries

*The agreement did not end all boundary problems between Mali and Mauritania. Another meeting between President Ould Daddah and the Mali head of state, Lieutenant Traore, took place at Kayes in July 1970. At that time they decided to establish a joint technical commission to examine "outstanding problems with a view of finding a solution which fits in with the fraternal relations between the two countries." (See *ARB*, July 1970, p. 1805.)

broke relations over alleged Algerian complicity in a plot to assassinate President Bourguiba. Diplomatic relations were restored by an agreement of July 26, 1963. This was accompanied by a series of conventions on other matters: on legal and judicial questions, frontier regulations (but not border delimitation), cultural relations, postal services, customs, tourism, electrical power, commerce and economic cooperation, railways cooperation and air transport.[9]

The conclusion of these agreements suggests that by this time President Bourguiba had already decided not to press Tunisian territorial claims against Algeria. Additional indications of the shift in Tunisia's policy soon became apparent. Thus, in referring to the border problem, Tunisian spokesmen ceased to demand ownership of the disputed territory, emphasizing instead economic agreements to assure joint exploitation of the mineral resources of the area. As the minister of state at the presidency, Bahi Ladgham, said during a visit to Algiers in November 1963, Tunis did not attach much importance to the territory in dispute, and would be content with joint development of the area's resources.[10]

Tunisia's new policy of playing down its territorial claims was restated by President Bourguiba with his customary eloquence in an interview published in December 1963. He said:

> Why put soldiers in the Sahara? To do what? To count the stars? No, frankly, I do not anymore see any reason for us to make territorial claims to Algeria. There is no question about it anymore. This problem has today been completely superseded, and I am fully satisfied. Since we now talk of joint exploitation of our wealth and of gradual economic integration, what is the importance of these kilometers of sand?

Bourguiba also referred to his meeting with Algeria's President Ben Bella at Bizerta, from December 12 to 15, 1963, on the occasion of the festivities marking France's evacuation of the Bizerta base, which had, he said, helped to clear the air of misunderstandings.[11]

The statements were apparently intended to indicate that

Tunisia would be willing to renounce its territorial claims if compensated by receiving a share of the income from the natural resources assumed to exist in the Sahara.

The change in Tunisian attitudes signified by the above discussion in late 1963 was gradual. The Tunisian claims, first raised in Tunisian-French negotiations over issues outstanding at Tunisia's attainment of independence, were restated with renewed vigor when it became clear that French withdrawal from Algeria was near. As long as President Bourguiba believed that there was a chance of French concessions to Tunisia, he presented its claim as being of first-rate importance. Tunisia's commitment was for example demonstrated in July 1961 by the vain attempt of Tunisian volunteers to "plant the flag" on Beacon 233,* in the course of which the volunteers attacked the French post at Fort Thiriet (near Fort Saint), and suffered heavy casualities.[12] Since the territorial claim involved a confrontation with France, it was relatively easy to justify it ideologically as consistent with the prevailing anticolonial atmosphere.

When Algeria became independent, however, President Bourguiba realistically recognized that Tunisia was unlikely to obtain territorial concessions from the new Algeria. While the agreements of July 26, 1963 indicated that Tunisia did not intend to pursue its claims, Tunisia did not at that stage formally recognize the *de facto* boundary. Instead, the Tunisian interest in the territory was deemphasized and the Saharan sands were described as "useless." At the same time, Tunisia hoped to be able to extract favorable terms of economic cooperation from Algeria, and perhaps to obtain Algeria's agreement for the construction of a pipeline to export Algerian oil through a Tunisian port.

Negotiations about economic cooperation were slowed down by the coup d'état in Algeria in June 1965. The new Algerian regime, headed by Colonel Boumedienne, included among deposed President Ben Bella's sins his alleged promise to President Bourguiba on the subject of the disputed area near Beacon 233, which was claimed by Tunisia. These accu-

---

*The Beacons are boundary markers going back to the Franco-Turkish boundary of 1910.

sations were accompanied by statements speaking emotionally of the "sanctity" of the national territory for which so much Algerian blood had been shed. Nevertheless the new regime also expressed its willingness for neighborly cooperation with Tunisia.[13]

The matter remained in suspension until January 1967, when agreement was reached on a provisional boundary in the El Borma region, where oil had been discovered on both sides of the disputed frontier. The agreement left unresolved the question of Beacon 233, which Tunisia had claimed. This, and other problems were settled by subsequent agreements in 1968, 1969, and 1970, according to which Beacon 233 remained well inside Algerian territory, and Tunisia accepted the border as interpreted by France and by Algeria at the time of Algeria's accession to independence.[14]

The relative ease with which the Tunisian government was able to deemphasize its claim and abandon it without being restricted by the public opinion which it had previously aroused, suggests that there was considerable public apathy on the issue. The sympathy of some sections of the public toward revolutionary Algeria may have facilitated the shift. Also important was the government's ability to direct and control public opinion, and to turn it on or off in accordance with policy needs.

Perhaps the most important factor enabling Tunisia to abandon its territorial claim was, however, President Bourguiba's pragmatism, which was reflected in the flexibility of his policies. It was made possible by his prudence in not defining the territorial claim as a core value. While assuming the posture of firm commitment, Bourguiba based the Tunisian claim on legal arguments concerning the border delimitation made by France, on the rights acquired by Tunisia through the participation of Tunisian laborers in road construction and other work in the Sahara, and upon equity—Tunisia's right for a share in the Sahara. The status quo was illegal and unjust according to the Tunisian view. But Tunisia's existence and the Tunisian nation were in no way endangered by it. Having refrained from defining the issue in terms of core values, Bourguiba was free to yield.

The Tunisian government's freedom of action does not by

itself explain the settlement. A most important factor which
served as an incentive to both sides to resume negotiations
and to seek a settlement was the practical question of the
development of the oil fields. As early as 1964 oil was discovered at El Borma, on the Tunisian side of the de facto
line, and commercial production began in 1966. The discovery of oil on the Algerian side in early 1967, at one place
only 2 kilometers from the Tunisian border, necessitated
urgent negotiations to delimit the border and also to coordinate production.[15]   Both Algeria and Tunisia therefore became
interested in a speedy settlement.

2. *Morocco abandons its claims against Algeria and Mauritania.*   Between September 1968 and June 1970, Morocco
concluded a series of agreements with Algeria and Mauritania,
by which Moroccan territorial claims against both countries
were abandoned and its disputes with them settled. How can
one explain this transformation in Morocco's policy after the
lengthy disputes and the repeated attempts at settlement
which had failed?

The Moroccan-Algerian territorial dispute can be divided
into two periods. The first (1961-1963), was characterized by
Moroccan pressure and by escalating tension in October 1963
culminating in a brief war. Following the war the parties
gradually disengaged from the dispute and relations slowly
improved, with Morocco finally abandoning its claims.

At the start of the first phase, Morocco negotiated about its
claims with France. But these negotiations were gradually
abandoned for, on the one hand, the French refused to offer
concessions and, on the other, Morocco came under Algerian
criticism for cooperating with France in designs to partition
Algeria. (A proposal considered by France at that time was
that independence be granted to the three northern depart-
ments, with the Sahara remaining French.)

In these circumstances Morocco sought to assure the Algerians that it would not make a deal with France behind their
backs. The issue seems to have been raised during private
discussions between Moroccan and Algerian representatives at
the Casablanca conference in January 1961. The phrase in
the resolution on Algeria which declared that the conference

"opposes the partition of Algeria" reflects Algerian concern over this problem.[16]

Moroccan attempts to induce the nationalists' provisional government to recognize Moroccan claims failed, however, because the Algerians refused to commit themselves. The most that Morocco was able to obtain at this time was an Algerian promise to negotiate the problem after independence. For its part, Morocco pledged itself to oppose French plans for partition. An agreement to this effect, dated July 6, 1961, was signed on behalf of the Algerians by Ferhat Abbas, then head of the Provisional Algerian Government.[17]

Despite Moroccan urging, Algeria did not fulfill its commitment to open negotiations on the border problem after independence. When French forces were withdrawn from the border area, following Algeria's independence in 1962, both Algeria and Morocco sent troops to occupy positions in the disputed territory. Further advances by Morocco in October led to fighting that threatened to escalate into a full-scale war.

Soon after the fighting began, mediation offers began pouring into Rabat and Algiers. The most persevering in such efforts were President Bourguiba of Tunisia and Emperor Haile Selassie of Ethiopia.[18] The emperor could hardly avoid the mediator's role, especially since he happened to be on a visit to Morocco and to Algeria while the fighting was in progress. Moreover, he had an interest in the outcome of the conflict and in the procedures and principles applied in its resolution, since parts of Ethiopia, too, were the objects of territorial claims.

Since apparently both Algeria and Morocco realized that they could not hope to benefit much from a protracted war, the problem for them became how to gain from the restoration of peace. Morocco hoped to press Algeria into entering on the promised negotiations about Morocco's territorial claims. Algeria wished to obtain the withdrawal of Moroccan forces from the positions they occupied and to gain recognition of the border held by France prior to Algeria's independence as the legitimate border with Morocco.

First, agreement had to be reached on the form of peace negotiations, the possible participation and identity of mediators, and the venue of a conference. Morocco preferred direct negotiations. Such negotiations actually did take place during the early stage of the fighting; they were assisted by the Ethiopian emperor. However, the negotiations were discontinued on October 18, 1963, after they had reached a deadlock.[19]

The OAU was first brought into the picture by Algeria. As early as October 8, Algeria had justified its refusal to negotiate about Moroccan claims by arguing that the OAU charter had confirmed the territorial status quo in Africa.[20] A formal Algerian appeal for an emergency meeting of the OAU Council of Ministers was announced on October 19. As the provisional secretariat of the organization had been entrusted to the Ethiopian government, Algeria's appeal strengthened the hand of the Ethiopian emperor, who continued in his mediation efforts, both in his personal capacity and, now, also on behalf of the OAU. At this stage, however, the attempts to refer the dispute to the OAU failed to win Morocco's consent. Considering the views favoring the preservation of colonial boundaries expressed at the Addis Ababa summit conference, Morocco felt that its position was not likely to gain support at an OAU forum. Morocco's misgivings about the OAU had already been expressed a month earlier, when it adhered to the organization; at that time Morocco had attached a reservation stating that its signature should not be interpreted as a recognition of existing borders nor as a renunciation of its rights.[21]

After some feverish diplomatic activity concerning various mediation proposals, King Hassan and President Ben Bella on October 26 accepted an invitation from President Modibo Keita of Mali to meet in Bamako, with Emperor Haile Selassie and President Keita present as informal mediators. Both Algeria and Morocco could find reasons to feel satisfied with the mediating team. The president of Mali was welcome to Algeria because of his recently proclaimed support for the principle of status quo.[22] Moreover, since Mali was at that time seeking Algerian cooperation in its efforts to control the nomadic Touareg dissidents, Algeria could expect that Mali would adopt a sympathetic attitude. Moroccan relations with Mali had cooled considerably since Mali had withdrawn from their common front against Mauritania and had ended its dispute with Mauritania. But its past association with Mali apparently encouraged Morocco to assume that its arguments against the Saharan boundaries imposed by France would meet with sympathy. Ethiopia's strong opposition to the redrawing of African borders influenced Algeria's ready acceptance of Emperor Haile Selassie as mediator; the emperor's conservative inclinations probably encouraged Morocco to do the same.

The meeting in Bamako lasted two days, October 29 and 30. It took considerable effort by the mediators to bring the two sides to an agreement. The joint communiqué made the following points: 1) a cease-fire was accepted; 2) a demilitarized zone was created, its limits to be determined by a commission of Algerian, Moroccan, Malian, and Ethiopian officers and its observance to be supervised by Malian and Ethiopian officers; 3) hostile propaganda and interference in internal affairs were to cease on a reciprocal basis; 4) an early meeting of the OAU Council of Ministers was requested, in order to establish an arbitration commission which would be charged with (a) ascertaining responsibility for the outbreak of hostilities; (b) examining the border problem and submitting recommendations to Algeria and Morocco for a definite settlement of their dispute.[23]

Both sides could claim gains. Morocco obtained Algeria's agreement to an examination of the border problem, and an Algerian undertaking to cease its propaganda attacks on the regime. Algeria obtained Moroccan withdrawal from the positions occupied during the fighting and Moroccan agreement that the dispute be settled within the framework of the OAU.

An extraordinary session of the Council of Ministers was held in Addis Ababa from November 15 to 18, 1963. It was a solemn occasion, the delegates being highly conscious of the responsibility placed on them. Both sides reiterated their positions and exchanged accusations. An additional point emphasized by the Algerian representative was that the council's decisions would have far-reaching implications for all African borders. Most delegations refrained from discussing the conflict and the substantive issues involved and, in the end, the council confined itself to the task assigned to it by the Bamako communiqué. The council designated Ethiopia, the Ivory Coast, Mali, Nigeria, Senegal, Sudan, and Tanganyika to serve on an ad hoc commission, and it defined the commission's terms of reference as those laid down in Article 4, subparagraphs (a) and (b) of the Bamako communiqué. The commission was further requested to report back to the Council on the results of its work. To the Council's contributions one must add that, by declaring its support for the Bamako agreement, it endowed the agreement with its own prestige and authority, and thus helped to strengthen it and to stabilize the cease-fire. An important principle proclaimed by the Council on this occasion was the "determination" of the African states always to seek solution to their differences "within the framework of the principles and the institutions prescribed by the Charter of the Organization of African Unity."[24]

The next step toward a settlement was taken not by the OAU commission but by the cease-fire commission set up in accordance with the Bamako communiqué. On February 20, 1964 it was announced that at last agreement had been reached on the thorny question of defining the demilitarized zone from which forces would be withdrawn and that the withdrawal of forces had been completed accordingly.[25] With this task accomplished, the cease-fire commission was dissolved in April by mutual agreement. It did not stay on to supervise the observance of the demilitarization agreement, as originally envisaged by the Bamako communiqué.[26] Presumably these agreements were made possible by the progress of direct negotiations between King Hassan and President Ben Bella at the Arab League summit conference in Cairo in January 1964.

With the immediate crisis resolved and the demilitarized zone separating the two parties, the OAU *ad hoc* commission met periodically in attempts to fulfill the mandate with which it had been charged. Yet it was unable to make progress. The commission submitted periodic reports to the OAU Council of Ministers, which thereupon formally resolved to "take note" of the report, to congratulate the commission for its work, and to request it to continue.[27]

In May 1966 the calm routine of the commission's work

was broken by a new crisis. It started when Algeria's nationalization of mines came to include a mine at Gara Djebilet, an area claimed by Morocco.[28]

When the ad hoc commission met in July, the crisis already belonged to the past. But Morocco succeeded in impressing on the commission that the unresolved dispute was a danger to peace. As a result, a new effort was made to break the deadlock.

The commission's discussions this time brought into the open a basic disagreement concerning its original terms of reference: was the commission authorized to arbitrate the dispute or merely to engage in mediation and conciliation? Significantly, Algeria favored arbitration and Morocco opposed it. Faced with this situation, the commission decided that arbitration would require a new mandate from the Council of Ministers. On the one hand the procedural debate reflected Algeria's expectation that arbitration would support the status quo, and on the other Morocco's hope that, in the processes of mediation and conciliation, Algeria would be asked to make concessions and to meet Moroccan claims part of the way.

When the OAU Council of Ministers met in Addis Ababa in November 1966, it again decided to ask the commission to continue its work, but refrained from ruling on the disputed interpretation of the terms of reference. The heads of state approved the council's resolution at their meeting a few days later.[29]

Although unable to resolve the dispute, the OAU performed important functions with respect to it. Its initial contribution had been that its authority had helped to stabilize the cease-fire in 1963. It also played an important role subsequently. It was Algeria which had first been interested in OAU intervention, whereas Morocco was reluctant to accept it because it feared the organization would support the principle of status quo. Thereafter, the initiative for continued OAU involvement came from Morocco. Since Morocco was frustrated in its attempts to obtain any Algerian concession and even to induce Algeria to enter into negotiations, the OAU commission became for Morocco a convenient outlet and an instrument by which Morocco could keep the issue alive. It also became a substitute for any real action directed toward the realization of Morocco's territorial claim. Any measures which could hurt Algeria or weaken its position would have encountered a strong Algerian response. Discussion alone by the OAU commission was relatively harmless and did not necessitate strong countermeasures. But, most important in the longer run, the work of the OAU ad hoc commission served to cool off the dispute, and thus it created conditions for disengagement and settlement.

An indication that the two sides were ready to open a new stage in their relations was provided in early 1968 by progress in negotiations for joint development of Algerian mineral resources. Morocco's willingness to bury past quarrels was reflected by King Hassan's trip to Algiers in September 1968, to attend the OAU summit conference. In the course of the visit, the king and President Boumedienne held talks through which progress toward an improvement in relations seems to have been made.[30]

The Algiers meeting was followed by President Boumedienne's state visit to Morocco in January 1969. The communiqué marking the end of the visit announced the conclusion of a "Treaty of Solidarity and Cooperation." Significantly, no mention was made in the joint communiqué, nor in the treaty, of the territorial dispute.

It is probable, however, that the territorial dispute occupied a prominent place in the discussions. By all indications Morocco did not press its territorial claim, and the two sides agreed, either tacitly or by an explicit but secret accord, to bypass the heart of the issue—the location of the frontier line. They concentrated instead on a number of matters surrounding the dispute on which agreement seemed possible. Thus, the two sides renounced the use of force in disputes between them. They also agreed to limit the arms race, a subject on which they had exchanged accusations in early 1967. Probably the most important agreements were on economic matters. These provided for increased trade, Moroccan purchase of Algerian oil and, most significantly, for cooperation in the development of mineral resources in the frontier zone. The projected cooperation called for the export of iron ore from the disputed Tindouf region via Morocco's

Atlantic ports. The possibility of processing the ore at Agadir was also mentioned.[31]

The process of rapprochement did not stop here. Rather, the Ifarne treaty (as the January 1969 agreement came to be called) served as a stepping stone toward the settlement of the territorial dispute. Another landmark on the road to a settlement was the meeting between King Hassan and President Boumedienne in Tlemcen (Algeria), in May 1970. The joint communiqué published at the conclusion of the meeting declared that the two governments agreed to form a mixed commission charged with delimiting the border.

Although nothing explicit was said, the establishment of the joint commission was generally understood to indicate that Morocco had renounced its territorial claims and that it had come to accept the de facto line inherited from France. In any event, it is clear that this time the two parties addressed themselves directly to the boundary question, and that agreement on the principles that would guide delimitation had been reached. The significance attached to the agreement was reflected in the optimistic atmosphere surrounding the meeting and in the assessment of an Algerian official, who told a journalist that this was the most important event in the history of the Maghreb since Algeria's independence.[32] By the time of writing Morocco had not yet *publicly* renounced its claims. Nevertheless, by all indications, the Tlemcen meeting signified Morocco's abandonment of its territorial claims against Algeria.

3. *The Moroccan-Mauritanian dispute.* After Morocco had in 1960 failed to prevent Mauritania's independence, several attempts were made to establish normal relations between the two countries. Although tension subsided, attempts at normalization repeatedly failed until 1969, when renewed negotiations speedily brought about a settlement.

Attempts to settle the dispute began soon after King Hassan's ascension to the throne, following the sudden death of his father, King Mohamed V, in 1961. According to President Ould Daddah, Senegal tried to mediate the dispute in June 1961. This attempt failed because Mauritania insisted that if Morocco wished to break the deadlock, it was indispensable that it first recognize Mauritanian independence. Morocco responded that it was unable to offer de jure recognition and suggested that Mauritania satisfy itself with de facto recognition. Morocco also requested that Mauritania commit itself to entering into a special relationship with Morocco, either federal or confederal. As the conditions were mutually unacceptable, the proposed high-level negotiations did not take place. An approach by Morocco seems to have been made a few months later, but failed again for the same reasons.[33]

Early in 1963 fresh attempts at conciliation were made. Again Senegal was involved as a mediator, but the position of both sides remained essentially unchanged.* Morocco offered to recognize Mauritanian sovereignty if Mauritania simultaneously signed cooperation agreements with Morocco. The Mauritanian response was conciliatory in form but unyielding in substance. Ould Daddah told the government party congress that he hoped for the establishment of normal relations but that no dialogue was possible and no technical cooperation agreements could be signed, as long as Morocco did not unconditionally and unequivocally recognize Mauritanian sovereignty. This exchange was accompanied by the return from exile in Morocco of several opposition leaders. There was much speculation that their return was part of a tacit agreement intended to facilitate conciliation between Morocco and Mauritania.[34]

Even if such an agreement had actually been reached, relations soon began to worsen. In Morocco, domestic political considerations inhibited the course toward conciliation. In the election campaign, in May 1963, the government was attacked by the opposition for its alleged readiness to yield on the Mauritanian question. This prompted the government

*It is interesting to speculate about Senegal's motives in lending its services as mediator. On the one hand, Senegal's interest stemmed from the fact that sections of some Senegalese tribes live across the border in Mauritania. On the other hand, Senegal's mediation was related to its quarrel with Mali, which had followed the break-up of their short-lived federation. While Mali sought to insure consideration of its interests in the event of Mauritania's dissolution by allying itself with Morocco, Senegal served notice of its interest in Mauritania's fate by offering its services as intermediary.

to show that it was as uncompromising as ever and, in protest against Mauritania's presence, King Hassan refused to attend the Addis Ababa summit conference (at which the OAU was established). In Mauritania the returned opposition leaders were arrested in August and charged with subversive activities. Morocco responded to the arrests by reappointing one of these opposition leaders, the emir of Trarza, to the post of minister of Mauritanian and Saharan affairs in the Moroccan government—a purely symbolic gesture, since the emir was at that time imprisoned in Mauritania.[35]

During 1964 mutual hostility moderated somewhat and it appeared that both sides desired to establish normal relations. Thus, King Hassan made a conciliatory speech in Dakar, on the occasion of his visit to Senegal, and Ould Daddah responded in a message to the National Assembly welcoming Hassan's words, and stating that as always Mauritania was ready to establish "relations of cooperation" with Morocco. In July King Hassan attended the OAU summit meeting in Cairo and did not object to being seated, in alphabetical order, next to President Ould Daddah of Mauritania. But the two did not speak to each other and the attempts of Presidents Bourguiba and Sékou Touré to arrange talks between them failed. However, the Moroccan and Mauritanian ministers of information did meet and agreed to put an end to the radio propaganda war waged by their respective broadcasting services. Observers detected a further sign of moderation on Morocco's part when in a government reshuffle in August 1964 the emir of Trarza was taken off the list of ministers.[36]

If there was some readiness for accomodation, however, it soon ceased to be evident. In January 1965, Prince Moulay Hassan was appointed to fill the vacant post of minister of Saharan and Mauritanian affairs. A further symbol of Morocco's continued commitment to the thesis that Mauritania was part of Morocco was the appointment in April 1967 of an exiled Mauritanian leader, Dey Ould Sidi Baba, as minister of the Royal Cabinet.[37]

In September 1969, a conciliatory gesture by King Hassan indicated that Morocco was prepared to abandon its claim. The gesture came in the form of an invitation to President Ould Daddah to attend a summit conference of Moslem states (September 22-25), convened in Rabat following the fire in the Al Aqsa mosque in Jerusalem. Ould Daddah reciprocated by accepting. The conference provided an opportunity for Hassan and Ould Daddah to confer. The first meeting was arranged by Algeria's President Boumedienne and attended by him. It apparently went well, as Ould Daddah extended his visit to Rabat in order to continue the talks.

That Morocco was now actively seeking reconciliation, and that it had renounced its claim to Mauritania, was indicated by King Hassan at his news conference on September 26. At the news conference, the king made an extraordinary public admission. He said that he had never been satisfied with Morocco's policy on Mauritania, that loyalty to his father had prevented him from changing it, but that a change had now become possible.[38]

The next steps followed rapidly. On October 30 a Mauritanian mission arrived in Rabat for talks and was received by the king. In January 1970, a Moroccan delegation went to Nouakchott for a return visit. At the conclusion of the visit, it was announced that Mauritania and Morocco would establish diplomatic relations. And, indeed, soon thereafter ambassadors were exchanged.[39] The reconciliation was sealed by another visit by President Ould Daddah to Morocco in June 1970, on which occasion a "Treaty of Solidarity, Good Neighborliness and Cooperation" was signed by the two heads of state. By the treaty Morocco and Mauritania agreed to respect each other's territorial integrity, to refrain from interfering in each other's internal affairs, to settle disputes peacefully, to reenforce political, economic, social and cultural relations, and to establish a joint commission, at the ministerial level, for the purpose of developing relations.[40]

Thus, with Morocco's recognition of Mauritania, and the conclusion of the treaty, Morocco publicly and formally gave notice that it had renounced its claims. This dispute, too, had been settled by the acceptance of boundaries established by the departing colonial power.

Why did Morocco's disputes with both Algeria and Mauritania defy solution for so long, and why did the disputes lend themselves to speedy settlement after 1968? Although the policies of all three states underwent changes over the years, the sharpest policy change was undertaken by Morocco between 1968 and 1970. For seven years after the death of King Mohamed V, Morocco had followed the irredentist course set for it by the late king. Although King Hassan II, who succeeded to the throne in 1961, did not share his father's approach to the problem of boundaries, he refrained from altering the course of Moroccan policies, because of, according to Hassan, feelings of filial loyalty. It is impossible to judge to what extent Hassan's policies were influenced by such sentiments. But his disinclination to change the policy was strengthened by the political advisability of avoiding unnecessary conflict with the Istiqlal party, which, despite the obvious failure of Morocco's policy on Mauritania, remained adamantly committed to irredentism. In June 1965 it called for "resolute steps to be taken by direct or diplomatic means to recover Mauritania." When in August 1965 an official Mauritanian delegation participated in a UNESCO conference in Tangier, the Moroccan press speculated as to whether this signified a modification of policy. But the Istiqlal party newspaper criticized the government for its acquiescence in Mauritanian participation, thus indicating again the Istiqlal's vehement opposition to normalization of relations.[41] To be sure, the Istiqlal was unable to influence the king to pursue the claim to Mauritania actively; yet it did inhibit him from pursuing the course of conciliation.

By 1968 internal political developments in Morocco enabled King Hassan to gain the freedom of action he needed, and he was no longer inhibited by the fear of the Istiqlal. The failure of the irredentist policy had become obvious, and it is unlikely that its continuation had influential supporters.

Against this background, Algeria took the initiative for a détente. According to some press reports, Egypt's defeat in the Six Day War with Israel in 1967 moved President Boumedienne to mend Algeria's relations with its Maghreb neighbors as a step which would place him in a position to challenge President Nasser's claim for leadership of the Arab world. To this political motive an economic incentive was added. Collaboration with Morocco offered favorable prospects for the development of the Tindouf region. While the export of the Tindouf ore through Algerian ports was impractical because of prohibitive costs, its shipment via Morocco's Atlantic ports appeared to offer advantages to both countries.

By this time, Morocco was receptive to the Algerian initiative. King Hassan was by then both inclined and able to abandon the irredentist course. Moreover, Moroccan participation in the development of the mineral resources of the disputed area offered a mode of settlement that would minimize the damage to Morocco's prestige and, at the same time, provide substantial economic advantages. Finally, an important incentive spurring Morocco toward a rapprochement with Algeria was the problem of Rio de Oro (Spanish Sahara). This Spanish dependence had been claimed by both Morocco and Mauritania. Spain had for years successfully played Morocco and Mauritania against each other, while developing the enormous phosphate deposits in the territory and preparing the basis for granting the territory autonomy while preserving its close links with Spain. As a showdown over the future of this territory approached, Morocco was eager to obtain Algeria's neutrality, if not support, in its rivalry with Mauritania over succession to the territory. Hints that Algeria too was interested in the territory, and that Algeria's Tindouf ore could be exported by way of the Spanish territory, as the coast there was closer to Tindouf than the Moroccan seashore, further stimulated Moroccan desire for a rapprochement with Algeria.[42]

The progress of the Moroccan-Algerian talks and Morocco's appeal for Algerian neutrality or support on Rio de Oro, inevitably raised the question of Mauritania. All three—Morocco, Mauritania, and Algeria—now came to regard the settlement of the Moroccan-Mauritanian dispute as a matter of urgent interest. While Mauritania became concerned at the possibility of a Moroccan-Algerian agreement disregarding its interests, Algeria was, for its part, reluctant to align itself with Morocco to the exclusion of Mauritania. Morocco realized that the progress of agreement with Algeria depended upon the normalizaiton of its relations with Mauritania. The three relationships—Algerian/Moroccan, Algerian/Mauritanian, and Moroccan/Mauritanian—were interdependent.[43]

Thus, the need for further progress in Morocco's talks with Algeria influenced King Hassan to take advantage of the Islamic summit conference to attempt to establish normal relations with Mauritania. The king justified his invitation to the Mauritanian president by saying that Moslems should bury their quarrels and join forces to solve their common problems.[44] The staging for the reconciliation—an Islamic summit—could hardly have been more propitious for Hassan in his attempt to neutralize the Istiqlal, which had always been an Islamic-traditionalist party. Criticism of the rapprochement policy by Istiqlal newspapers was met by the arrest of their editors. Hassan was free to act, both Morocco and Mauritania were willing, and Algeria's Boumedienne helped by inviting Hassan and Ould Daddah to meet in his residence.

Morocco's abandonment of a claim which had once been regarded as a core value was made possible by the change in the person of the ruler. Still, the change of policy was gradual and it took place only after changes in the domestic environment and in the Algerian attitude to Morocco. No less important was the emergence of issues that helped to round off the bargain and, at the same time, served as incentives for a settlement: the requirements of mineral development and the ripening of the Rio do Oro problem. Last, the availability of an ideological common denominator in the ideas of Islamic, Maghreb, and African solidarity, helped to smooth the process and to legitimize the rapprochement.

A REVIEW OF THE DISPUTES

A combination of circumstances contributed to the possibility of boundary agreements. The leaders of one side, at least, did not regard the issue at stake as involving a core value. Kenyan leaders' views of the Gadaduma wells, Ould Daddah's view of the territories claimed by Mali, Bourguiba's of Tunisia's claims on Algeria, and Hassan's view of Moroccan claims on Algeria and Mauritania can all be described as devoid of a rigid indentification of these territories with their countries' most cherished values. The freedom of action enjoyed by these leaders was an additional factor contributing to the agreements. Ould Daddah gained this freedom by suppressing the opposition, and Hassan by overcoming the Istiqlal, while the apathy of the Tunisian and Kenyan publics toward the territorial issue rendered Bourguiba and Kenyatta free to act. Finally, in each case, a new factor appeared that served as an incentive for a settlement, in the sense that the sides came to believe that they had more to gain from an agreement, even if it involved abandoning some claims, than from continued deadlock. Kenya was interested in Ethiopian support against Somalia, Mauritania wanted to disrupt the Mali-Morocco alliance, Tunisia and Algeria were spurred by the requirements of oil field development at El Borma, and Morocco, Algeria, and Mauritania by the prospect that Rio de Oro would become autonomous under Spanish tutelage. All three factors—a flexible image of the issue, freedom to act, and an inducement to alter existing policies—seem to have been necessary prerequisites, without which agreement would have been impossible.

Chapter **11** *Prospects*

It is tempting to speculate about the future of boundary politics. Assuming that the past provides some indication of future trends, we shall attempt to assess the prospects for the outbreak of new border and territorial disputes and for the revival of disputes that have been suspended or formally resolved.

Although boundary and territorial disputes in Africa have not assumed the major proportions that had been expected, the potential for conflict remains great. The basic elements for the making of border and territorial disputes are present in Africa in abundance. One element is ideological. The feeling prevails that the borders were arbitrarily imposed by the colonial powers. Anticolonialism can carry the corollary of territorial revisionism. Second, the borders are artificial—they correspond poorly with the facts of human and economic geography. Ethnic and tribal groups by the hundreds are divided by borders, and may create boundary claims or attempt secession. The interference of borders with the migrations of nomadic tribes in search of water and grazing land, and the obstacles these borders may pose for the utilization and development of natural resources may also cause conflict, as may the obstacles posed to communications. The existence of land-locked states is an additional potentially unsettling factor. Finally, the multi-ethnic and inchoate character of most states is itself another source of instability, especially since it carries the potential for the development of separatist movements. A third element making for border conflicts is of a technical nature: the imprecise formulation of many delimitation documents.[1]

Despite the existence of this high potential for conflict, relatively few disputes have actually erupted. The general tendency of African governments has been to refrain from posing territorial claims and to respect the status quo. As for the divided tribes, the overwhelming majority have accepted the fact of their division and have not given rise to irredentism or separatism. A consideration of the prospects for new disputes must address itself to the factors that might induce changes in existing attitudes and policies.[2]

POSSIBILITY OF NEW DISPUTES

Changes leading to new disputes may develop at two levels: the level of popular or tribal attitudes and the level of governmental policies. Tribes or peoples may come into conflict with governments over secessionist and separatist attempts; governments may enter into disputes with each other over claims for boundary rectification and territorial cession.

Changes in popular attitudes can come about in two ways: as the result of a political upheaval in a state that upsets an existing political balance; or by the slow and gradual change that comes with development, improved communications, and political awareness. In the first, political upheaval may produce feelings of alienation, leading to secessionist sentiments. Nigeria is the notable example. The military coup of July 1966, directed against the Ibo officers who had carried out the first coup in January 1966, and the anti-Ibo massacres that followed the coup, led to the alienation of the Ibos and to Biafra's secession. Another example is Chad, where the establishment of southern dominance in the government after 1959 induced the growth of separatist sentiment in the north. In view of the endemic political instability of most African states, drastic changes in the relative political influence of tribal groups which would induce the growth of secessionist sentiments can be expected to take place.

As part of the second way in which popular attitudes change, the growth of political consciousness may sharpen awareness of particular tribal interests and increase friction with rival groups and with the central government. Uneven rates of economic development within the country may contribute to the process. It is conceivable that such friction may develop into separatist sentiment. Development processes also imply more effective administration of outlying areas, more effective collection of taxes, customs control of the border, veterinary supervision over cattle, and marketing regulations for agricultural products. While such measures may be essential for development, for the effective utilization of natural resources, and for state-building in general, they are also apt to provoke resentment among people unaccustomed to these blessings of civilization. Frontier populations in particular, whose commercial and other contacts across hitherto unadministered borders would be affected by the tightening of administration, might become restive and develop secessionist sentiments. The case of the Touareg in Mali is an example of separatism developing in reaction to more effective administration. The pursuit of policies of national integration by governments might induce similar separatism elsewhere as well.

In addition, governments might alter their policies and demand border rectifications or raise territorial claims. Some such changes might develop in response to secessionism in a contiguous country. If the secessionists proclaim that they wish to join the contiguous state, that state might be tempted to give such a movement its blessing and support. Another inducement for governments to abandon their respect for the status quo might be the discovery of mineral resources across the border in the neighboring territory. This was the case in several disputes occurring in the early years of independence. Mauritania has enormous deposits of iron in the north. There is iron in the Tindouf area of Algeria, which was claimed by Morocco. The potential wealth of the Sahara was one object of Tunisia's claims. The Haut-Ogooué area of Gabon, which was claimed by Congo, contains uranium and manganese mines. The eastern region of Nigeria disputed the manner in which the Nigerian federal government apportioned the revenues from oil production in the east. And Katanga's

immense riches in copper and other minerals were an inducement for the attempt to secede from Congo. It is unlikely
that the discovery of new mineral resources would by itself
provoke border and territorial claims, but it might contribute
to and reinforce other revisionist tendencies.

The prospects for new border and territorial disputes are
greatly increased by the general volatility of interstate relations in Africa. Changes in regimes, the advent of new men,
competition for regional or continental influence, the manip-
ulation of African governments by the great powers, all may
lead to friction among neighboring states. When confidence
between neighbors is undermined, and when antagonism
develops between them, boundary and territorial claims may
be produced. Such situations have indeed developed in the
past, as between Dahomey and Niger, Ghana and Upper
Volta, or Malawi and Tanzania. In a sense, the border or
territorial dispute in such cases is merely a symptom of the
bad relations between neighbors, or a secondary dispute
stemming from some primary conflict. In view of the instability of African politics, there seems to be a high propensity
for this kind of dispute, especially where the borders are
uncertain and the delimitation agreements imprecise.

To the extent that governments and political movements
choose their options by calculating their capacity to attain
revisionist goals, the temptations to raise boundary or territorial claims may be moderated. The demonstrated advantage
of mutual respect for the status quo may be an additional
restraining influence. But since calculated choice of options is
not the dominant characteristic of political behavior, the
likelihood of new disputes seems considerable.

SUSPENDED AND RESOLVED DISPUTES

By definition, *suspended disputes* are disputes which have
not been resolved. The suspension of the dispute reflects an
ambivalence in the attitudes of the revisionist parties. On the
one hand, they realize that no advantage is likely to accrue
from the continued pursuit of their revisionist goals. Yet,
either because of their own deep commitment to those goals

or because of the political hazards involved, they do not formally and publicly abandon them but on the contrary proclaim continued dedication to them.

The fragility of such situations is obvious. Unless the détente has been accompanied by the development of intensive economic and political cooperation and cultural as well as personal understanding, the conflict may be renewed at any time.

The factors that may end the suspension and renew the conflict are several. The ouster of ruling politicians may be accompanied by charges that the deposed politicians "betrayed" the national interest and the new government may revert to the pursuit of revisionist goals. Even governments that favored the suspension of the dispute and wished to follow a policy of détente, may be forced by domestic political pressures to reverse their stand. In a way, the Somali government invited such pressures by raising the expectation that progress toward the realization of Somali unity could be made by the policy of détente. The Dahomey-Niger dispute and the Congo-Gabon dispute are less likely to be revived, primarily because the issues in these quarrels have not been regarded as core values. The likelihood of their revival also seems low because no rosy expectations accompanied their suspension.

The stability and durability of formal boundary agreements is also uncertain. Although, for example, the Moroccan government has formally recognized the status quo, irredentism still prevails among some Moroccan political groups. As long as irredentism continues to appeal to opposition groups, internal political upheavals might bring about the resumption of irredentist policies.

A potential problem likely to put boundary settlements to a severe test is that of the succession to colonial territories. The prospect of Spain's retaining control over Rio de Oro served to stimulate Morocco, Mauritania, and Algeria to settle their disputes. But, if Spain were to announce plans for withdrawal from the territory, conflict over succession to the territory might erupt. Similarly, if the French Territory of the Afars and the Issas makes progress toward independence, the suspended Somali-Ethiopian dispute is likely to be resumed with great fervor.

Finally, both suspended and resolved disputes may be revived by accident. Clashes between tribesmen across the border, or between migrating nomads from one country and the authorities on the other side of the line, may start a chain reaction, or at least contribute to pressures for the resumption of conflict. The renewed strains in 1970 between Mali and Mauritania illustrate such dangers.

It is extremely risky to forecast political developments, but nevertheless, it can be ventured that if new disputes erupt, or if suspended or resolved disputes are resumed, their course is likely to resemble the course of past disputes. The capacity of states to realize revisionist goals remains low and after a while frustration and fatigue are likely to set in. The ideological atmosphere extolling African solidarity will probably continue to prevail. In these circumstances, the factors that have brought about the suspension of disputes in the past are likely to influence the course of new or resumed disputes as well. Such a pattern would, of course, be modified if the great powers were to become deeply involved in African affairs. But as long as great power involvement does not assume major proportions, this pattern of boundary politics is likely to prevail.

Appendix, Notes,
and Index

This list summarizes information drawn from the sources
mentioned in the text. It outlines those disputes that have
caused domestic strife or have had international ramifications. It is not inclusive. There are other borders that have
not been agreed upon by the states concerned but have
caused no serious problems. For another list see R. Waters,
"Inter-African Boundary Disputes," in C. G. Widstrand, ed.,
African Boundary Problems (Uppsala: Scandinavian Institute
of African Studies, 1969), pp. 183-185. In addition to the
disputes listed, several significant claims have been raised by
unofficial bodies, but not supported by the governments
concerned:

Botswana: In the early 1960's some political leaders raised
a claim to the Caprivi strip; claims to former British Bechuanaland, transferred by Britain to the Cape Colony in 1895
have also been mentioned.

Cameroon: in 1958, some political leaders spoke of recon-
stituting the borders to their outlines of 1911-1914. During
this period Cameroon comprised not only the territories that
are formally claimed from Nigeria (the former British Northern Cameroons), but also portions of Congo (Brazzaville).

Lesotho: Political leaders have occasionally referred to
"lost territories" that ought to be claimed from South Africa.

Morocco: Allal el Fasi's image of a "greater Morocco"
initially comprised parts of northern Mali.

Nigeria: In the late 1950s some Nigerian Action Group

leaders propagated the idea that the Yorubas in Dahomey should join Nigeria.

1. Algeria and Tunisia

   Territorial goals: Tunisia wanted to revise borders in its favor and acquire part of the Sahara. Algeria wanted to preserve borders inherited from France.

   Claim or dispute: Tunisia's claim was based on interpretation of treaties and rights to Sahara of riparian states.

   Starting date: 1956.

   Was violence used? Against the French.

   Formal negotiations: Yes.

   Status as of January 1972: Tunisia gave up its claims by a series of agreements confirming the status quo, 1967-1970.

2. Cameroon and Nigeria

   Territorial goals: Cameroon claimed the former Northern British Cameroons. Nigeria wanted to retain the territory that joined Nigeria as a result of a plebiscite in 1961.

   Claim or dispute: Historical; Cameroon's claim was based on reference to the 1914 borders of German Kamerun.

   Starting date: 1960; but unification movement dates back to 1948.

   Was violence used? No.

   Formal negotiations: None.

   Status as of January 1972: Dormant, though Cameroon repeats the claim periodically for the record.

3. Chad and the secessionist movement

   Territorial goals: Secessionist tendencies occasionally ascribed to sections of the Moslem opposition to the regime. Goals, whether independence or union with Sudan, have been unclear.

Claim or dispute: Ethnic and religious.
Starting date: 1963.
Was violence used? Yes.
Formal negotiations: Yes.
Status as of January 1972: Area remains disaffected.

4. Congo (Brazzaville) and Gabon

Territorial goals: Congo claimed parts of the Upper
Ogooué region of Gabon. Gabon wanted to retain
borders inherited at independence.
Claim or dispute: Congo's claim was based on the borders
that had existed during part of the colonial per-
iod; mineral resources were another inducement;
ethnic factors were also present.
Starting date: 1962.
Was violence used? No.
Formal negotiations: Yes.
Status as of January 1972: Suspended following Douala
conference, 1962.

5. Congo (Kinshasa) and Katanga

Territorial goals: Katanga wished to secede and become
an independent state. Congo wanted to retain the
borders inherited at independence.
Claim or dispute: Economic interest and ethnic animos-
ities.
Starting date: 1960.
Was violence used? Yes.
Formal negotiations: Yes.
Status as of January 1972: Attempt crushed; Katanga
reintegrated in Congo.

6. Dahomey and Niger

Territorial goals: Both claimed exclusive jurisdiction over
Lété island in the Niger river.
Claim or dispute: Disagreement about the interpretation
of the administrative delimitation by France. This

was a secondary dispute, inflamed by political antagonism between the governments.

Starting date: 1963; but disagreement dates back to the colonial period.

Was violence used? No.

Formal negotiations: Yes.

Status as of January 1972: Suspended following the restoration of political confidence between the governments in 1965.

7. Egypt and Sudan

Territorial goals: Egypt demanded the return of certain areas north of the twenty-second parallel, which were placed under Sudanese administration in 1902. Sudan wished to retain jurisdiction over the same areas.

Claim or dispute: Secondary dispute. The question of the validity of the 1899 line (twenty-second parallel), claimed by Egypt, or of the 1902 line, claimed by Sudan, was raised by Egypt to support bargaining on other issues.

Starting date: 1958.

Was violence used? Egyptian forces crossed into the disputed territory in 1958.

Formal negotiations: Yes.

Status as of January 1972: Suspended.

8. Eritrean secessionists and Ethiopia

Territorial goals: Movement among some Moslem Eritreans to secede from Ethiopia; unclear whether they wished to join Sudan or whether they wanted independence for Eritrea. Ethiopia wanted to retain Eritrea, and to integrate it within Ethiopia.

Claim or dispute: Ethnic and religious.

Starting date: Traditional; revived 1948.

Was violence used? Yes.

Formal negotiations: No.

Status as of January 1972: Insurgents wage guerrilla war.

9. Ethiopia and Kenya

Territorial goals: Both sides claimed Gadaduma wells.
Claim or dispute: Interpretation of agreements reached
between Britain and Ethiopia.
Starting date: Colonial period.
Was violence used? No.
Formal negotiations: Yes.
Status as of January 1972: Settled by border agreements
in 1963 and 1970.

10. Ethiopia and Sudan

Territorial goals: Mutual claims to small areas along an
imprecisely delimited border.
Claim or dispute: Secondary dispute; differences over the
interpretation of the 1902 Anglo-Ethiopian delimitation agreement developed into a heated dispute following the growth of mutual suspicions
that the other side was aiding separatist insurgents.
Starting date: 1965.
Was violence used? No.
Formal negotiations: Yes.
Status as of January 1972: Generally quiescent, with
occasional arguments.

11. A. Ghana and Ivory Coast

Territorial goals: Ghana wished to annex Sanwi area.
Ivory Coast wished to retain Sanwi, and to pre-
serve borders inherited at independence.
Claim or dispute: Ethnic. Secondary dispute, a symptom
of antagonism between governments.
Starting date: 1959.
Was violence used? No.
Formal negotiations: None.
Status as of January 1972: Following deposition of Presi-
dent Nkrumah in 1966, the new Ghanaian regime
assured the Ivory Coast that Ghana had no terri-
torial ambitions.

B. Ivory Coast and the Sanwi secessionist movement

Territorial goals: The Sanwi were vague and unclear
whether they aimed at independence, or wanted
union with Ghana. Ivory Coast wanted to preserve borders inherited from France.

Claim or dispute: Ethnic, alienation of the Agni people of
Sanwi.

Starting date: Colonial period; resurgence of Sanwi secessionism in 1959.

Was violence used? Minor disturbances.

Formal negotiations: None.

Status as of January 1972: Sanwi movement suppressed.

12. A. Ghana and Togo

Territorial goals: Ghana wanted to annex Togo Republic.
Togo wanted to annex the Ewe-inhabited area of
Ghana; and to annex former British Togoland.

Claim or dispute: Ethnic—Ewe unification. Historic—
restoration of Togo's boundaries as they were
before 1914.

Starting date: Colonial period (1919), but began in earn-
est in 1958.

Was violence used? No.

Formal negotiations: Yes.

Status of January 1972: Ghanaian claim dropped following deposition of Nkrumah in 1966. Togo's claim
suspended.

B. Ghana and secessionist movement in British Togoland

Territorial goals: Ewes in British Togoland wanted to
prevent the integration of the region in Ghana,
and to join it with the Togo Republic. Ghana
wanted to integrate former British Togoland with
Ghana.

Claim or dispute: Ethnic—Ewe unification movement;
historic—to restore Togoland as it had existed
before 1914.

Starting date: 1957.

Was violence used? Insurrection was attempted.

Formal negotiations: None.
Status as of January 1972: Movement suppressed by
Ghana.

13. Ghana and Upper Volta

Territorial goals: Dispute over small areas along their
border.
Claim or dispute: Secondary dispute: disagreement over
interpretation of delimitation agreements assumed major proportion as a result of the political antagonism between the governments.
Starting date: 1963.
Was violence used? No.
Formal negotiations: Yes.
Status as of January 1972: Boundary settled by agreement in 1966 after President Nkrumah was over-
thrown.

14. Guinea and Liberia

Territorial goals: Liberia claimed small area near iron-rich
Nimba mountain.
Claim or dispute: Historic: Liberia claimed territories
allegedly usurped by France.
Starting date: Colonial period.
Was violence used? No.
Formal negotiations: None.
Status as of January 1972: Liberia withdrew its claim
when Guinea became independent in 1958.

15. Ivory Coast and Liberia

Territorial goals: Liberia claimed areas east of the Cavally
River. Ivory Coast wished to retain the right
(western) bank of the Cavally River as the border,
as it was during French rule.
Claim or dispute: Historic—Liberia claimed territories allegedly usurped by France. Disputed interpretation
of border agreements between Liberia and France.

Starting date: Colonial period.
Was violence used? No.
Formal negotiations: None.
Status as of January 1972: Liberia withdrew its
claim after the Ivory Coast became inde-
pendent.

16. Malawi and Tanzania

Territorial goals: Tanzania claimed part of lake Nyasa.
Malawi wanted border to remain on the Tanzanian shore.
Claim or dispute: Secondary dispute—the economic problem of access and use of the lake by Tanzanians
living on its shores became an angry territorial
dispute as a result of the political antagonism
between the two governments.
Starting date: 1967.
Was violence used? No.
Formal negotiations: Yes.
Status as of January 1972: Quiescent after angry exchanges in 1967.

17. Mali and Mauritania

Territorial goals: Mali claimed the Eastern Hodh and
areas administered by Mauritania along the western sector of the border. Mauritania wanted to
retain the border inherited from the French administration.
Claim or dispute: Disagreement over interpretation of the
administrative delimitation by the French colonial authorities. Historical—Mali resented the transfer of territory to Mauritania in 1944.
Starting date: 1960.
Was violence used? Yes.
Formal negotiations: Yes.
Status as of January 1972: Border settled by agreement
in 1963.

18. Mali and Targui secessionists

> *Territorial goals:* Touareg movement to secede from Mali;
> ultimate goals vague. Mali wanted to integrate the
> Touareg within Mali.
> *Claim or dispute:* Ethnic.
> *Starting date:* 1963.
> *Was violence used?* Yes.
> *Formal negotiations:* None.
> *Status as of January 1972:* Movement suppressed.

19. Morocco-Algeria

> *Territorial goals:* Morocco claimed large portions of
> Algerian held Sahara. Algeria wanted to retain the
> border inherited from the French administration.
> *Claim or dispute:* Morocco claimed that the areas had
> been part of the Moroccan state in precolonial
> times. Algeria claimed that the territories had
> been administered by France as part of Algeria,
> and that the National Liberation Front (FLN)
> fought for them, as it had for the rest of Algeria.
> *Starting date:* Colonial period; Morocco revived its claim
> in 1956.
> *Was violence used?* Yes.
> *Formal negotiations:* Yes.
> *Status as of January 1972:* Morocco gave up its claim,
> recognizing Algeria's sovereignty over the areas.

20. A. Morocco and Mauritania

> *Territorial goals:* Morocco wanted to annex Mauritania;
> Mauritania wanted to preserve independence.
> *Claim or dispute:* Morocco claimed that Mauritania had
> been part of the Moroccan state in precolonial
> times.
> *Starting date:* Colonial period; Morocco revived its claim
> in 1956.
> *Was violence used?* Yes.
> *Formal negotiations:* Yes.

Status as of January 1972: Settled by Morocco's recognition of Mauritania's independence, 1969-1970.

B. Morocco and Mauritania

Territorial goals: Both Morocco and Mauritania claim the Spanish Sahara.

Claim or dispute: Morocco's claim—historical, as above; Mauritania's—ethnic. Both were interested in the mineral wealth assumed to exist in the territory.

Starting date: 1956.

Was violence used? Yes.

Formal negotiations: Yes.

Status as of January 1972: Attempts to coordinate policy against Spain.

21. Nigeria and Biafra

Territorial goals: Biafra wanted to secede from Nigeria and become independent; Nigeria wanted to preserve the integrity of the Nigerian state within the boundaries inherited at independence.

Claim or dispute: Ethnic.

Starting date: 1967.

Was violence used? Yes.

Formal negotiations: Yes.

Status as of January 1972: Secession crushed by Nigerian army, 1970.

22. A. Somalia and Ethiopia

Territorial goals: Somalia wanted to annex the Somali-inhabited areas of Ethiopia. Ethiopia wanted to retain the borders established by the relevant Anglo-Ethiopian and Italian-Ethiopian agreements.

Claim or dispute: Ethnic.

Starting date: 1948.

Was violence used: Yes.

Formal negotiations: Yes.

Status as of January 1972: Suspended, following 1967 talks.

B. Somalia and Ethiopia

Territorial goals: Competition for succession to the
French Territory of Afars and Issas (French
Somaliland).

Claim or dispute: Somali's claim was ethnic; Ethiopia's,
economic involving outlet to sea through the port
of Djibouti.

Starting date: Latent for years; intensified since 1960.

Was violence used: Minor.

Formal negotiations: Yes.

Status as of January 1972: Suspended following 1967
talks.

23. Somalia and Kenya

Territorial goals: Somalia wanted to annex the Somali-
inhabited areas of northern Kenya. Kenya wanted
to retain the borders inherited at independence.

Claim or dispute: Ethnic.

Starting date: 1948.

Was violence used: Yes.

Formal negotiations: Yes.

Status as of January 1972: Suspended since the 1967
talks.

24. Sudan and the secessionists in the southern Sudan

Territorial goals: The southerners wanted to secede from
Sudan and establish an independent state. Sudan
wanted to retain borders inherited at independence and to integrate the south within the
Sudan.

Claim or dispute: Ethnic and religious.

Starting date: Gradual growth and spread after 1955.

Was violence used? Yes.

Formal negotiations: Yes.

Status as of March 1972: An agreement between the
government and the insurgents, granting the south
regional autonomy, was reportedly concluded in
February—March 1972.

25. Uganda and Buganda

> *Territorial goals:* Buganda wanted to secede from
>   Uganda, and to preserve its distinct personality.
>   Uganda wanted to retain borders inherited at
>   independence and to integrate Buganda within
>   Uganda.
> *Claim or dispute:* Ethnic and historic—Buganda wanted to
>   preserve its autonomy and dominant status.
> *Starting date:* Colonial period; flared up in 1966.
> *Was violence used?* Yes.
> *Formal negotiations:* None.
> *Status as of January 1972:* Suppressed.

26. Uganda and Ruwenzururu secessionist movement

> *Territorial goals:* Ruwenzururu movement of Baamba
>   and Bakonjo tribesmen initially demanded to be
>   detached administratively from Toro kingdom in
>   Uganda; secession from Uganda added subse-
>   quently.
> *Claim or dispute:* Ethnic and tribal animosities.
> *Starting date:* 1962.
> *Was violence used?* Yes.
> *Formal negotiations:* Yes.
> *Status as of January 1972:* Suppressed.

27. Zambia and the Lozi people of the Barotse Province

> *Territorial goals:* Movement among some of the Lozi
>   (Barotse) people aiming to secede from Zambia
>   and establish an independent state. Zambia
>   wished to retain borders inherited at indepen-
>   dence and to integrate the Barotse within Zambia.
> *Claim or dispute:* Ethnic and historical; reenforced by
>   economic grievances.
> *Starting date:* Since colonial days.
> *Was violence used?* No.
> *Formal negotiations:* None.
> *Status as of January 1972:* Continued existence of
>   secessionist sentiments.

Notes

Preface

1. All African Peoples Conference, *Speeches by the Prime Minister of Ghana at the Opening and Closing Sessions on December 8th and 13th, 1958* (Accra: Government Printer, n.d.), pp. 5-6; Kwame Nkrumah, *Address to the Nationalists' Conference* (Accra: Bureau of African Affairs, 1962), p. 11; and R. J. Harrison Church, *West Africa* (London: Longmans, Green and Co., 1957), p. 533. For a view that the conflict potential was actually low, see R. L. Kapil, "On the Conflict Potential of Inherited Boundaries in Africa," *World Politics*, 18 (July 1966), 656-673.

2. For a list, see Appendix.

3. Quoted from Jacques Ancel, *Les frontières* (Paris, 1938), p. 196, seen in B. W. Hodder and D. R. Harris, *Africa in Transition* (London: Methuen and Co., 1967), p. 22.

4. For a description of the African system, see I. W. Zartman, "Africa as a Subordinate State System in International Relations," *International Organization*, 21 (1967), 545-564.

5. On the concept of "core value," see K. E. Boulding, *Conflict and Defense* (New York: Harper & Row, 1963), pp. 311-312.

Chapter 1. The Drawing of Colonial Boundaries

1. That African divisions have facilitated the establishment of European control has sometimes been argued in support of the Pan-African plea for solidarity and unity. See, for example, Julius K. Nyerere, *The Second Scramble*, speech delivered at the opening of a world assembly of youth seminar in Dar es Salaam in 1961 (Dar es

Salaam: 1962), p. 1. Nkrumah expressed a similar assessment of the African role in the "scramble" in his speech at the opening of the All African Peoples Conference in Accra in December 1958. See All African Peoples Conference, *Speeches by the Prime Minister of Ghana at the Opening and Closing Sessions on December 8th and 13th, 1958* (Accra: Government Printer, n.d.).

2. For an elaboration and illustrations of this point and of the discussion which follows see Saadia Touval, "Treaties, Borders, and the Partition of Africa," *Journal of African History*, 7, (1966), 279-292.

3. Information Services of the Somali Government, *The Somali Peninsula: A New Light on Imperial Motives* (Mogadishu, 1962), p. 59. On the Sanwi appeal in 1959, see A. L. Zolberg, *One Party Government in the Ivory Coast* (Princeton: Princeton University Press, 1964), pp. 289-294. The story of the appeal of Attanlé II, chief of Agoué in 1959-1960, was related to me in Togo in January 1966. On Buganda, see D. E. Apter, *The Political Kingdom in Uganda* (Princeton: Princeton University Press, 1961), pp. 176-177, 185, 209, 283-284, 385.

4. For example, the British claim at the Berlin Conference to exclude the Niger from international control was based on treaty rights British agents had acquired in the region. See S. E. Crowe, *The Berlin West African Conference, 1884-1885* (London: Longmans, Green & Co., 1942), pp. 125-126, 223-224.

5. See the views of Lord Salisbury, then British Prime Minister, on the rules for such bargaining, in G. P. Gooch and H. W. V. Temperley, eds., *British Documents on the Origin of the War* (London: H.M.S.O., 1927), I, 132, 140.

6. A. J. Wills, *An Introduction to the History of Central Africa* (London: Oxford University Press, 1964), pp. 164, 167-168; and Gervas Clay, *Your Friend, Lewanika* (London: Chatto & Windus, 1968), p. 137. Lewanika, the Barotse ruler, was greatly disappointed, and complained that his domain was cut in half. For a somewhat different case concerning the Chad-Sudan border and involving British obligatons toward the ruler of Darfur, see A. B. Theobald, *'Ali Dinar, Last Sultan of Darfur, 1898-1916* (London: Logmans, 1965).

7. Quoted in David Kimble, *A Political History of Ghana, 1850-1928* (Oxford: Oxford University Press, 1963), p. 280, n. 3.

8. Margery Perham, *Lugard* (London: Collins, 1956), I, 708-709.

9. Lord Hailey, *An African Survey* (London: Oxford University Press, 1957), pp. 500-501; and J. L. Garvin, *The Life of Joseph Chamberlain*, (London: Macmillan & Co., 1934), III, 40-41.

10. League of Nations, Permanent Mandates Commission, *Minutes of the Second Session*, August 9, 1922, p. 72. See also Pierre Jentgen, *Les frontières du Ruanda-Urundi et le régime international de tutelle* (Brussels: Académie Royale des Sciences Coloniales, 1957), pp. 39-40.

11. Examples of boundary agreements providing for such population movements are the Anglo-French Convention concerning the transfer of Iles de Los and portion of Gambia from Britain to France (Article 7 of the Anglo-French Convention of 1904, reproduced in Gooch & Temperley, *British Documents*, II, 380); the Anglo-Belgian Agreement of 1915 concerning the Congo-Uganda border (Cmd. 517); the Anglo-Italian Agreement of 1927 concerning the Kenya-Italian Somaliland border (Cmd. 4230); and the Anglo-French Agreement on the border between British and French Togoland (Togoland Boundary Commission, 1927-1929, *Protocol with the Description of the Frontier* [Lomé: September 21, 1929]).

12. An example are the grazing rights in Ethiopia accorded by the 1897 Anglo-Ethiopian Treaty to tribes from British Somaliland. For the treaty, see Sir Edward Hertslet, ed., *The Map of Africa by Treaty*, 3rd ed. (London: H.M.S.O., 1909), II, 423-429. An example of the preservation of hunting and fishing rights is the Anglo-Belgian Agreement delimiting the border between Tanganyika and Ruanda. See S. B. Jones, *Boundary Making* (Washington: Monograph Series of the Carnegie Endowment for International Peace, 1945), p. 134.

13. Article 3, Agreement between the British and German Governments respecting Africa and Heligoland, July 1, 1890, reproduced in Hertslet, *Map of Africa* III, 899-906.

14. For example: Article 4 of the Anglo-German Agreement of 1890 (ibid.); the Franco-German Protocol of 1885 concerning the Dahomey-Togo border (Jones, *Boundary Making*, p. 40); The Anglo-Belgian Agreement of 1927 concerning the Congo-Northern Rhodesia border (ibid., pp. 190-191, 195-196).

15. Soudan, "Rapport Politique Annuel, 1949," mimeo., pp. 36-38.

16. Speech by the governor-general of French West Africa, M. J. Brévié, December 9, 1933, reproduced in Institut Colonial International, *Annuaire de Documentation Coloniale Comparée, 1933* (Brussels: Etabblissements Généraux d'imprimerie, n.d.), II, 409.

17. Virginia Thompson and Richard Adloff, *French West Africa* (London: George Allen & Unwin, 1958), pp. 173-175.

18. Kenneth Ingham, "Uganda's Old Eastern Province: The Transfer to East Africa Protectorate in 1902," *Uganda Journal*, 21, (March 1957), 41-46.

19. George Bennett, "The Eastern Boundary of Uganda in 1902," *Uganda Journal*, 23 (March 1959), 69-72.

20. J. Brasnett, "The Karasuk Problem," *Uganda Journal*, 22, (September 1958), 113-122.

21. The governor's letter, dated May 15, 1949, is quoted in Soudan, "Rapport Politique Annuel, 1949," mimeo., pp. 39-40.

22. Ibid., pp. 40-43.

23. Robert E. Sherwood, *Roosevelt and Hopkins* (New York: Harper & Brothers, 1948), p. 710.

Chapter 2. *Sources of Status-Quo and Revisionist Policies*

1. H. R. Lynch, *Edward Wilmot Blyden* (London: Oxford University Press, 1967), p. 197. The 1903 quotation is from Blyden's *Africa and the Africans* (London: C. M. Phillips, 1903), p. 34.

2. For background on the Ewe problem see Claude E. Welch, Jr., *Dream of Unity* (Ithaca, N.Y.: Cornell University Press, 1966), pp. 37-64.

3. Quoted in Gold Coast, Sessional Paper VII, 1919-1920, *Correspondence Relating to the National Congress of British West Africa* (Accra: Government Press, 1920), p. 15.

4. Ibid., p. 38.

5. Kimble, *Political History of Ghana*, pp. 384-385. For further background on the NCBWA and the 1920 conference, see ibid., pp. 374-389.

6. George Padmore, *The Gold Coast Revolution* (London: D. Dobson, 1953), p. 47. See also Padmore, *Pan Africanism or Communism?* (London: D. Dobson, 1956), p. 129.

7. See George Shepperson, "Pan-Africanism and pan-Africanism," *Phylon*, 23 (1962), 357. For a biography of Du Bois see E. M. Rudwick, *W. E. B. Du Bois* (Philadelphia: University of Pennsylvania Press, 1960). For histories of Pan-Africanism during this early period, see Padmore, *Pan-Africanism or Communism?* and Colin Legum, *Pan-Africanism* (London and Dunmow: Pall Mall Press, 1962).

8. George Padmore, ed., *History of the Pan-African Congress* (London: Hammersmith Bookshop, 1963), p. 55.

9. Quoted by Welch, *Dream of Unity*, p. 66.

10. Padmore, *History of the Pan-African Congress*, p. 63.

11. Ibid., p. 45.

12. Cameroon, although formally unreconciled to the integration of British Northern Cameroons within Nigeria, has not in practice pursued irredentist policies, and is therefore not listed as an irredentist state.

13. Lord Curzon of Kedleston, *Frontiers*, Romanes Lecture (Oxford: The Clarendon Press, 1908), pp. 7-8.

14. See I. William Zartman, "Characteristics of Developing Foreign Policies," in W. H. Lewis, ed., *French Speaking Africa* (New York: Walker & Co., 1965), p. 192.

15. On the Somalis, see Saadia Touval, *Somali Nationalism* (Cambridge, Mass.: Harvard University Press, 1963); on the Ewes, see Welch, *Dream of Unity*, pp. 37-102. Concerning the Yorubas and Ibos there is

some evidence of such trends in the pre-independence thinking of nationalist leaders. See Obafemi Awolowo, *Path to Nigerian Freedom* (London: Faber and Faber, 1947), pp. 47-55; and Nnamdi Azikiwe, *Zik* (Cambridge, Eng.: Cambridge University Press, 1961), pp. 242-246. For an interesting comparative discussion see Otto Pflanze, "Nationalism in Europe, 1848-1871," and Philip D. Curtin, "Nationalism in Africa, 1945-1965," both in *Review of Politics*, 28, (April 1966), 121-153.

16. See S. P. Huntington, "The Political Modernization of Traditional Monarchies," *Daedalus*, Summer 1966, p. 769. On tribalism, see also Immanuel Wallerstein, "Ethnicity and National Integration in West Africa," *Cahiers d'Etudes Africaines*, no. 3 (October 1960); A. R. Zolberg, "Ethnicity and National Integration: The Ivory Coast and Mali," paper prepared for delivery at the 1966 Annual Meeting of the African Studies Association, University of Indiana, Bloomington, Ind., October 26-29, 1966; and Paul Mercier, "Remarques sur la signification du 'Tribalisme' actuel en Afrique Noire," *Cahiers Internationaux de Sociologie*, 31 (July-December 1961), 61-80.

17. See L. W. Pye, *Aspects of Political Development* (Boston: Little, Brown, 1966), p. 23. See also J. F. A. Ajayi, "The Place of African History and Culture in the Process of Nation Building in Africa South of the Sahara," reprinted in Immanuel Wallerstein, ed., *Social Change; The Colonial Situation* (New York: John Wiley and Sons, 1966), pp. 606-616.

18. See *A. B. A. K. O., 1950-1960*, ed. Benoît Verhaegen (Brussels: Centre de Recherche et d'Information Socio-Politiques, 1962).

19. See J. Brasnett, "The Karasuk Problem," 120-121.

20. The view that the border had been altered was denied by the Tanganyikan prime minister in a statement in parliament on June 11, 1962. See, Tanganyika, *Parliamentary Debates*, 1st sess., June 11, 1962, cols. 263-264. The border between Tanganyika and Malawi was defined by the Anglo-German Agreement of July 1, 1890, Article 1, Section 2. See Sir Edward Hertslet, *The Map of Africa by Treaty* III, 899-906. It placed the border on the Tanganyikan shore of the lake. For a discussion of conflicting and confusing descriptions of this border in colonial times see A. C. McEwen, *International Boundaries of East Africa* (London: Oxford University Press, 1971) pp. 170-206.

21. Rupert Emerson, *Self-Determination Revisited in the Era of Decolonization* (Cambridge, Mass.: Harvard University, Center for International Affairs, Occasional Papers in International Affairs, No. 9, December 1964).

22. Touval, *Somali Nationalism*.

23. Allal el Fassi in *Al Istiqlal*, September 17, 1960, quoted in Mauritania, *The Islamic Republic of Mauritania and the Kingdom of Morocco* (1961), p. 58. (This is the Mauritanian "Green Book.")

24. Welch, *Dream of Unity*, pp. 121-126.

25. Ghana, *Government Proposals for a Republican Constitution* (Accra: Government Printer, March 7, 1960, W. P. No. 1/60), pp. 4-5. For the origins of the Ghanaian attitude to the Ewe problem see also George Padmore, *The Gold Coast Revolution* (London: Dennis Dobson, 1953).

26. Nkrumah's interest in the Nzima partition is reflected in his autobiography. See Kwame Nkrumah, *The Autobiography of Kwame Nkrumah* (Edinburgh: Thomas Nelson & Sons, 1957), p. 264 and map on p. 263.

27. The above account is based on Zolberg, *One Party Government in the Ivory Coast*, pp. 289-294.

28. *Ghana Today*, March 23 and April 20, 1966.

29. See A. A. Castagno, "The Political Party System in the Somali Republic," in J. S. Coleman and Carl Rosberg, eds., *Political Parties and National Integration in Tropical Africa* (Berkeley and Los Angeles: University of California Press, 1964), pp. 533, 539-540, 554. See also R. L. Kapil, "On the Conflict Potential of Inherited Boundaries in Africa," p. 656-673.

30. D. E. Ashford, "The Irredentist Appeal in Morocco and Mauritania," *Western Political Quarterly*, 15 (December 1962) 641-651; Doudou Thiam, *The Foreign Policy of African States* (London: Phoenix House, 1965), pp. xi-xii; Philippe Husson, *La Question des Frontières terrestres du Maroc* (Paris, 1960), pp. 44-49.

31. Castagno, "The Political Party System," p. 548. See also I. M. Lewis, "Pan-Africanism and Pan-Somalism," *Journal of Modern African Studies*, 1, (June 1963), 156-157.

32. On Somali nationalism, see Lewis, "Pan-Africanism and Pan-Somalism;" I. M. Lewis, *The Modern History of Somaliland* (London: Widenfeld and Nicolson, 1965), p. 16 and passim; and Touval, *Somali Nationalism*. On the origins of Moroccan irredentist aspirations, see I. W. Zartman, "The Sahara—Bridge or Barrier," *International Conciliation*, no. 541 (January 1963), pp. 42-43; and Ashford "The Irredentist Appeal." See also D. E. Ashford, *Political Change in Morocco* (Princeton: Princeton University Press, 1961).

Chapter 3. Border Problems at Conferences, 1958-1963

1. For the history and evolution of AAPSO see Colin Legum, *Pan Africanism* (London: Pall Mall, 1962), pp. 39-40; Paul F. Smets, *De Bandoeng à Moshi* (Brussels: Institut de Sociologie de l'Université Libre de Bruxelles, 1964), pp. 28-39; Odette Guitard, *Bandoung et le Réveil des Peuples Colonisés* (Paris: Presses Universitaires de France, 1965),

pp. 64-78; and G. H. Jansen, *Afro-Asia and Non-Alignment* (London: Faber and Faber, 1966), pp. 250-268. See also Charles Neuhauser, *Third World Politics: China and the Afro-Asian People's Solidarity Organization 1957-1967*, Harvard East Asian Monographs, no. 27 (Cambridge, Mass.: Harvard University, 1968).

2. On the Istiqlal's criticism of the Democratic Independence Party's participation at the conference, see Ashford, *Political Change in Morocco*, pp. 102, 316, 333.

3. *Afro-Asian Peoples' Solidarity Conference* (Moscow: Foreign Languages Publishing House, 1958), p. 14.

4. Ibid., pp. 217-218.

5. The speech was reprinted in A. K. Barden, *Awakening Africa: Conferences of Independent African States* (Accra: Bureau of African Affairs, n.d. [1962]), p. 31. See also *Conference of Independent African States, Speeches Delivered at the close of the Conference* (Accra: 1958), p. 24.

6. The resolutions are reprinted in full in Legum, *Pan-Africanism*, pp. 139-148.

7. A. K. Barden, Foreword to *Awakening Africa*.

8. W. Scott Thompson, *Ghana's Foreign Policy* (Princeton: Princeton University Press, 1969), pp. 50-51; Legum, *Pan-Africanism*, pp. 42-45; Philippe Decraene, *Le Panafricanisme* (Paris: Presses Universitaires de France, 1964), pp. 49-55; Immanuel Wallerstein, *Africa: The Politics of Unity* (New York: Random House, 1967), pp. 33-35, 38-39.

9. *Resolutions of the All-African Peoples Conference*, pp. 4-5; reprinted also in Legum, *Pan Africanism*, p. 231.

10. *All-African Peoples Conference, Speeches by the Prime Minister*, p. 5.

11. E. S. Munger, *African Field Reports, 1952-1961* (Capetown: C. Struik, 1961), pp. 75, 77-79.

12. Thompson, *Ghana's Foreign Policy*, pp. 58-64.

13. Ibid., pp. 60-61.

14. According to Ezekiel Mphahlele, who headed the South African delegation at the conference, the draft resolutions which emerged from the committees were discussed by the heads of the delegations before being passed on to the plenary. See Ezekiel Mphahlele, "Accra Conference Diary," in Langston Hughes, ed., *An African Treasury* (New York: Crown Publishers, 1960), pp. 37-40. See also Catherine Hoskyns, "Tunis Diary," *Africa South in Exile*, 4 (July-September 1960), 110-111; Guitard, *Bandoung et le Réveil*, p. 93, n. 1.

15. For Nkrumah's speech, see Barden, *Awakening Africa*, pp. 149-150; for Tubman's speech, see Lawrence A. Marinelli, *The New Liberia* (New York: Praeger, 1964), p. 126. See also Thiam, *The Foreign Policy of African States*, p. 44.

16. For the texts of the communiqué and declaration, see Marinelli, *The New Liberia*, pp. 194-198. For a detailed account of the conference and an assessment of its results see J. Gus Liebenow, "Which Road to African Unity? The Sanniquellie Conference, 1959," in Gwendolen M. Carter, ed., *Politics in Africa: Seven Cases* (New York: Harcourt, Brace & World, 1966), pp. 1-32.

17. *Afro-Asian Bulletin* (February-March 1960), pp. 72-73. See also Hoskyns, "Tunis Diary."

18. Reprinted in Legum, *Pan-Africanism*, p. 246.

19. Ibid., p. 242.

20. Ibid., p. 243.

21. *Second Afro-Asian Peoples' Solidarity Conference* (Cairo: The Permanent Secretariat of the Organization for Afro-Asian Peoples' Solidarity, n.d.).

22. Ibid. A further expression of support for Somali claims was contained in a press release of the secretary-general of AAPSO, Youssef el Sebai (Egypt) on May 28, 1960, welcoming the forthcoming independence of British Somaliland and Italian-administered Somalia. It referred to the "artificial division" of the Somalis, and called "upon all Asian and African States and peoples to support the independence and unification" of the Somalis. See *Afro-Asian Bulletin*, nos. 11-12 (September-October 1960), pp. 34-35.

23. Ibid.

24. *Second Conference of Independent African States, Addis Ababa, 14-26 June 1960* (Addis Ababa: Ministry of Information of the Imperial Ethiopian Government, n.d.), pp. 89-90.

25. Ibid., p. 73.

26. Ibid., pp. 31-35.

27. Barden, Foreword to *Awakening Africa*, n. p.

28. Among previous Moroccan diplomatic successes were the Tangiers conference of Maghreb political parties in April 1958, and the Arab League meeting in Lebanon in August 1960. Moroccan claims were supported by both gatherings. See Jamal Sa'd, *The Problem of Mauritania*, (New York: Arab Information Center, n.d.); and Kingdom of Morocco, Ministry of Foreign Affairs, *Livre Blanc sur la Mauritanie* (Rabat, 1960), p. 117.

29. The participating states were: Cameroon, Central African Republic, Chad, Congo (Brazzaville), Dahomey, Gabon, Ivory Coast, Mauritania, Niger, Senegal, and Upper Volta. The Malagasy Republic joined the group at its subsequent meeting in Brazzaville. See Hella Pick, "The Brazzaville Twelve and How They Came to Be," *Africa Report*, 6 (May 1961) 2, 8, 12, 15; and *Africa Digest*, 8 (December 1960), 121-122.

30. United Nations General Assembly, *Official Records (GAOR)*,

15th Session, First Committee, 1109th meeting, November 15, 1960, pp. 131-133. For a summary of Morocco's historical and legal arguments, see Saadia Touval, "The Moroccan-Algerian Territorial Dispute," *Africa Research Bulletin*, (October 1966), pp. 631-633.

31. *GAOR*, 15th Session, First Committee, 1114th and 1116th meetings, November 23 and 25, 1960. In supporting Morocco, India argued that boundaries imposed by colonial powers could not be accepted without reservations. Presumably, India would have been more cautious in its argumentation two years later, when India's own colonial borders came under attack from China.

32. *GAOR*, 15th Session, First Committee, 1109th meeting (November 15), 1111th meeting (November 16), and 1113th—1119th meetings (November 23-26, 1960). Since no resolution was adopted by the First Committee, the General Assembly decided without a vote to take note of the First Committee's report. See *GAOR*, 15th Session, 954th meeting, December 18, 1960. By then, Mauritania was already an independent state, having acceded to full independence on November 28, 1960.

33. The attitude of Nigeria was stated by Prime Minister Abubakar Tafawa Balewa in his address to the General Assembly on the occasion of Nigeria's admission to membership (*GAOR*, 15th Session, 893d meeting, October 7, 1960). He said:

> The colonizing Powers of the last century partitioned Africa in a haphazard and artificial manner and drew boundaries which cut right across former groupings. Yet, however artificial those boundaries were at first the countries they have created have come to regard themselves as units independent of one another . . . It is, therefore, our policy to leave those boundaries as they are at present and to discourage any adjustment whatsoever. I hope that this policy will bring about an atmosphere of trust and that if each country is given proper recognition and respect as a sovereign State it will be possible to have effective co-operation on all matters of common concern to us.

34. United Nations Security Council, *Official Records (SCOR)*, 911th meeting, December 3, 1960.

35. Ministère de l'Information, République du Congo-Brazzaville, *La Conference de Brazzaville* (Brazzaville: December 1960), p. 22. An English translation was published in Legum, *Pan-Africanism*, p. 179.

36. *Le Monde*, December 28, 1960.

37. Legum, *Pan-Africanism*, p. 189.

38. Ibid., p. 187. Italics added.

39. For the text of the Cairo communiqué see Legum, *Pan-Africanism*, pp. 195-197. On the 1962 meeting, see Thomas Hovet, Jr., *Africa and the United Nations* (London: Faber and Faber, 1963), p. 59. On the

Yaoundé and Tananarive conferences, see ibid., pp. 49-50, 52. For the Monrovia resolutions see Legum, *Pan-Africanism*, pp. 198-200.

40. UN Doc. A/L. 335.

41. *GAOR*, 15th Session, 989th meeting, April 19, 1961; Resolution 1602 (XV).

42. *SCOR*, 971st meeting, October 25, 1961.

43. *GAOR*, 16th Session, 1043rd meeting, October 27, 1961; Resolution 1631 (XV).

44. The text of the resolution is reproduced in Jules Gérard-Libois and Benoît Verhaegen, *Congo 1960* (Brussels: Centre de Recherche et d'Information Socio-Politiques, n.d.), II, 632. Italics in the original. See also Legum, *Pan-Africanism*, p. 48; Wallerstein, *Africa, The Politics of Unity*, pp. 44-45.

45. Legum, *Pan-Africanism*, pp. 192, 195, 199.

46. Ibid., pp. 258-259. A measure of Soviet influence at the third AAPC in Cairo seems to be reflected in the bizarre assertion that there were West German military bases in Cameroon. The objection of the Brazzaville states to the referendum, and their support for the restoration of Cameroon to its pre-World War I borders was reflected in the resolution of the Yaoundé conference (March 26-28, 1961), and a draft resolution submitted by the Brazzaville states at the resumed 15th session of the UN General Assembly, proposing that a commission be established to investigate the circumstances in which the referendum was held. (UN Docs. A/C. 4/L. 684, 684 Rev. 1, 684 Rev. 2, April 15 and 19, 1961. The draft resolution was not put to a vote. See *GAOR*, 15th Session resumed, Fourth Committee, 1153d meeting, April 20, 1961, p. 384.)

47. *GAOR*, 16th Session, 1066th meeting. The draft resolution by the Brazzaville states calling for self-determination in West Irian (UN Doc. A/L. 368), was defeated in the General Assembly on November 27, 1961.

48. African states were nearly unanimous on two other issues. Both the Casablanca and Brazzaville states expressed opposition to an alleged French plan to separate the Saharan regions from Algeria when Algeria attained independence. The Brazzaville states were somewhat slower and more moderate in expressing themselves on the subject. But the positions of the two blocs were essentially the same. References to Algeria's territorial integrity were made at the AAPC, Tunis (Legum, *Pan-Africanism*, p. 242), Casablanca (ibid., p. 191), AAPC, Cairo (ibid., p. 248), Yaoundé (Thomas Hovet Jr., *Africa and the United Nations*, p. 49), and Monrovia (Legum, *Pan-Africanism*, p. 199). With respect to the question of Ruanda-Urundi, African states were in agreement in their preference that the territory's unity be preserved, rather than its being

split in two. See the nineteen nations' draft resolution endorsing the Trusteeship Council's recommendation that the territory's unity be preserved. UN Doc. A/C. 4/L. 664.

49. Legum, *Pan-Africanism*, pp. 255-256.

50. Information gathered in interviews with participants. See also Lewis, "Pan-Africanism and Pan-Somalism," p. 154; AAPC, *Meeting of the Steering Committee at Dar es Salaam*, January 26-30, 1961.

51. On the proceedings see *Afrique Nouvelle* (Dakar), May 24, 1961. The information on the conference was supplemented by interviews. For the full text of the resolutions, see Legum, *Pan-Africanism*, pp. 198-201. See also Marinelli, *The New Liberia*, pp. 129-134, 198-209.

52. Legum, *Pan-Africanism*, p. 198.

53. *The Conference of Heads of State and Government of Non-Aligned Countries, Belgrade, September 1-6, 1961* (Belgrade: Publičističko-Izdavački Zavod "Jugoslavija," 1961), pp. 228-229. See also Peter H. Lyon, *Neutralism* (Leicester: Leicester University Press, 1963) pp. 185-186. Additional information was supplied by interviews.

54. *The Conference of Heads of State*, p. 207.

55. Ibid., pp. 253, 257.

56. *West Africa*, February 3, 1962, p. 115; C. A. Johnson, "Political and Regional Groupings in Africa," *International Organization*, 16 (1962), 442. In this connection it seems relevant to note that the charter of the UAM (as the organization of the Brazzaville states came to be called), adopted at Tananarive in September 1961, did not include among the goals of the organization the usual reference to the preservation of the territorial integrity of states. The UAM charter is reproduced in Albert Tevoedjre, *Pan-Africanism in Action*, Occasional Papers in International Affairs, no. 11, November 1965 (Cambridge, Mass.: Harvard University, Center for International Affairs), p. 61.

57. For the text see Marinelli, *The New Liberia*, pp. 209-220.

58. Lewis, "Pan-Africanism and Pan-Somalism."

59. Manfred Halpern, "Afro-Asians at Moshi," *Africa Report* (March 1963), pp. 21-22.

60. For the text of the resolution see *The Third Afro-Asian Peoples' Solidarity Conference* (Cairo: Permanent Secretariat of the Afro-Asian Peoples' Solidarity Organization, n.d.), p. 84, or Smets, *De Bandoeng à Moshi*, p. 114.

61. *The Third Afro-Asian Peoples', Solidarity Conference*, p. 90.

62. Ibid., p. 89.

Chapter 4. Norms and Politics: Confirmation of the Status Quo

1. Members of the OAU were:

Algeria	Guinea	Senegal
Burundi	Ivory Coast	Sierra Leone
Cameroon	Liberia	Somalia
Central African Republic	Libya	Sudan
Chad	Madagascar	Tanganyika
Congo (Brazzaville)	Mali	Togo
Congo (Leopoldville)	Mauritania	Tunisia
Dahomey	Morocco	Uganda
Ethiopia	Niger	United Arab
Gabon	Nigeria	Republic
Ghana	Rwanda	Upper Volta

Morocco is listed among the states that established the OAU in May 1963, but it formally adhered to the organization only in September 1963. The list is taken from the Summit Conference of Independent African States, *Proceedings of the Summit Conference of Independent African States* (hereafter cited as *Proceedings*), I, sec. 1 (Addis Ababa, May 1963).

2. See Immanuel Wallerstein, "The Early Years of the OAU: The Search for Organizational Preeminence," *International Organization*, 20 (1966), 774-787.

3. See Boutros Boutros-Ghali, "The Addis Ababa Charter," *International Conciliation*, no. 546 (January 1964); Jorge Castañeda, "The Underdeveloped Nations and the Development of International Law," *International Organization*, 15 (1961), 38-48; and A. A. Mazrui, "The United Nations and Some African Political Attitudes," *International Organization*, 18 (1964), 499-520.

4. On revolutionary and conservative views of the OAU see Wallerstein, *Africa, The Politics of Unity*, pp. 94-95.

5. *Proceedings*, I, sec. 1, Document AGENDA/CONF/5, May 15, 1963. In the final agenda of the foreign ministers' conference, the Somali proposal was included under item VII, "Establishment of Permanent Conciliation Commission" (Document AGENDA/12, May 17, 1963). However, it was not listed on the agendas of the two committees set up by the foreign ministers as the establishment of a conciliation commission was subsumed under the discussion on the "Establishment of Organization of the African States" (item I of Committee I, Document CIAS/Plen./3, May 22, 1963).

6. The Somali president's address and the Ethiopian prime minister's reply can be found in *Proceedings*, I, sec. 2, Documents CIAS/GEN/INF/25 and CIAS/GEN/INF/43. See also Norman J. Padelford, "The Organization of African Unity," *International Organization*, 18 (1964), 527.

7. Memorandum submitted to the summit by the Kenya African National Union (KANU). I am indebted to Professor Joseph S. Nye, Jr.,

for providing me with a copy of the memorandum.

8. *Proceedings*, I, sec. 2, Document CIAS/GEN/INF/29, p. 4.

9. *Proceedings*, I, sec. 2, Document CIAS/GEN/INF/36, p. 7.

10. *Proceedings*, I, sec. 2, Document CIAS/GEN/INF/33, p. 2. For the views of the president of the Malagasy Republic and the prime minister of Nigeria see ibid., Documents CIAS/GEN/INF/14, p. 4, and CIAS/GEN/INF/35, p. 2, respectively.

11. See the discussion in Boutros Boutros-Ghali, "The Addis Ababa Charter," pp. 29-30. See also N. J. Padelford, "The Organization of African Unity," pp. 525-536; and T. O. Elias, "The Charter of the Organization of African Unity," *American Journal of International Law*, 59 (April 1965), 243-267.

12. Ibid., p. 248.

13. The author was impressed by Tanzania's interest in the problem when he visited the country in 1960, 1963, and 1965. In 1960 he talked with Julius Nyerere, whose interest in the Somali disputes was stimulated by his attendance at Somalia's independence celebrations in July 1960. Tanzania's advocacy of the status quo began to weaken in 1965. Tanzania began to press for the revision of its border with Malawi, and in 1968, Tanzania was the first state to recognize Biafra. For President Nyerere's changed views, see *Africa Research Bulletin* (hereafter cited as *ARB*), April 1968, p. 1031.

14. Also interesting for their comments about border problems were the speeches of the emperor of Ethiopia, the presidents of Dahomey, the Malagasy Republic, and Tanzania, the prime minister of Nigeria, and the representatives of the Ivory Coast, Somalia, and Upper Volta. All the speeches are printed in *Conference des Chefs d'Etat et du Gouvernement de l'OUA* (Cairo: Administration de l'Information, 1964).

15. Ibid., p. 229; and *The Somali Republic and the Organization of African Unity* (Mogadishu: Ministry of Foreign Affairs, 1964), pp. 15-18.

16. Ibid., p. 19.

17. OAU Document AHG/Res. 16 (I).

18. *Somali News* (Mogadishu), October 9, 1964; and *The Somali Republic and the Organization of African Unity*, pp. 16-24.

19. Ibid., p. 18.

20. See Emerson, *Self-Determination Revisited in the Era of Decolonization.*

21. The African states present were: Algeria, Burundi, Cameroon, Central African Republic, Chad, Congo (Brazzaville), Dahomey, Ethiopia, Ghana, Guinea, Kenya, Liberia, Libya, Malawi, Mauritania, Mali, Morocco, Nigeria, Senegal, Sierra Leone, Somalia, Sudan, Tanzania, Togo, Tunisia, Uganda, U.A.R. and Zambia. In addition, Angola was the single nonindependent country accorded the full status of a participating state.

22. For the text of the speech, see the *National Review*, published by the Ministry of Information, Mogadishu, No. 4, November 1964, pp. 13-19.

23. The account which follows is based on the report delivered by Prime Minister Abdirazaq Haji Hussein to the Somali National Assembly, as published in the *Somali News*, November 6, 1964, and on information from interviews. See also *Somali News*, October 16, 23, and 30, 1964.

24. The doctrine that the right of self-determination should be qualified was incorporated in the joint communiqué issued by the emperor of Ethiopia and the president of India on October 13, 1964. In the context of the Kashmir problem, the communiqué declared the emperor's support for "the principle that self-determination should apply only to colonial territories which have not yet attained their independence and not to parts of sovereign or independent states" (Press release of the Ethiopian Foreign Ministry).

25. This was the argument of Somali Prime Minister Abdirazaq Haji Hussein. See *Somali News*, October 16, October 30, and November 6, 1964.

26. For these resolutions see *Review of International Affairs* (Belgrade), 15 (November 5, 1964), 82-84.

27. *Resolutions of the Fourth Afro-Asian Peoples' Solidarity Conference, May 9-16, 1965, Winneba, Ghana* (Cairo: Permanent Secretariat of the Afro-Asian Peoples' Solidarity Organization, 1965), p. 23.

28. Ibid., p. 50.

29. Ibid., p. 52.

30. Ibid., p. 81.

31. Ibid., p. 71.

32. *ARB*, August 1967, p. 834, and September 1967, pp. 855-856.

33. Ibid., November 1967, p. 901.

34. Ibid., April 1968, p. 1031.

35. Ibid., December 1969, pp. 1613-1615, and January 1970, pp. 1643-1644.

Chapter 5. The Use of Force

1. Information about the Anya-Nya is scarce. See G. W. Shepherd, Jr., "National Integration and the Southern Sudan," *Journal of Modern African Studies*, 4 (October 1966), 193-212; and Keith Kyle, "The Southern Problem in the Sudan," *The World Today*, December 1966, pp. 512-520.

2. Ashford, *Political Change in Morocco*, pp. 175-184, 204-206. Ashford implies that there was *governmental* decision concerning the

operations (p. 205). See also I. W. Zartman, *Morocco: Problems of New Power* (New York: Atherton Press, 1964), pp. 63-86.

3. Patrick Seale in *The Observer* (London), February 9, 1964.

4. Kenya, *Kenya-Somalia Relations* (Nairobi: Government Printer, April 1967), pp. 60-61.

5. *Jeune Afrique*, September 10, 1967.

6. Gil Dugué, *Vers les Etats-Unis d'Afrique* (Dakar: Editions Lettres Africaines, 1960), pp. 55-62. On incidents between the Royal Moroccan Army and the MLA see Zartman, *Morocco*, pp. 85-86. For King Mohamed V's speech at M'Hamid, see *Le Monde*, February 27 and 28, 1958.

7. *Kenya-Somalia Relations*, p. 37.

8. Interviews, Mogadishu, November 1965.

9. *Kenya-Somalia Relations*, pp. 37, 45. Tom Stacey, *Summons to Ruwenzori* (London: Secker and Warburg, 1965); M. O. Beshir, *The Southern Sudan* (London: C. Hurst and Co., 1968), p. 84 and passim; Shepherd, "National Integration," *ARB*, January 1967, p. 703.

10. Interviews, Mogadishu, November 1965.

11. Interviews, Nairobi, October 1965, and Kampala, December 1965; Kyle "The Southern Problem," and Shepherd, "National Integration."

12. Joseph Oduho and William Deng, *The Problem of the Southern Sudan* (Oxford: Oxford University Press, 1963), pp. 59-60.

13. Because of the arrangements for maximum press coverage of President de Gaulle's tour, the Djibouti riots were extensively reported in the press. See *Le Monde*, August 27 and 28-29, 1966.

14. *The Issue of the Northern Frontier District* (Mogadishu: Government of the Somali Republic, May 1963), pp. 31-33.

15. *East African Standard* and *Daily Nation* (both published in Nairobi), June 30, and July 1, 1963; *ARB*, May 1968, pp. 1074 and 1076; *Le Monde*, November 11, 1960.

16. *Kenya-Somalia Relations*, p. 16.

17. Welch, *Dream of Unity*, p. 135.

18. Saadia Touval, "The Organization of African Unity and African Borders," *International Organization*, 21 (1967), 111-113.

19. Kyle, "The Southern Problem," pp. 512-520. See also *The Reporter* (Nairobi), January 5, 1963.

20. Touval, "The Organization of African Unity," pp. 107-108.

21. This analysis owes much to T. C. Schelling, *Arms and Influence* (New Haven: Yale University Press, 1966), Chap. i.

22. The Mali-Mauritania agreement is discussed in I. W. Zartman, "A Disputed Frontier is Settled," *Africa Report*, 8 (August 1963), 13-14, and correction, ibid. 9, (March 1964), 31. See also *Le Monde*, February 16-17, 19, 1963 and April 6, 1965. On Mali-Moroccan cooperation, see *Le Monde*, February 17 and June 3, 1961; and *Christian Science*

Monitor, September 16, 1961. Mauritania's charges that Morocco and Mali intended to partition Mauritania between them were reported in *Le Monde*, April 13, 1962. The Moroccan-Algerian agreement at Bamako is discussed in Chapter 10.

23. Information on the rebellion and its suppression is scarce. See *Le Monde*, October 13-14, and December 10, 1963; July 30, August 16-17, September 15, 24, and December 10, 1964. See also *New York Herald Tribune* (European edition), January 27, 1964.

24. The UN and OAU roles in the Somali disputes are discussed in Chapter 9. On the Khartoum conference, see Chapter 7. Among the Uganda government's measures exerting pressure on the southern Sudanese was legislation prohibiting the harboring of refugees without permit, enacted in December 1964, while an internal debate was taking place within SANU about whether to negotiate with the Sudanese government; *ARB*, December 1964, p. 203.

25. The change in the Kenyan mood was reflected by the debates in the House of Representatives. The debate on July 25, 1963, after the murder of the Boran chief and the Isiolo D.C., but before the commencement of large scale shifta activity, was very quiet. On the other hand, the debate on November 28, 1963, after wide-scale shifta operations had been launched, was a stormy occasion. See Kenya. House of Representatives, 1963, First Session, cols. 339-340, 1368-1385 (July 25), and cols. 2400-2428 (November 28).

26. A newspaper correspondent who visited with the Touareg early in 1958 reported them as saying that they were free people and that the Negroes from the south could not reach them because they could not penetrate the desert. The French kept them from slave raiding; but when the French left, they would resume raiding and dominate the slaves; they would not permit the slaves to dominate them; Max Olivier-Lecamp in *Le Figaro*, March 5, 1958.

27. See for example *ARB*, April 1968, p. 1043, for a report on Colonel Ojukwu's press conference, at which he accused the federal government of being a British instrument.

Chapter 6.   The Roles of Friends and Allies

1. On Mauritania's internal politics, see A. G. Gerteiny, *Mauritania* (London: Pall Mall Press, 1967), pp. 126-135, 147-162; and C. H. Moore, "One-Partyism in Mauritania," *Journal of Modern African Studies*, 3 (October 1965), 409-420.

2. Quoted in *Keesing's*, p. 16227. See also Zartman, "The Sahara— Bridge or Barrier?" p. 38.

3. For the full text of the Arab League's resolution see *Livre blanc sur la Mauritanie*, p. 117. See also Sa'd, *The Problem of Mauritania*. On King Mohamed's tour, see *Middle East Record, 1960* (published for the Israel Oriental Society, Reuven Shiloah Research Center, by Weidenfeld and Nicolson, London), pp. 161-162.

4. "Accord de défense entre les Gouvernements de la République française et de la République islamique de Mauritanie," in France, Ministère des affaires étrangères, *Recueil des Traités et Accords de la France, Année 1962* (Paris: Imprimerie Nationale, 1963), pp. 288-289. The agreement also contained annexes on a joint defense committee and on raw materials and strategic goods. Another agreement signed on that occasion was a treaty on technical military assistance (ibid., pp. 291-299). For a report on the negotiations leading to these agreements see *Le Monde*, June 18-19, 1961.

5. Maurice Ligot, "La Coopération militaire dans les Accords passés entre la France et les Etats africains et malgache d'Expression française," *Revue Juridique et Politique d'Outre Mer*, 17 (October-December 1963), 517-532.

6. As part of the reorganization of French forces and the reduction in the number of French bases in Africa, French troops were withdrawn from Mauritania in December 1965. It was explained at the time that this did not affect French commitments, and that French forces remained available on call. See *ARB*, January 1966, p. 456; *Le Monde*, September 19, 1964 and September 11, 1965.

7. The Mauritanian leaders' reserve toward the rest of French Africa during the colonial period is reflected in their not having joined any of the interterritorial political parties. See R. S. Morgenthau, *Political Parties in French-Speaking West Africa* (Oxford: Oxford University Press, 1964), pp. 307, 314. This contrasts sharply with the close links established among the political leaders from the other territories.

8. *Middle East Record, 1960*, p. 313 and *Middle East Record, 1961* (published for Tel-Aviv University, Reuven Shiloah Research Center, by the Israel Program for Scientific Translations, Jerusalem), pp. 169-170; *Le Monde*, November 29, 1960.

9. *Le Monde*, May 29, July 9, November 28, 1963, and October 22, 1964. For some Negro-Mauritanian reactions to Ould Daddah's policy of rapprochement with the UAR see Gerteiny, *Mauritania*, pp. 153-154.

10. *Le Monde*, December 10, 1964; *ARB*, July 1964, p. 110 and August 1964, p. 130.

11. *The Times* (London), October 21 and 22, 1963; *Le Monde*, October 23, 1963.

12. See *Mizan Newsletter*, November 1963, pp. 22-25.

13. *Afro-Asian Solidarity Against Imperialism*, a collection of documents, speeches and press interviews from the visits of Chinese leaders

to thirteen African and Asian countries (Peking: Foreign Languages Press, 1964), pp. 90, 104.

14. The arms race was intensified in 1967. See *New York Times,* February 10, 11, 1967. On military aid and arms deliveries prior to 1967 see M. J. V. Bell, *Military Assistance to Independent African States*; David Wood, *The Armed Forces of African States*; John L. Sutton and Geoffrey Kemp, *Arms to Developing Countries 1945-1965* (all published by the Institute for Strategic Studies, London, as *Adelphi Papers*, no. 15, December 1964; no. 27, April 1966; and no. 28, October 1966, respectively).

15. *New York Times,* May 2, 1967. In response to a Kenyan protest the UAR assured Kenya that it was no longer supplying arms to Somalia, *ARB* (May 1967), p. 773.

16. Somalis attached particular significance to statements of support by Sadiq al Mahdi (who was at the time president of the Umma party and served subsequently as prime minister of the Sudan) during his visit to Mogadishu in July 1965. In August 1968 it was reported that Sudan-Somali Friendship Associations were formed in Mogadishu and Khartoum. The Khartoum group proclaimed that it would work for "the liberation of Somali territories now enslaved by imperialism." See *The National Review* (published by the Ministry of Information, Mogadishu), no. 5 (July 1965), pp. 12 and 27; *ARB*, August 1968, p. 1144. See also *Somali News* (Mogadishu), July 1, 1966; *ARB*, July 1966, pp. 568, 576; and April 1967, p. 754.

17. Quoted in *Ghana Today* (published by the Information Section of the Ghana Office, London), 5 (November 8, 1961).

18. *Daily Graphic* (Accra), October 23, 1961.

19. *The Somali Republic and the Organization of African Unity*, p. 19.

20. Thomspon, *Ghana's Foreign Policy 1957-1966*, pp. 202, 252-253; *ARB*, March 1966, p. 486.

21. Interview, Dar es Salaam, August 1963. There are small immigrant Somali communities living in Tanzania.

22. On the strengthening of Somali-Tanzanian ties following the visit, see the *East African Standard,* December 15, 1965 and *The National Review* (Mogadishu), January 1967.

23. *Somali News,* December 4, 1964; *ARB*, November 1964, p. 192, April 1965, pp. 273, 283. Also of interest is a pamphlet, *Somalia a Divided Nation Seeking Reunification* (published by the Ministry of Information, Mogadishu, in collaboration with the Somali Embassy in Bonn, April 1965).

24. Somalia's alliances were discussed above. As for the Eritreans, Ethiopia reported that an Eritrean separatist leader who defected

named Syria, Iraq, Saudi Arabia, and Sudan as providing arms and financial assistance to the movement. According to the same report Syria and Sudan also provided training facilities, and the guerrillas were operating from bases in Sudan. See *ARB*, May 1967, pp. 781-782. See also *Jeune Afrique*, no. 494 (June 23, 1970), p. 61. In September 1966 it was reported that President Aref of Iraq had promised a delegation of the Eritrean Liberation Front that he would raise the Eritrean problem with Emperor Haile Selassie, who was scheduled to visit Iraq the following month. Subsequently, the emperor cancelled his visit. The formal reason given for the cancellation was "an outbreak of cholera" in Iraq. See *ARB*, September 1966, p. 621 and October 1966, p. 644.

25. I happened to be in Addis Ababa at the time of Tom Mboya's visit in October 1960, and recall the warm welcome he was accorded on that occasion.

26. *ARB*, January 1964, p. 10; June 1964, p. 90.

27. *Ethiopia Observer*, 8, no. 2 (1964), 134.

28. *ARB*, July 1965, p. 331.

29. *Le Monde*, August 28-29, 30; September 18-19, 29; October 12, 21, 22, 1966; and *New York Herald Tribune* (European edition), September 3-4, 1966.

30. For this correspondence, see the *East African Standard*, May 1, 1963.

31. The British offer, by Secretary of State for the Colonies Alan Lennox-Boyd, is quoted in *Commonwealth Survey*, 5, no. 4 (February 17, 1959), pp. 178-179. On subsequent friction, see *The Times* (London), February 11 and 19, 1959.

32. Bell, *Military Assistance*; Wood, *The Armed Forces*.

33. Some information on British aid to Kenya can be found in Bell, *Military Assistance*, p. 11; and Wood, *The Armed Forces*, p. 15. See also Great Britain, House of Commons, *Parliamentary Debates*, 695, cols. *176-178* (written answers), June 3, 1964.

34. *Department of State Bulletin*, October 28, 1963, p. 675.

35. Khrushchev's messages were dated February 10, 1964. They were circulated as UN documents S/5538 and S/5539. On the Soviet attitude to the Somali problem, 1945-1948, see Touval, *Somali Nationalism*, pp. 173-175.

36. On Kenyan resentment at Soviet aid to Somalia and suspicions of Chinese support see *Kenya-Somalia Relations*, pp. 7-8. On the Kenyan government's suspicions of Soviet assistance to the domestic opposition, see *ARB*, March 1966, p. 498; charges of Chinese interference in Kenya's domestic politics, *ARB*, March 1966, p. 498, July 1966, p. 580, February 1967, p. 726, June 1967, p. 805, July 1967, p. 826.

37. *Afro-Asian Solidarity Against Imperialism*, p. 259.

38. Ibid., pp. 287-288; and see also pp. 265, 269, 300.

39. *National Review* (Mogadishu), no. 5 (July 1965), p. 5.

40. *ARB*, July 1968, p. 1117; December 1969, p. 1616; February 1970, p. 1666; July 1970, p. 1814.

41. On Sudan's sources of military aid see Bell, *Military Assistance*, pp. 14-15; Wood, *The Armed Forces*, p. 24; *New York Times*, August 10, 1967; *ARB*, February 1970, pp. 1677-1678.

42. George Modelski, "Kautilya: Foreign Policy and the International System in the Ancient Hindu World," *American Political Science Review*, 58 (September 1964), 549-560. On Kautilyan alliances in Africa, see Zartman, "Africa as a Subordinate State System in International Relations," pp. 545-564.

43. A reference to this claim can be found in Virginia Thompson, "Dahomey," in Carter, *Five African States*, p. 250. The Dahomeyan suspicion was fed also by minor incidents such as the following related to me in Lomé in January 1966: in 1960, around the time of Dahomey's independence, Atanlé II, chief of Agoué, a town on the Dahomey-Togo border, asked President de Gaulle that the town be united with its brethren in Togo. The French authorities forwarded the chief's letter to President Maga of Dahomey, and as a result the chief was arrested, and remained in prison till 1963. (There was a sequel: President Olympio of Togo whose family was from Agoué refused to intervene in Atanlé's favor lest this irritate President Maga. After Olympio's assassination his family wanted him to be interred in Agoué, but the local population at first refused, arguing that he had denied his kinsmen and now they deny him. The burial was finally arranged following the intervention of the local priest.)

44. *New York Times*, January 14, 1963. See also Thompson, *Ghana's Foreign Policy*, pp. 246-248.

45. *Le Monde*, May 2, 18-19, August 2, 1958; and *The Guardian*, March 2, 1960.

46. *Le Monde*, July 9, 11, and December 6, 1963. A list of the Franco-Togolese cooperation agreements was published on the occasion of their ratification in the *Journal Officiel de la République Francaise*, December 22, 1963 (Loi no. 63-1253). But, significantly, the text of the defense agreement was omitted when the texts of the other agreements were published in the *Journal Officiel*, June 10, 1964 (*Décret* 64-523). See also Maurice Ligot, "La Coopération militaire."

47. *ARB*, January 1966, p. 442; Arpil 1966, p. 507; and June 1966, pp. 547-548.

48. The alliances in which Ghana, Ivory Coast, and Upper Volta participated are discussed in detail in I. W. Zartman, *International Relations in The New Africa* (Englewood Cliffs, N.J.: Prentice Hall, 1966), pp. 17-26.

49. The assumption of a French guarantee (not aimed specifically at Ghana), was reconfirmed by the scenario of the Franco-Ivoirien war games named Alligator III. See *Le Monde*, September 13, 1967. For the text of the treaty, see France, *Recueil de Traités 1962*, pp. 280-284.

50. For a general discussion of the functions of such relationships, see George Liska, *Alliances and the Third World* (Baltimore: Johns Hopkins Press, 1968).

51. See Aristide Zolberg, *One Party Government in the Ivory Coast*, pp. 289-294. Significantly, the Ivory Coast press was restrained in discussing Ghana's role in the affair. For a report on President Nkrumah's statement claiming that the Sanwi wish to join Ghana see *Abidjan-Matin*, April 24, 1960. Some information on Ghanaian assistance to the Sanwi movement was presented to the Extraordinary Session of the OAU Council of Ministers in Lagos on June 11, 1965.

52. See L. Gray Cowan, "Political Determinants," in Vernon McKay, ed., *African Diplomacy* (London: Pall Mall Press, 1966), p. 134.

53. Unpublished Summary Record of the Third Ordinary Session of the Council of Ministers, held in Cairo on July 13-17, 1964, First Committee (Political), July 14, 1964.

54. A. A. Mazrui, *Towards a Pax Africana* (London: Weidenfeld and Nicolson, 1967), p. 185.

55. C. T. Thorne, Jr., "External Political Pressures," in McKay, ed., *African Diplomacy*, p. 157.

56. The expectation that the Soviet Union would favor territorial revisions in Africa was based in part upon interpretations of Professor I. I. Potekhin's writings which were believed to be in accord with official policy. See "Africa's Future: The Soviet View," an abridgement of I. I. Potekhin's *Afrika Smotrit v Budushcheye* (Africa Looks Ahead), Moscow 1960, in supplement to *Mizan Newsletter*, no. 4 (April 1961), pp. 10-15; *A Soviet Primer on Africa*, translation of I. I. Potekhin's *Afrika 1956-1961*, translation published by U.S. Dept. of Commerce, Joint Publications Research Service (JPRS 14232), June 25, 1962, pp. 58, 111-115, 171. For views carrying the opposite implication, of support for the status quo, see I. I. Potekhine, "L'Intelligentsia et l'éveil de la conscience nationale des peuples," in *Des Africanistes russes parlent de l'Afrique* (Paris: Présence Africaine, 1960), pp. 185-195.

Of greater political importance was Nikita Khrushchev's message to all governments, dated December 31, 1963, calling for the conclusion of a treaty renouncing the use of force in the settlement of territorial and frontier disputes. See UN Docs. A/5751, (September 21, 1964) and A/5740, (October 8, 1964). The Soviet proposal was not discussed because the 19th session of the General Assembly did not hold any debates.

57. Details on the organization and tasks of the police can be found

in *The Somali Republic Police Force 12th Anniversary* (an illustrated brochure published by the police force in 1962).

Chapter 7. Negotiations and Their Results

1. My debt to the analyses of negotiation and bargaining by F. C. Iklé and T. C. Schelling is obvious. See Iklé's *How Nations Negotiate* (New York: Frederick A. Praeger, 1964); and Schelling's *Strategy of Conflict* (Cambridge, Mass.: Harvard University Press, 1960); and *Arms and Influence.*

2. See classifications of outcomes suggested by Kenneth Boulding, *Conflict and Defense* (New York: Harper & Row, 1963), pp. 309-310; and by K. J. Holsti, "Resolving International Conflicts: A Taxonomy of Behavior and Some Figures on Procedures," *Journal of Conflict Resolution*, 10 (1966), 272-296. These classifications were stimulating, but inapplicable to the cases and processes discussed here. Still, "disengagement" comes close to Boulding's "reconciliation."

3. On the difficulties of reconciling "core values," see Boulding, *Conflict and Defense*, pp. 311-312. See also his "National Images and International Systems," *Journal of Conflict Resolution*, 3 (1959), pp. 120-131.

4. Boulding, *Conflict and Defense*, pp. 323-324; Schelling, *Arms and Influence*, chap. i.

5. Quoted from President Tubman's annual message to the legislature, November 1960, reprinted in *Liberia Annual Review 1960-1961* (London and Monrovia: Consolidated Publications Co., n.d.), p. 72. See also Zartman, *International Relations in the New Africa*, pp. 115-116.

6. Tanganyika, National Assembly, *Parliamentary Debates*, Official Report, First Session, second meeting, June 11, 1962, cols. 263-264. Tanzania (as Tanganyika came to be called), raised the matter with Malawi (formerly Nyasaland), in 1965 and 1967, but failed to obtain satisfaction. See *The Guardian*, July 18, 1966 and *ARB*, July 1967, p. 817.

7. André de Laubadère, "Le statut international du Maroc depuis 1955," in *Annuaire Français de Droit International, 1956* (Paris: C.N.R.S., 1957), pp. 133-134, n. 14.

8. *Le Monde*, June 17-18, 1956.

9. Morocco, Ministry of Foreign Affairs, *Livre blanc*, p. 102.

10. *Le Monde*, February 20, 25, 26; March 7; April 12, 13, 1957.

11. Morocco, *Livre blanc*, pp. 104-120.

12. *Keesing's Contemporary Archives*, pp. 18341-18342.

13. Ibid., p. 18348.

14. Abdirashid Ali Shermarke, then prime minister, to the KADU delegation, August 17, 1962, quoted in Somalia, *The Somali Republic and African Unity*, p. 21.

15. *The Issue of the Northern Frontier District*, pp. 20-21, 47-48; and John Drysdale, *The Somali Dispute* (London: Pall Mall Press, 1964), p. 130.

16. Great Britain, *Kenya: Report of the NFD Commission* (London: H.M.S.O., 1962), Cmnd. 1900, pp. 1, 18. The terms of reference are dated October 5, 1962.

17. *The Issue of the Northern Frontier District*, pp. 48-49.

18. Ibid., p. 53.

19. Ibid., pp. 53-71; Drysdale, *Somali Dispute*, pp. 130-145.

20. Great Britain, *Kenya Preparations for Independence* (London: H.M.S.O., 1963), Cmnd. 2082. The document relates that the Kenya ministerial delegation visiting London informed the British government of its talks with the Somali foreign minister and its intention of having further talks with him. Somalia's insistence that Britain remained responsible for the problem was conveyed to London through the good offices of the U.S. See Drysdale, *Somali Dispute*, p. 149.

21. Quoted in Drysdale, *Somali Dispute*, pp. 155-156.

22. Ibid., pp. 156-157. *The East African Standard* (Nairobi), August 13, 24, 27, 29, 30, 1963.

23. *Sunday Nation* (Nairobi), August 25, 1963.

24. For a history of the problem, see Beshir, *Southern Sudan*; Shepherd, "National Integration," pp. 194-200.

25. *ARB*, September 1964, p. 151. See also Beshir, *Southern Sudan*, pp. 86-87.

26. The letter is reproduced in full in Beshir, *Southern Sudan*, Appendix 10, pp. 154-158.

27. Ibid., p. 155 (italics added).

28. On the negotiations preceding the conference, and the Khartoum conference itself, see *ibid.*, pp. 88-97; *ARB*, December 1964, p. 203, January 1965, p. 222, February 1965, p. 241. See also Shepherd, "National Integration."

29. *Voice of the Southern Sudan*, 3 (May 1965), pp. 1-2. (Published by SANU in England.)

30. *The Times* (London), May 30, 1966.

31. Uganda's pressure on the southerners to attend the talks is evident also from a statement in Parliament by the Minister of Internal Affairs, Felix Onama, on January 3, 1965, reproduced in Beshir, *Southern Sudan*, pp. 163-164. On Uganda's policy see also Shepherd, "National Integration," pp. 204-205.

32. See *ARB*, September 1965, p. 365 and February 1966, p. 463.

A report on the activities of William Deng at the 1966 OAU summit in Addis Ababa was carried by Agence France Press, November 4, 1966.

Chapter 8. Disengagement, I

1. See Kenneth Boulding, *Conflict and Defense*, pp. 308-311; K. J. Holsti, "Resolving International Conflicts: A Taxonomy of Behavior and Some Figures on Procedures," pp. 275-281.

2. Boulding, *Conflict and Defense*, pp. 311-312.

3. The handling of the dispute by the United Nations is conveniently summarized in *International Organization*, 12, (Summer 1958), pp. 333-335.

4. P. M. Holt, *A Modern History of the Sudan* (London: Weidenfeld & Nicolson, 1961), pp. 164-165.

5. *The Guardian*, July 19, 1966.

6. Tevoedjre, *Pan-Africanism in Action*, p. 38.

7. Ibid.

8. Ibid., p. 39.

9. Republic of Dahomey, *Ce qu'il faut savoir sur la crise daho-nigerienne* (Cotonou: December 24, 1963), and Republic of Niger, *The Relations of Niger and Dahomey at the End of 1963* (Niamey: n.d. [1964]).

10. Agence Ivoirienne de Presse, January 16, 1964.

11. *ARB*, January 1964, p. 4.

12. *ARB*, March 1964, pp. 36-37; Fondation Nationale des Sciences Politiques, Centre d'Etude des Relations Internationales (Paris), *Chronologie Politique Africaine*, 5, (March-April 1964), pp. ii, 2.

13. *ARB*, July 1964, p. 110; *West Africa*, July 18, 1964, p. 799.

14. Before independence, Justin Ahomadegbé had been the head of the Dahomey section of the RDA, the interterritorial party led by Houphouët-Boigny. On the other hand, Sourou-Migan Apithy had been associated with Houphouët-Boigny's political enemies, and in 1959 advocated Dahomey's affiliation with the Mali federation. For a convenient account of the background personal-political relationships, see Virginia Thompson, "Dahomey," in Carter, ed., *Five African States*, pp. 173-262.

15. Agence Ivoirienne de Presse, January 19, 1965; *Afrique Nouvelle* (Dakar), week of January 21-27, 1965; *ARB*, January 1965, p. 221.

16. *ARB*, June 1965, p. 313.

17. *Manchester Guardian*, February 17, 1958.

18. *Le Monde*, May 2, 1958; *Combat*, May 3-4, 1958.

19. *The Times* (London) and *Manchester Guardian*, May 27, 1958.

20. *Le Monde*, August 2, 1958.

21. *New York Times*, October 19, 1958.

22. *The Times* (London), October 30, 1959.

23. Ibid., November 2, 1959.

24. *New York Times*, February 5, 1960.

25. Ibid., February 5, March 19, 1960; *The Guardian*, March 2, 1960; *Daily Telegraph*, March 19, 1960.

26. *New York Times*, March 16, 1960; *The Times* (London), March 16, 1960; *Le Monde*, March 17, 1960. Exchanges on these accusations continued for several weeks.

27. W. S. Thompson, *Ghana's Foreign Policy 1957-1966*, pp. 85-87, 229-230; *Le Monde*, September 17, 1960; *New York Times*; September 17, October 23, 1960.

28. *Le Monde*, January 9, December 25, 28, 1962, *The Observer*, January 6, 1963; *The Times* (London), January 7, 1963. See also Ghana, *Statement by the Government on the Recent Conspiracy*, (Accra: Ministry of Information and Broadcasting, December 11, 1961), pp. 1, 23-24.

29. There is an interesting account of Dahomey's mediation attempt in Tevoedjre, *Pan-Africanism in Action*, pp. 41-50. Ghana's maneuvers in this case seem to have been influenced more by the Monrovia group's conference in Lagos in January 1962, than by the Togolese problem. But a full evaluation of this episode must await the publication of additional versions. On Dahomey's relations with Togo, and their effect of encouraging collaboration between Dahomey and Ghana see Chapter 6. See also W. S. Thompson, *Ghana's Foreign Policy*, pp. 231-237, 308-311.

30. *Le Monde*, January 22, 23, February 9, June 13, July 17, 1963.

31. *ARB*, August 1964, p. 130; September 1964, p. 146; January 1965, p. 222; February 1965, pp. 238, 239; March 1965, p. 257; July 1965, p. 332. See also W. S. Thompson, *Ghana's Foreign Policy*, pp. 313-315, 367-369.

32. *ARB*, September 1965, p. 361.

33. *Ghana Today*, 10, March 23, 1966, and April 20, 1966.

34. *ARB*, April 1966, p. 509.

Chapter 9. Disengagement, II: The Somali Case

1. *The Ethio-Somalia Frontier Problem* (Addis Ababa: Ethiopian Ministry of Information, n.d. [1961]), p. 26.

2. Somalia. *The Somali Republic and African Unity* (1962), pp. 17, 21.

3. For a history of the Pan-African Freedom Movement for East, Central and Southern Africa see Joseph S. Nye Jr., *Pan-Africanism and East African Integration* (Cambridge, Mass.: Harvard University Press, 1966), pp. 119-123. See also Richard Cox, *Pan-Africanism in Practice: PAFMECSA 1958-1964* (London: Oxford University Press, 1964).

4. *Pan-African Freedom Movement for East Central and Southern Africa* (Addis Ababa: Ministry of External Affairs, n.d. [1962]), pp. 81-82.

5. *The Somali Republic and African Unity* (1962), p. 13. The same condition was stipulated by the Somali observer attending the session of the East African Central Legislative Assembly in Kampala, on November 29, 1962. He said:

We, in the Somali Republic, visualize a Federation in which the Somali people will form one constituent unit in a federation of East and Central African States. In so far as my country is concerned, it would be necessary, therefore, that before embarking upon Federation, the Somali people should be reunited. In my view, boundary revision between existing States must come *before* and not after Federation.

Italics in the original. I am indebted to Joseph S. Nye, Jr. for the text of this speech. The Central Legislative Assembly was composed of representatives of the legislatures of Kenya, Uganda, and Tanganyika and was the legislative authority for the East African Common Services Organization.

6. See Chapter 7.

7. Some information on these talks was revealed in the course of two debates in the Kenya parliament. See Kenya, House of Representatives, 1963 First Session, cols. 2400-2428 (November 28, 1963), and ibid. 1963 Second Session (vol. 2), cols. 8-47 (December 31, 1963). See also *Kenya-Somalia Relations*, pp. 12-13.

8. *ARB*, April 1964, p. 52.

9. UN Doc. S/5536. The Somali government's message was dated February 9, 1964.

10. *New York Times*, February 10, 1964.

11. The account which follows is based on the unpublished Summary Record of the Second Extraordinary Session of the Council of Ministers, held in Dar es Salaam from February 12 to 15, 1964.

12. *The Times* (London) and *Le Monde*, February 13, 1964.

13. UN Doc. S/5542. The prime minister's message was dated February 13, 1964.

14. OAU Doc. ECM/Res. 3 (II).

15. OAU Doc. ECM/Res. 4 (II).

16. *The Observer* (London) and *New York Times*, February 16, 1964.

Following the Council of Ministers meeting other African states, including Ghana, Morocco, and Tanganyika, also tried to mediate in the dispute. See *Le Monde*, February 20 and 25, 1964.

17. The account which follows is based on the unpublished Summary Record of the Second Ordinary Session of the Council of Ministers, held in Lagos from February 24 to 29, 1964. See also *Somali News* (Mogadishu), March 13, 1964.

18. OAU Doc. CM/Res. 16 (II), and CM/Res. 17 (II).

19. *The National Review*, (Mogadishu: Ministry of Information, March 1964), no. 2, p. 1.

20. The full text of the communiqué was published in the *OAU Review*, 1 (May 1964), pp. 40-41.

21. An agreement to this effect was reached between the Somali, Ethiopian, and Kenyan representatives, in the presence of the provisional secretary-general. For the text see *The Somali Republic and the Organization of African Unity* (1964), pp. 39-40.

22. Ibid., pp. 25-27.

23. Unpublished Summary Record of the Third Ordinary Session of the Council of Ministers, held in Cairo from July 13 to 17, 1964.

24. *ARB*, March 1965, pp. 256-257. See also Somalia. *The Somali Peoples' Quest for Unity* (Mogadishu: Ministry of Foreign Affairs, 1965), pp. 9-10.

25. *ARB*, October 1965, p. 381.

26. The reconstruction of the preparations for the conference is based on interviews conducted in Nairobi and in Dar es Salaam in November and December 1965.

27. This assessment is based on the analysis of the two sides' proposals which follows below, and on my impressions from an interview with former Prime Minister Abdirazaq Haji Hussein, on November 10, 1965.

28. The Somali proposals at Arusha were published in *The National Review*, no. 6 (April 1966), p. 9.

29. *East African Standard*, December 14, 15, 1965; *ARB*, December 1965, p. 426.

30. For example, Radio Mogadishu March 8, 9, 10, 16, 24, 1966, as reported by the BBC's *Summary of World Broadcasts*, nos. ME/2108, ME/2109, ME/2110, ME/2115, ME/2122, respectively.

31. Mogadishu Radio, April 5, 1966 (as reported by *Foreign Radio Broadcasts*, April 6, 1966).

32. *ARB*, April 1966, p. 507. See also *The National Review*, no. 6, April 1966, p. 40.

33. *ARB*, July 1966, p. 575; *Kenya-Somalia Relations*, pp. 64-65; *ARB*, April 1967, pp. 755-756; *New York Times*, May 3, 1967.

34. *ARB*, January 1965, pp. 227-228.

35. *ARB*, June 1965, p. 321, and June 1966, p. 558; *The Somali Peoples' Quest for Unity*, p. 18. For a convenient summary see *Yearbook of the United Nations 1966* (New York: UN Office of Public Information, 1966), pp. 581-583.

36. *Le Monde*, September 18-19, and October 12, 1966; *ARB*, September 1966, pp. 618-619, and October 1966, p. 643.

37. On the Franco-Ethiopian talks, *Le Monde*, August 28-29, 30, 31, and October 21, 22, 1966; *ARB*, August 1966, pp. 597, 599-600. On the Franco-Somali talks, *ARB*, October 1966, p. 645, November 1966, pp. 666-667. See also *French Somaliland: A Classic Colonial Case* (Mogadishu: Ministry of Foreign Affairs, March 1967), pp. 24-27.

38. This account is based on *Le Monde*, November 1, 5 and 10, 1966 and the news bulletins of Agence France Press.

39. Res. 2228 (XXI), December 20, 1966. The resolution as a whole was adopted by a vote of 95 to 1 with 18 abstentions. The paragraph calling for international supervision of the referendum was passed by 72 to 2, with 39 abstentions. On the bargaining between Somalia and Ethiopia and their agreement concerning the draft resolution, see *French Somaliland: A Classic Colonial Case*, pp. 19-20.

40. *ARB*, March 1967, p. 742.

41. For some reactions see *ARB*, March 1967, pp. 744-745; April 1967, p. 766; June 1967, p. 804.

42. OAU Doc. AHG/ST. 1 (IV).

43. *ARB*, September 1967, p. 859.

44. *ARB*, October 1967, p. 881, and *Somali News*, November 3, 1967.

45. The summary that follows is based on the *ARB*. For a vivid account, see Raymond Thurston, "Detente in the Horn," *Africa Report*, 14 (February 1969), 6-13.

46. "How the Arusha Understanding Works, by a spokesman of the Foreign Affairs Ministry," *Somali News*, November 3, 1967, p. 12.

47. *ARB*, September 1967, p. 859.

48. *Somali News*, November 3, 1967, p. 2.

49. Speech by Prime Minister Egal on October 14, 1968. See *ARB*, October 1968, p. 1210.

50. "How the Arusha Understanding Works . . .," *Somali News*, November 3, 1967, p. 12.

51. Prime Minister Egal stated in his radio broadcast on October 31 that the initiative came from Somalia; see *Somali News*, November 3, 1967.

52. The editorial in the *Somali News* of November 3, 1967 (p. 3), defending the Arusha agreement with Kenya against criticism, described the restoration of normalcy to the lives of the Somalis in the NFD as

the "most important achievement" of the entire agreement. Prime Minister Egal, in his radio broadcast, credited the agreement with achieving "that the problem of the NFD be kept alive on the conference table without making the people of the NFD a sacrificial lamb." See *Somali News*, November 3, 1967, p. 2.

53. *ARB*, October 1967, p. 881.

54. *ARB*, November 1967, p. 907.

55. *ARB*, November 1967, p. 907; December 1967, p. 931. After Abdirazaq Haji Hussein resigned as Secretary-General, the party's institutional and hierarchical structures were changed, and the new post of "party leader" was created. See *ARB*, February 1968, p. 981. On the elections, see *ARB*, April 1969, p. 1378.

56. *ARB*, November 1967, p. 907.

57. *ARB*, November 1967, p. 903.

58. I am indebted to Mr. John Drysdale for sharing with me some of the information available to him about these events.

59. *The Times* (London), October 30, 1967.

60. That the question of French aid was brought up is evident from the joint communiqué issued after the talks. See *ARB*, September 1968, p. 1196.

61. Editorial, *Somali News*, November 3, 1967, p. 3. But it is significant to note that the more prominent argument in defense of the government's policy was that it is consistent with Somali *national* goals. The Pan-African argument was given secondary place.

62. *ARB*, November 1967, pp. 903, 907.

63. *ARB*, October 1969, p. 1551, and November 1969, pp. 1581-1582.

64. Somali irredentist goals were reiterated on the occasions of the Republic's tenth anniversary of independence in July 1970, and the first anniversary of the revolutionary regime in October 1970. See *ARB*, June 1970, p. 1784 and October 1970, p. 1895. A reminder that clashes between Somali tribesmen and Ethiopian authorities might lead to friction between governments was provided in July 1969. See *ARB*, July 1969, p. 1461, and August 1969, p. 1489.

Chapter 10. Boundary Agreements

1. On "compromise" see Boulding, *Conflict and Defense*, pp. 310-313; F. C. Iklé, *How Nations Negotiate*, pp. 206-210; K. J. Holsti, "Resolving International Conflicts: A Taxonomy of Behavior and Some Figures on Procedures," pp. 276-280.

2. Virginia Thompson and Richard Adloff, *French West Africa*, p. 147; Gerteiny, *Mauritania*, pp. 202-203.

3. On the agreement, see Republic of Kenya, National Assembly, *House of Representatives Offical Report*, vol. 5, July 27, 1965, cols. 1409-1411, and vol. 6, September 22, 1965, cols. 445-454. For a detailed discussion of this border see McEwen, *International Boundaries of East Africa*, pp. 102-112.

4. Interviews at Isiolo, Kenya, November 1960.

5. *Le Monde*, January 20, July 2, 1960.

6. *Le Monde*, April 1-2, 13, 21, May 12, 23, 29, 1962.

7. *Le Monde*, November 25-26, 28, 1962.

8. *Le Monde*, February 16-17, 19, 1963. For details of the agreement see I. W. Zartman, "A Disputed Frontier is Settled," *Africa Report*, 8 (August 1963), 13-14, and correction, *Africa Report*, 9 (March 1964), 31; A. G. Gerteiny, *Mauritania*, pp. 203-204.

9. For the texts of the agreements, see *Annuaire de l'Afrique du Nord 1963*, (Paris: C.N.R.S., 1965), pp. 993-1013.

10. *Le Monde*, November 7, 1963.

11. *Jeune Afrique*, no. 164 (December 30, 1963-January 5, 1964). The translation is mine.

12. *Keesing's*, pp. 18342-18343.

13. *ARB*, April 1966, p. 509; June 1966, p. 548; January 1967, p. 696.

14. *Le Monde*, January 23, May 19, 1967; April 24, 27, 1968; *ARB* January 1967, p. 696; March 1967, p. 734; May 1967, p. 774; April 1968, p. 1033; December 1969, p. 1604; and January 1970, p. 1633; May 1970, p. 1748. Also *Jeune Afrique*, no. 472 (January 20, 1970), p. 20.

15. *ARB*, January 1967, p. 696; March 1967, p. 734. Also, *ARB* (economic series), March-April 1967, p. 722. An agreement for the construction of a pipeline for the transport of the oi! from the Algerian side of the El Borma field through Tunisia was announced in February 1969. See *ARB* (economic series), January-February 1969, p. 1249.

16. See Hovet, *Africa in the United Nations*, p. 56.

17. For the text of the agreement, see *Le Monde*, October 23, 1963.

18. Tunisian mediation seemed unacceptable to both contestants. Morocco resented Tunisia's early recognition of Mauritania, whereas Algeria was antagonized by Tunisia's claims to portions of the Algerian Sahara. See *Le Monde*, October 15, 17, 20-21, 22, 25, and November 6, 1963.

19. *New York Times*, October 6, 1963; *Le Monde*, October 12 and 19, 1963.

20. *Le Monde*, October 8, 16, 1963.

21. *New York Times*, October 15, 1963; *The Times* (London), Octo-

ber 21, 1963; *Le Monde*, October 22, 1963. For the text of the Moroccan reservation see *Maghreb* (Paris), 1 (March-April 1964), p. 12.

22. Modibo Keita defended the preservation of the territorial status quo in his speech at the African summit in May 1963. See Chapter 4.

23. For the full text, see *Le Monde*, November 1, 1963.

24. OAU Doc. ECM/Res. 1 (I). See also *The Observer*, November 17, 1963 and *Le Monde*, November 17-18, 1963.

25. *Le Monde*, February 21, 1964. For details of the demilitarization agreement, see *Le Monde*, March 10, 1964.

26. *Le Monde*, April 26-27, 1964.

27. OAU Documents CM/Res. 37 (III), CM/Res. 53 (IV), AHG/Res. 32 (II). For a more detailed discussion, see Saadia Touval, "The Organization of African Unity and African Borders," pp. 108-110.

28. *ARB*, May 1966, p. 529; *New York Times*, May 21, 1966. For the Algerian version of the negotiations concerning the crisis, see the speech of Foreign Minister Abdelaziz Bouteflika reproduced in *Revue Algérienne des Sciences Juridiques, Politiques et Economiques*, no. 1 (March 1967), pp. 108-127.

29. *ARB*, July 1966, pp. 568-569; *Maghreb Digest* (Los Angeles), vol. 4, nos. 7-8 (July-August 1966), p. 92; *Le Monde*, October 21 and November 10, 1966.

30. *ARB* (Economic series), February-March 1968, pp. 939-940. At the Foreign Ministers conference, a few days before the summit, Morocco had still requested that the Moroccan-Algerian dispute remain on the OAU agenda. See *ARB*, September 1968, p. 1173.

31. *Le Monde*, January 18, 1969; *ARB*, January 1969, pp. 1290-1291. See also *Jeune Afrique*, no. 421 (Week of January 27-February 2, 1969). On the exchanges concerning the arms race, see *Le Monde*, March 4, 1967; *New York Times*, March 3 and 4, 1967.

32. *Le Monde*, May 27 and 29, 1970; *Jeune Afrique*, no. 492 (June 9, 1970), pp. 27-28.

33. Ould Daddah's interview, in *Le Monde*, May 29, 1962. See also Zartman, *International Relations in the New Africa*, pp. 29-30.

34. *Le Monde*, March 24-25, 28, 30, April 5, and 26, 1963.

35. *Le Monde*, August 14, November 22, 1963, May 12, July 9, 1965. The emir was never able to resume his duties because he became ill in jail, and was transferred to a hospital in Dakar, where he died in May 1965.

36. *Le Monde*, April 8, July 13-14, August 5 and 22, 1964.

37. *ARB*, January 1965, p. 223; April 1967, p. 757; May 1967, p. 786.

38. *Le Monde*, September 28-29, 1969; *Arab Report and Record* (London), 1969/17 (1-15 September), p. 365, and *ARB*, September 1969, p. 1519. For the text of the king's statement see BBC, *Summary*

of World Broadcasts, part 4, *The Middle East and Africa*, September 30, 1969, pp. ME/3190/E/5-6.

39. *ARB*, October 1969, p. 1544; November 1969, p. 1576; January 1970, pp. 1635-1636; *Le Monde*, February 3, 1970.

40. *Le Monde*, June 9, 10, 1970; *ARB*, June 1970, p. 1776; and *Jeune Afrique*, no. 494 (June 23, 1970), pp. 22-25.

41. *ARB*, June 1965, p. 317; *Le Monde*, August 7 and 10, 1965.

42. *Le Monde*, June 9, 10, 1970; *Jeune Afrique*, no. 477, (February 23, 1970), pp. 32-33; no. 494 (June 23, 1970), pp. 22-25; no. 490 (May 26, 1970), pp. 22-23; and *ARB*, December 1969, pp. 1603-1604; June 1970, pp. 1776-1777.

43. As early as February 1968, at the OAU Council of Ministers conference in Addis Ababa, Algeria had proposed that the Foreign Ministers of Algeria, Morocco, and Mauritania meet to consult "so as to expedite the liberation of Spanish Sahara." See Council of Ministers, Political Committee, *Report of the Rapporteur*, OAU Doc. CM(Cttee A/Draft. Rpt.1).

44. *Arab Report and Record*, 1969/18 (September 15-30, 1969), p. 389.

Chapter 11. Prospects

1. For information on the status of delimitation and demarcation, see A. S. Rayner, "The Length and Status of International Boundaries in Africa," in C. G. Widstrand, ed., *African Boundary Problems*, (Uppsala: Scandinavian Institute of African Studies, 1969), pp. 186-189.

2. For a prediction that the acceptance of the status quo will be abandoned, see Walker Connor, "Self-Determination: The New Phase," *World Politics*, 20 (October 1967), 30-53. For a more optimistic assessment, see Zartman, "The Foreign and Military Politics of African Boundary Problems," in Widstrand, *African Boundary Problems*, pp. 96-100.

Index

AAPC, *see* All-African Peoples Conference
AAPSO, *see* Afro-Asian Peoples' Solidarity Organization
ABAKO, *see* Bakongo Alliance
Abbas, Ferhat, 256
Abboud, General Ibrahim, 42, 143, 219
Abidjan, conference of French-speaking states at, 66, 67, 68
Abrahams, Peter, 24
Accra, OAU summit conference at (October 1965), 223, 230
Achimota (school), 22
Action Group, 31
Addis Ababa: summit conference at (May 1963), 44, 83, 213; Conference of Independent States at (June 1960), 64-66, 75-76, 213
Aden, Mahamoud Yusuf, 65
Adjei, Ako, 207
Afar (Danakil) tribe, 243
Afar and Issa Territory (formerly French Somaliland), 144, 226-229, 236, 243, 274-275
Afghanistan, 92
Afro-Asian Peoples' Solidarity Organization (AAPSO), 62, 80-81; first conference of

(Cairo, 1957), 51-53, 72; second conference of (Conakry, 1960), 63-64; third conference of (Moshi, 1963), 78-79; fourth conference of (Winneba, 1965), 93-95
Afro-Malagasy Union (UAM), 131n, 157, 164; and Congo-Gabon dispute, 196-198; and Dahomey-Niger dispute, 199-201
Agni tribe, 37, 38
Agoué, chief of, in Dahomey, 7
Ahidjo, Ahmadu, 75, 97
Ahomadegbé, Justin, 200, 201
ALF, *see* Azania Liberation Front
Algeria: border dispute with Tunisia, 54, 182, 251-255; AAPC resolution on, 62; and Conference of Nonaligned States, 77; and Moroccan-Mauritanian dispute, 125-126, 127; and Targui separatism, 131-132. *See also* Algerian-Moroccan dispute
Algerian-Moroccan dispute, 24, 26, 34, 86, 87; and AAPSO conference, 94-95; and the use of force, 112-113, 114-115, 119, 120, 124; described, 132-133; settlement of, 255-262, 265-269

323

*Publications Written under the Auspices of the
Center for International Affairs,
Harvard University*

Created in 1958, the Center for International Affairs fosters advanced study of basic world problems by scholars from various disciplines and senior officials from many countries. The research at the Center focuses on economic, social, and political development, the management of force in the modern world, the evolving roles of Western Europe and the Communist bloc, and the conditions of international order. Books published by Harvard University Press are listed here in the order in which they have been issued. A complete list of publications may be obtained from the Center. Out-of-print titles are indicated by an asterisk.

The Soviet Bloc: Unity and Conflict, by Zbigniew K. Brzezinski (jointly with the Russian Research Center), 1960. Revised and enlarged edition, 1967.
Rift and Revolt in Hungary: Nationalism versus Communism, by Ferenc A. Váli, 1961.*
The Economy of Cyprus, by A. J. Meyer, with Simos Vassiliou (jointly with the Center for Middle Eastern Studies), 1962.
Entrepreneurs of Lebanon: The Role of the Business Leader in a Developing Economy, by Yusif A. Sayigh (jointly with the Center for Middle Eastern Studies), 1962.*
Communist China 1955-1959: Policy Documents with Analysis, with a foreword by Robert R. Bowie and John K. Fairbank (jointly with the East Asian Research Center), 1962.
In Search of France, by Stanley Hoffmann, Charles P. Kindleberger, Laurence W. Wylie, Jesse R. Pitts, Jean-Baptiste Duroselle, and François Goguel, 1963.*
Somali Nationalism: International Politics and the Drive for Unity in the Horn of Africa, by Saadia Touval, 1963.
The Dilemma of Mexico's Development: The Roles of the Private and Public Sectors, by Raymond Vernon, 1963.
The Arms Debate, by Robert A. Levine, 1963.
Africans on the Land: Economic Problems of African Agricultural Development in Southern, Central, and East Africa, with Special Reference to Southern Rhodesia, by Montague Yudelman, 1964.
Public Policy and Private Enterprise in Mexico, edited by Raymond Vernon, 1964.*
Democracy in Germany, by Fritz Erler (Jodidi Lectures), 1965.
The Rise of Nationalism in Central Africa: The Making of Malawi and Zambia, 1873-1964, by Robert I. Rotberg, 1965.
Pan-Africanism and East African Integration, by Joseph S. Nye, Jr., 1965.
Germany and the Atlantic Alliance: The Interaction of Strategy and Politics, by James L. Richardson, 1966.
Political Change in a West African State: A Study of the Modernization Process in Sierra Leone, by Martin Kilson, 1966.
Planning without Facts: Lessons in Resource Allocation from Nigeria's Development, by Wolfgang F. Stolper, 1966.

Export Instability and Economic Development, by Alasdair I. MacBean, 1966.

Europe's Postwar Growth: The Role of Labor Supply, by Charles P. Kindleberger, 1967.

Pakistan's Development: Social Goals and Private Incentives, by Gustav F. Papanek, 1967.

Strike a Blow and Die: A Narrative of Race Relations in Colonial Africa, by George Simeon Mwase, edited by Robert I. Rotberg, 1967. Second printing, with a revised introduction, 1970.

Development Policy: Theory and Practice, edited by Gustav F. Papanek, 1968.*

Korea: The Politics of the Vortex, by Gregory Henderson, 1968.

The Brazilian Capital Goods Industry, 1929-1964 (jointly with the Center for Studies in Education and Development), by Nathaniel H. Leff, 1968.

The Process of Modernization: An Annotated Bibliography on the Sociocultural Aspects of Development, by John Brode, 1969.

Taxation and Development: Lessons from Colombian Experience, by Richard M. Bird, 1970.

Lord and Peasant in Peru: A Paradigm of Political and Social Change, by F. LaMond Tullis, 1970.

Agricultural Development in India's Districts, by Dorris D. Brown, 1971.

The Kennedy Round in American Trade Policy: The Twilight of the GATT? by John W. Evans, 1971.

Korean Development: The Interplay of Politics and Economics, by David C. Cole and Princeton N. Lyman, 1971.

Political Mobilization of the Venezuelan Peasant, by John Duncan Powell, 1971.

Studies in Development Planning, edited by Hollis B. Chenery, 1971.

Development Policy II: The Pakistan Experience, edited by Walter P. Falcon and Gustav F. Papanek, 1971.

Peasants against Politics: Rural Organization in Brittany, 1911-1967, by Suzanne Berger, 1972.

Transnational Relations and World Politics, edited by Robert O. Keohane and Joseph S. Nye, Jr., 1972.

Latin American University Students: A Six Nation Study, by Arthur Liebman, Kenneth N. Walker, and Myron Glazer, 1972.

The Politics of Land Reform in Chile, 1950-1970: Public Policy, Political Institutions, and Social Change, by Robert R. Kaufman, 1972.

The Boundary Politics of Independent Africa, by Saadia Touval, 1972.